Virginia with love from Mum & Daddy.

Xmas 1940

£2-20

LH48

D0875324

*

MEMORY
HOLD-THE-DOOR

BOOKS BY JOHN BUCHAN

SCHOLAR-GIPSIES, 1896
JOHN BURNET OF BARNS, 1898
A HISTORY OF BRASENOSE COLLEGE, 1898
GREY WEATHER, 1899
A LOST LADY OF OLD YEARS, 1899
THE HALF-HEARTED, 1900
THE WATCHER BY THE THRESHOLD, 1902
THE AFRICAN COLONY, 1903
THE TAXATION OF FOREIGN INCOME, 1905
A LODGE IN THE WILDERNESS, 1906
SOME EIGHTEENTH CENTURY BY-WAYS, 1908
PRESTER JOHN, 1910
SIR WALTER RALEIGH, 1911
THE MOON ENDURETH, 1912
SALUTE TO ADVENTURERS, 1915
THE THIRTY-NINE STEPS, 1915
GREENMANTLE, 1916
POEMS, SCOTS AND ENGLISH, 1917
MR. STANDFAST, 1919
THE SOUTH AFRICAN FORCES IN FRANCE, 1920
FRANCIS AND RIVERSDALE GRENFELL, 1920
THE PATH OF THE KING, 1921
A HISTORY OF THE GREAT WAR, 1921-22

HUNTINGTOWER, 1922
MIDWINTER, 1923
THE THREE HOSTAGES, 1924
LORD MINTO : A MEMOIR, 1924
JOHN MACNAB, 1925
THE ROYAL SCOTS FUSILIERS, 1925
THE DANCING FLOOR, 1926
HOMILIES AND RECREATIONS, 1926
WITCH WOOD, 1927
THE RUNAGATES' CLUB, 1928
MONTROSE, 1928
THE COURTS OF THE MORNING, 1929
CASTLE GAY, 1930
THE KIRK IN SCOTLAND, 1930 (With Sir George Adam Smith)
THE BLANKET OF THE DARK, 1931
SIR WALTER SCOTT, 1932
JULIUS CAESAR, 1932
THE GAP IN THE CURTAIN, 1932
THE MAGIC WALKING-STICK, 1932
THE MASSACRE OF GLENCOE, 1933
A PRINCE OF THE CAPTIVITY, 1933
GORDON AT KHARTOUM, 1934
THE FREE FISHERS, 1934
OLIVER CROMWELL, 1934
THE KING'S GRACE, 1935
THE HOUSE OF THE FOUR WINDS, 1935
THE ISLAND OF SHEEP, 1936
AUGUSTUS, 1937
MEMORY HOLD-THE-DOOR, 1940
CANADIAN OCCASIONS, 1940

SICK HEART RIVER *
THE LONG TRAVERSE *

* To be published in 1941

J.B., 1938

MEMORY
HOLD-THE-DOOR

By

JOHN BUCHAN

LONDON

HODDER AND STOUGHTON LTD.

ST. PAUL'S HOUSE, WARWICK SQUARE, E.C.4

1940

First printed . . June 1940
Reprinted . . August 1940
Reprinted . September 1940
Reprinted . October 1940
Reprinted . October 1940
Reprinted . October 1940
Reprinted . November 1940

Made and Printed in Great Britain for HODDER AND STOUGHTON LTD., London
by T. AND A. CONSTABLE LTD., Printers, Edinburgh

PREFACE

THIS book is a journal of certain experiences, not written in the experiencing moment, but rebuilt out of memory. As we age, the mystery of Time more and more dominates the mind. We live less in the present, which no longer has the solidity that it had in youth; less in the future, for the future every day narrows its span. The abiding things lie in the past, and the mind busies itself with what Henry James has called "the irresistible reconstruction, to the all too baffled vision, of irrevocable presences and aspects, the conscious, shining, mocking void, sad somehow with excess of serenity."

Such a research is not a mere catalogue of memories. I have no new theory of Time to propound, but I would declare my belief that it preserves and quickens rather than destroys. An experience, especially in youth, is quickly overlaid by others, and is not at the moment fully comprehended. But it is overlaid, not lost. Time hurries it from us, but also keeps it in store, and it can later be recaptured and amplified by memory, so that at leisure we can interpret its meaning and enjoy its savour.

These chapters are so brazenly egotistic that my first intention was to have them privately printed. But I reflected that a diary of a pilgrimage, a record of the effect upon one mind of the mutations of life, might interest others who travel a like road. It is not a book

7

of reminiscences in the ordinary sense, for my purpose has been to record only a few selected experiences. The lover of gossip will find nothing to please him, for I have written at length only of the dead. Nor is it an autobiography, for I cannot believe that the external incidents of my life are important enough to be worth chronicling in detail. And it is only in a meagre sense a confession of faith. It is a record of the impressions made upon me by the outer world, rather than a weaving of such impressions into a personal religion and philosophy. Some day I may attempt the latter.

I have included one or two passages from a little book, *These for Remembrance*, of which a few copies were printed privately in 1919.

J. B.

CONTENTS

ILLUSTRATIONS

CHAPTER I

WOOD, WATER AND HILL

I

AS a child I must have differed in other things besides sanctity from the good Bernard of Clairvaux, who, we are told, could walk all day by the Lake of Geneva and never see the lake. My earliest recollections are not of myself, but of my environment. It is only reflection that fits my small presence into the picture.

When a few months old I was brought by my parents to a little grey manse on the Fife coast. It was a square, stone house standing in a big garden, with a railway behind it, and in front, across a muddy by-road, a linoleum factory, a coal-pit and a rope-walk, with a bleaching-works somewhere in the rear. To-day industry no longer hems it in, but has submerged it, and a vast factory has obliterated house and garden. The place smelt at all times of the making of wax-cloth; not unpleasantly, though in spring the searching odour was apt to overpower the wafts of lilac and hawthorn.

To the north, beyond the narrow tarnished strip, lay deep country. Two streams converged through "dens" to a junction below the rope-walk. Both were of small volume, and one was foul with the discards of the bleaching-works. There must have been a time when sea-trout in a spate ran up them from the Firth, but now in their lower courses they were like sewers, and finished their degraded life in a drain in the town harbour. There was no beauty in those perverted little

13

valleys, except in spring, when the discoloured and malodorous waters flowed through a mist of blue hyacinths.

Above the bleaching-works and the rope-walk the "dens" became woodland. At first the trees were all beeches and oaks whose roots corrugated the path. But presently these gave place to fir and pine with a carpet of bracken. The "dens" were cut at right-angles by a highway, beyond which lay the policies of an old country house. This highway was the end of one stream, which had its source in a pond; but the other had a longer course, coming from some distant spring through a big wood of close-set young spruces, where notices warned against trespass. Beyond that in turn was a wide grassy loaning where tinkers camped, and the well-tilled haughs of central Fife, and the twin nipples of the Lomonds.

Those woods, when the other day I revisited them, seemed slender copses with fields of roots and grain within a stone's throw. But to a child they were illimitable forests. The "dens" of the two streams I thought of as the White Woods, for they had sunlight and open spaces; but that beyond the highway was the Black Wood, to enter which was an adventure. As I grew older a passion for birds' eggs took me into its recesses, and in spring and summer it had no mystery. Moreover, at those seasons holidays were always in my mind, when I should go south to the Border hills, and except that they were the home of birds the woods had little charm for me. But in autumn and winter they recovered the spell which they laid on my earliest childhood.

They smelt differently from the clean Borderland, where the woods were only tiny plantings of fir and birch among the heather. To me as a child, autumn meant the thick, close odour of rotting leaves, varied by scents from the harvested stubble; glimpses of uncanny scarlet toadstools, which I believed to be the work of Lapland witches; acres of spongy ground which miraculously dried up at the first frosts. Winter meant vistas of frozen branches with cold blue lights between, tracks which had to be rediscovered among snowdrifts, and everywhere great pits of darkness. In winter especially I had an authentic forest to explore, which to me was a far more real world than the bustling town behind me, or the wide spaces of sea and open country.

Looking back I realise that the woodlands dominated and coloured my childish outlook. We were a noted household for fairy tales. My father had a great collection of them, including some of the ancient Scottish ones like *The Red Etin of Ireland*, and when we entered the woods we felt ourselves stepping into the veritable world of faery, especially in winter, when the snow made a forest of what in summer was only a coppice. My memory is full of snowstorms, when no postman arrived or milkman from the farm, and we had to dig ourselves out like hibernating bears. In such weather a walk of a hundred yards was an enterprise, and even in lesser falls the woods lost all their homely landmarks for us, and became a *terra incognita* peopled from the story-books. Witches and warlocks, bears and wolf-packs, stolen princesses and robber lords lurked in corners which at other times were too bare and familiar for the mind to play with. Also I had found in the library a book of Norse mythology which strongly captured my fancy. Norns and Valkyries got into the gales that blew up the Firth, and blasting from a distant quarry was the thud of Thor's hammer.

A second imaginative world overshadowed the woods, more potent even than that of the sagas and the fairy folk. Our household was ruled by the old Calvinistic discipline. That discipline can have had none of the harshness against which so many have revolted, for it did not dim the beauty and interest of the earth. My father was a man of wide culture, to whom, in the words of the Psalms, all things were full of the goodness of the Lord. But the regime made a solemn background to a child's life. He was conscious of living in a world ruled by unalterable law under the direct eye of the Almighty. He was a miserable atom as compared with Omnipotence, but an atom, nevertheless, in which Omnipotence took an acute interest. The words of the Bible, from daily family prayers and long Sabbath sessions, were as familiar to him as the story of Jack and the Beanstalk. A child has a natural love of rhetoric, and the noble scriptural cadences had their own meaning for me, quite apart from their proper interpretation. The consequence was that I built up a Bible world of my own and placed it in the woods.

From it I excluded the more gracious pictures, the rejoicing "little hills," the mountains that "clapped their hands," Elim with its wells and palm trees, the "streams of water in the south" of the 126th Psalm. These belonged properly to the sunny Border. But for the rest, Israel warred in the woods, Israelitish prophets kennelled in the shale of the burns, backsliding Judah built altars to Baal on some knoll under the pines. I knew exactly what a heathenish "grove" was: it was a cluster of self-sown beeches on a certain "high place." The imagery of the Psalms haunted every sylvan corner. More, as I struggled, a confused little mortal, with the first tangles of Calvinistic theology, I came to identify abstractions with special localities. The Soul, a shining cylindrical thing, was linked with a particular patch of bent and heather, and in that theatre its struggles took place, while Sin, a horrid substance like black salt, was intimately connected with a certain thicket of brambles and spotted toadstools. This odd habit long remained with me. When I began to read philosophy the processes of the Hegelian dialectic were associated with a homely Galloway heath, and the Socratic arguments with the upper Thames between Godstow and Eynsham.

Oddly enough, while as a child I hypostatised so many abstractions, I left out the Calvinistic Devil. He never worried me, for I could not take him seriously. The fatal influence of Robert Burns made me regard him as a rather humorous and jovial figure; nay more, as something of a sportsman, dashing and debonair. I agreed with the old Scots lady who complained that "if we were a' as eident in the pursuit o' our special callings as the Deil, puir man, it would be better for us." I would not have been afraid if he had risen suddenly out of the cabbage-garden at Hallowe'en. Sin was a horrid thing, but not the Arch-Sinner.

One other book disputed the claim of the Bible to people the woods—*The Pilgrim's Progress*. On Sundays it was a rule that secular books were barred, but we children did not find the embargo much of a penance, for we discovered a fruity line in missionary adventure, we wallowed in martyrologies, we had *The Bible in Spain*, and above all we had Bunyan. From *The Holy War* I acquired my first interest in military operations, which cannot have been the intention of the author, while *The Pilgrim's Progress* became my constant companion. Even to-day I think that, if the text were lost, I could restore most of it from memory. My delight

B

in it came partly from the rhythms of its prose, which, save in King James's Bible, have not been equalled in our literature; there are passages, such as the death of Mr. Valiant-for-Truth, which all my life have made music in my ear. But its spell was largely due to its plain narrative, its picture of life as a pilgrimage over hill and dale, where surprising adventures lurked by the wayside, a hard road with now and then long views to cheer the traveller and a great brightness at the end of it. John Bunyan claimed our woods as his own. There was the Wicket-gate at the back of the colliery, where one entered them; the Hill Difficulty—more than one; the Slough of Despond—various specimens; the Plain called Ease; Doubting Castle—a disused gravel-pit; the Enchanted Land—a bog full of orchises; the Land of Beulah—a pleasant grassy place where tinkers made their fires. There was no River at the end, which was fortunate perhaps, for otherwise my brothers and I might have been drowned in trying to ford it.

The woods, oddly enough, were an invitation to books. In summer, especially in the Borders, I loathed the sight of the printed word, and my ambitions were for a career of devastating bodily adventure. But the winter woods had a quaint flavour of letters. Always in our scrambles among them there was the prospect of a bright fire, curtains drawn, and a long evening to read in. At such seasons I desired nothing better than a bookish life, as scholar or divine. My aim was to be a country parson in some place where the winters were long and snowy, and a man was forced to spend much of his days and all his evenings in a fire-lit library.

But presently spring came, bookishness went by the board, and the only volume I could think of was a fly-book.

II

Our sea was the Firth of Forth. Twenty miles across, the butt-end of the Pentlands loomed over the smoke of Leith. The island of Inchkeith lay in the middle distance. To the east it was possible on a clear day to see the line of the Lammermoors, North Berwick Law and the Isle of May. But of this far prospect a child was scarcely aware. The castle of Edinburgh, an object of romance to me as a milestone on the way to the Borders, was not identified with the distant lump seen dimly above the spires of the capital. The Firth was a thing of short prospects for the eye and very long prospects for the fancy.

In the winter I was barely conscious of it, except as a fog-filled trench, or a yeasty desert of white-caps, from which came stories of wrecked fishing-boats. Once, when I had a notion of being a sailor, I played truant from school and spent a delirious afternoon at the end of the pier, buffeted by rain and drenched with spray. But in early summer it became an absorbing thing. The shore in the neighbourhood of the town was a foul place, smelling of drains and rotten fish, but to the east, beyond the scarp of Ravenscraig (famous from Sir Walter Scott's ballad of *Rosabelle*), there was a mile or two of clean coast, part of the demesne of Dysart House. It was possible to enter this by scrambling over rocks and scaling a wall, and we children came to regard it as our special preserve. There a succession of low reefs enclosed little sandy creeks, where we could bathe in a strong salt sea in the company of jelly-fish and sea-anemones. Behind lay a sea-wood of battered elders, and at the back of all great thickets of rhododendrons, which in May were towers of blossom. It was a perfect playground for children, for we were alone except for the gulls and a passing smack. Sometimes on a holiday we followed the coast eastward, past the once notable port of Dysart, to the fishing hamlets of the Wemysses and Buckhaven. Dysart in particular was a joy to us, for in its little harbour were to be found craft from foreign ports and sailormen speaking broken English. One especially I remember, a Dutch fore-and-aft schooner, painted green, with a cage of singing birds and a pot of tulips in the cabin, whose skipper gave us tea and mushrooms, and promised to all of us places in his crew.

Those summer afternoons on the shore opened up the world for me. In my father's congregation there were several retired ship-captains, who had sailed to outlandish spots and had on their walls ostrich eggs, and South Sea weapons, and ship models under glass. In such folk I had little interest in the winter time, but in summer I cadged greedily for invitations to tea, when I could ply them with questions and beg foreign curios. Under their tuition I learned to carve ship models for myself, and became learned in the matter of sails and rigging and types of vessels. But my interest was less in seamanship than in the unknown lands which could be reached by ships. I became aware of the largeness of the globe. At the time I collected foreign stamps, and to this day the smell of gum, with which I plastered them in an album, brings back to me that spacious awakening.

The woods were, on the whole, a solemn place, canopied by Calvinistic heavens. Their world was an arena of pilgrimage, romantic, exciting, mysterious, but governed by an inexorable law. The sea also invited to pilgrimage, but how different! It offered a world sunlit and infinitely varied. All the things which fascinated me in books—tropic islands, forests of strange

fruits, snow mountains, ports thronged with queer
shipping and foreign faces—lay somewhere beyond the
waters in which I swam with indifferent skill. I never
attempted to harmonise the two worlds—I never
wanted to. But that summer shore was a wholesome
emancipation. It seemed to slacken the bonds of
destiny and enlarge the horizon. It saved one small
mortal from becoming an owlish and bookish prig.

III

Each year from early summer until some date in
September we children dwelt in the Borders. It was
a complete break, for there seemed no link between
the Tweedside hills and either the woods or the beaches
of Fife. In those weeks we never gave our home a
thought, and with bitter reluctance we returned to it.
The Borders were to us a holy land which it would
have been sacrilege to try to join on to our common life.

We lived with our maternal grandparents in an old
farmhouse close to the main Edinburgh-Carlisle road,
where it descended from benty moorlands to the Tweed
valley. My father's family had been for the most
part lawyers in Edinburgh and in the little burgh of
Peebles, and owners of a small estate in Midlothian ;
my mother's had for generations been sheep-farmers on
the confines of three shires—Lanark, Midlothian and
Tweeddale. The whole countryside was dotted with our
relatives. My grandmother was a formidable old lady,
who ruled her household like a grenadier. She had
the hawk nose and the bright commanding eye of
her kinsman, Mr. Gladstone, and she did not readily
suffer the fool. But for us children she had an
infinite tolerance. "Never daunton youth," was
her favourite adage ; a text often on her lips was

"Fathers, provoke not your children to anger, lest they be discouraged."

The farm stood at the mouth of a shallow glen bounded by high green hills. The stream in the glen joined a "water" flowing from the west, which three miles off entered Tweed. We were therefore at the meeting-place of the plateau of the Scottish midlands and the main range of the southern hills which runs from the Cheviots to Galloway. North and west we looked to inconsiderable uplands and ploughlands; east was an isolated knot of respectable summits; but south, beyond the trench of Tweed, was a sea of broad, blue, heathy mountains, the highest in the Lowlands, rolling to the fastnesses of Ettrick and Moffatdale. We had for our playground both the desert and the sown.

Of the desert, till I had almost reached my teens, I was conscious only as a background; my business was with the immediate environment—the links of the burn, the fields of old pasture, certain ancient trees which had been standing when the vale was the demesne of a Jacobite laird, a seductive mill-dam lined with yellow flags, a water-meadow full of corncrakes, the confluence of the burn and the "water," and the progress of the said water by fir-clad knolls and young plantations and brackeny downs to Tweed.

A child's imagination needs something small which it can seize and adopt as its very own. The things I remember most vividly from those early days are tiny nooks of meadow, woodland and hill. One was beside the burn, where a half-moon of hill-turf fringed a pool occupied by a big trout. An ancient beech in the background cast its shadow and its nuts over the grass. The place strongly took our fancy, and it was a favourite stage for our make-believe—suitable alike for playing at keeping shop, house or castle, as the bridge of

Horatius (the pool being a satisfying end for False
Sextus) or as sanctuary for a Jacobite with a price on
his head. . . . Another was a hollow in a near-by hill,
from which stone had been taken long ago. It was
floored with thyme and milkwort, and fringed with
crimson bell-heather. It was of course the entrance to
King Arthur's sleeping-place, for Arthur and Merlin
were in every legend of the valley, and often of an
afternoon we laboured with fluttering hearts to enlarge
a fox's earth, expecting momentarily that the passage
would open and the magic horn dangle before our
eyes. . . . Still a third was in a fir wood, a mossy den
with a long prospect of the valley, where cushats,
plovers and curlews kept up a cheerful din, and hunger
could be sated by the largest and juiciest of blaeberries.

As I advanced in years I became less interested in those
fanciful nooks than in the hills themselves, where the
shepherds lived and wrought. I had my first introduction to an old and happy world. I would be out
at dawn to "look the hill," delighting in the task,
especially if the weather were wild. I attended every
clipping, where shepherds came from ten miles round
to lend a hand. I helped to drive sheep to the local
market and sat, heavily responsible, in a corner of the
auction-ring. I became learned in the talk of the trade,
and no bad judge of sheep stock. Those Border shepherds, the men of the long stride and the clear eye,
were a great race—I have never known a greater. The
narrower kinds of fanaticism, which have run riot elsewhere in Scotland, rarely affected the Borders. Their
people were "grave livers," in Wordsworth's phrase,
God-fearing, decent in all the relations of life, and
supreme masters of their craft. They were a fighting
stock because of their ancestry, and of a noble independence. As the source of the greatest ballads in any

literature they had fire and imagination, and some aptitude for the graces of life. They lacked the dourness of the conventional Scot, having a quick eye for comedy, and, being in themselves wholly secure, they were aristocrats with the fine manners of an aristocracy. By them I was admitted into the secrets of a whole lost world of pastoral. I acquired a reverence and affection for the "plain people," who to Walter Scott and Abraham Lincoln were what mattered most in the world. I learned the soft, kindly, idiomatic Border speech. My old friends, by whose side I used to quarter the hills, are long ago at rest in moorland kirkyards, and my salutation goes to them beyond the hills of death. I have never had better friends, and I have striven to acquire some tincture of their philosophy of life, a creed at once mirthful and grave, stalwart and merciful.

From that countryside an older world had not quite departed. On the green hill-roads drovers still passed with their herds of kyloes, moving from the north to the Border, and so blocking the bridge of Peebles that small boys could not get home from school. Falkirk Tryst still flourished; my youngest uncle used to drive sheep there, sleeping on the road beside his flock. Edie Ochiltree and the blue-gowns had gone, but the tramp might still be a professional man and no wastrel, one who peregrinated the country for seasonal jobs and could fascinate children with outland tales. Old folks had still stories to tell of James Hogg and Walter Scott. There was a great-uncle of ours who lived to be a friend of my own children, and who as a small boy had as his nurse an old woman who had been scared as a little girl by the clans passing in the 'Forty-five on their march to Derby. And the highroad, which now glistens with tarmac, was a thoroughfare only for sheep

and vagrants and an occasional farmer's gig or baker's
cart. In all its upper stretches, before it crossed the
watershed into Annandale, the space between the ruts
was shaggy with heather.

So there were stages in our Border childhood; first
the miniature world of nooks and playgrounds; then
the middle distance, the adjacent hills and the neighbouring glens; and last, as we grew older and stronger,
the high places, adventures and explorations. In the
first, I remember, a certain straight mile of highway
seemed an interminable thing, and was broken up for
me by gates—the White Yett, the Black Yett; in the
second, it was no more than a tiresome prologue; in
the third, it was scarcely even an episode. From constant scrambling we children became a clan of hardy
mountaineers who could ascend a steep face faster than
the shepherds. But our staying power was limited, and
after a long day we would crawl home very weary.
Our zest for the business never flagged, for our horizon
had suddenly widened. In Fife beyond the woods
there was nothing to explore except flat fields, while
what lay across the magical summer sea was in the
world of dreams. But in the Borders, just outside our
narrow range, lay a great back-country, whose inhabitants we sometimes met and about whose wonders
we were abundantly informed. If we could only cross
a ridge of hill or push beyond a turning in the road
our eyes would behold it.

There were two main arenas to explore: the Hills
and the Road. The first was the tangle of uplands to
the south beyond the Tweed valley. We knew that
they stretched for fifty miles to the English border.
They held in their recesses a hundred places whose
names were like music to us—Yarrow and Ettrick and
Eskdalemuir; legendary streams like Manor and Talla

and Megget and Gameshope; spots famous in history and familiar to us from Sir Walter and the Ballads. But they were all beyond our orbit. Even to come within sight of them meant ascending one of the long tributary glens of Tweed and crossing a formidable watershed. We could see from our home the summits of their guardian mountains, Scrape and Broad Law and Dollar Law and Cramalt Craig. At first it was the desire for trout that led us to the burns on the other side of Tweed. Gradually we passed from the pools at the foot, fringed with birches and rowans, to the upper courses where good fish could be taken in runnels a foot wide. Then came a day when fishing was unprosperous and we boldly climbed the ridge beyond the springs in the hope of surprising a new world. Alas! the Tweedside hills are not a sharp "divide," and there were hours of weary tramping over bent and bog before we got our prospect. But there were things to draw us on—cloudberries, which only grow on the high tops, and deep peat-haggs which were unknown on our familiar hills. Sometimes we were rewarded with a vision, though it meant a desperate journey back. I shall never forget one afternoon when from some ridge —I think it was Dollar Law—I saw a far gleam of silver, and with a beating heart knew that I was looking on St. Mary's Loch.

The Road also was an avenue for us into the unknown. It was the Great South Road from the Scottish capital to England. Armies had marched along it; Prince Charlie's ragged Highlanders had footed it; in my grandparents' memory coaches had jingled down it, and horns and bugles had woke the echoes in the furthest glens. Far more than the railway, it was for me a link with the outer world. It followed Tweed to its source, past places which captured my fancy—the little hamlet of Tweedsmuir where Talla Water came down from its linns; the old coaching hostelries of the Crook and the Bield; Tweedhopefoot, famous in Covenanting days; Tweedshaws, where the river had its source; and then, beyond the divide, the mysterious green chasm called the Devil's Beef Tub, and the Annan and the Esk, and enormous half-mythical England. Those upper glens had the general name of the "Muirs," and a shepherd from "up the water" was to me a potent figure of romance. Many a summer afternoon my feeble legs carried me up the valley, always a little further, till one day I had a glimpse of the steeple of Tweedsmuir kirk.

It was my furthest effort on foot, achieved when I must have been about twelve years of age. After that a craze for fishing took me in thrall, and I was sixteen and the possessor of a shabby bicycle before I next explored the Road. Now the business was easy. In a few hours I could be at the head of the valley, and look down into the pit of the Beef Tub and south over the blue champaign of Annandale. But a bicycle could be put to a nobler purpose than trundling along a highway, and I used it principally to take me to remote glens where I could fish unfrequented streams. So my frontier shifted from the Road back again to the Hills. It was in them that the true field for exploration lay, and I and my fishing-rod were soon making notable journeys, starting and returning in the small hours.

Wood, sea and hill were the intimacies of my childhood, and they have never lost their spell for me. But the spell of each was different. The woods and beaches were always foreign places, in which I was at best a sojourner. But the Border hills were my own possession, a countryside in which my roots went deep.

So strong did I feel my proprietary interest that I projected a history of our glen in the style of Gilbert White's *Selborne*, in which every trickle of a burn would have had its chronicle. This attachment to a corner of earth induced a love of nature in general, and from my early affection I have drawn a passion for landscapes in many parts of the globe, landscapes often little akin to the gentle Border hills.

Most of us have certain childish memories which we can never repeat, since they represent moments when life was in utter harmony and sense and spirit perfectly attuned. Such memories for me are all of Tweedside, and I have welcomed with delight any maturer experience which had a hint of their magic. Three I have always cherished. One was the waking on a hot July morning with a day of moorland wandering before me. Around me were the subtle odours of an old house, somewhere far off the fragrance of coffee, and the smell of new-mown hay drifting through the open window. Through the same window came a multitude of sounds —the clank of the neighbouring smithy, the clucking of hens, sheep fording the burn. From my bed I could see the sky blue as deep-sea water, and against it the bare green top of a hill. Even to-day a fine morning gives me something of the thrill of those summer awakenings.

Another memory is of a long tramp on a drove-road in the teeth of the wind, with the rain in my face and mist swirling down the glens. I felt that I was contending joyfully with something kindly at heart, something to stir the blood and at the same time instinct with a delicate comfort—the homely smell of sheep, the scent of peat-reek, the glimpse of firelight from a wayside cottage.

The third was family prayers of a Sabbath evening.

THE GATE OF TWEEDSMUIR

It was the custom to return from church through the fields, which lay yellow in the sunset. While our elders cast a half-ashamed sabbatical eye over the crops of meadow hay and the kyloes in the pastures, we children. feeling the bonds of the Sabbath ritual slackening, were hard at work planning enterprises for the morrow. Then in the dusky parlour, with its comforting secular aroma of tobacco, my grandfather read chapters of both Testaments and a lengthy prayer from some forgotten *Family Altar*. I did not follow one word, for my thoughts were busy with other things. He read in a high liturgical manner, his voice rising and falling in reverent cadences. It seemed to us children a benediction on the enforced leisure of the day and a promise of a new and glorious week of wind and sun.

All my life I have been haunted—and cheered—by these recollections: the green summit against the unclouded blue above a populous friendly world, the buffets of rain on the moorland road, the drone of my grandfather's voice in the Sabbath twilight. Each was a summons to action. But there was a fourth which spoke only of peace. This was the coming down from the hills, very hungry and foot-sore, to a whitewashed farm on the brink of the heather, where, in a parlour looking out on a garden of gooseberries and phloxes, with a glimpse beyond of running water, I was stayed with tea and new-baked scones and apple-and-rowan-berry jelly. Then I demanded nothing more of life except to be allowed to go on living in that quiet world of pastoral. The dying shepherd asked not for the conventional Heaven, but for "Bourhope at a reasonable rent," and, if Paradise be a renewal of what was happy and innocent in our earthly days, mine will be some such golden afternoon within sight and sound of Tweed.

CHAPTER II

PORTA MUSARUM

I

I NEVER went to school in the conventional sense, for a boarding school was beyond the narrow means of my family. But I had many academies. The first was a dame's school, where I learned to knit, and was expelled for upsetting a broth pot on the kitchen fire. The next was a board school in the same Fife village. Then came the burgh school of the neighbouring town, which meant a daily tramp of six miles. There followed the high school of the same town, a famous institution in which I believe Thomas Carlyle once taught. When we migrated to Glasgow I attended for several years an ancient grammar school on the south side of the river, from which, at the age of seventeen, I passed to Glasgow University.

Had I gone to a public school I might have developed into a useful wing three-quarter in the rugby game. Otherwise I do not think I missed much. I and my brothers were, I fear, incapable of what is called the public-school spirit. While devotees of the open air we lacked interest in games, and had few of the usual boyish ambitions. We had no wish to run with the pack, for we were absorbed in our private concerns. School to me was therefore only a minor episode. The atmosphere I lived in was always that of my home. I never felt the shyness and repression of the small boy which I have read of in school stories. At my various schools I had my ups and downs, but they mattered little and were forgotten in an hour. My interest in

30

the world at large was not checked by any artificial conventions, and, though I was afraid of many things, I had none of the social fears and resentments of the traditional schoolboy.

Yet, looking back, I seem to have enjoyed my schools enormously. There I mixed on terms of comradeship and utter equality with children from every kind of queer environment. At my village school my chief friend was the son of a notorious local ne'er-do-well, and the two of us captained a gang of barefooted ragamuffins who waged ceaseless war against the local "gentry," the sons of well-to-do manufacturers. With one especially, who seemed to us gigantic in height and ferocious in temper, we avoided close combat and engaged him at a distance with bows and arrows. I did not meet my antagonist again until one day in 1916 during the battle of the Somme—he was then a major-general and is now a peer—when I found him of modest stature and exceeding affability.

My lack of the usual code had one serious draw-back. Youthful high spirits had to be worked off somehow, and adventures—often unjustifiable adventures—took the place of games. As a family we were too easily "dared," as the phrase went, to attempt things dangerous or ridiculous. We were of Walter Bagehot's opinion that the greatest pleasure in life is doing what people say you cannot do, and the consequence was that we were an anxiety to our parents, and often, owing to bodily damage, an affliction to ourselves. At my later schools this foolishness abated and I fell more into the normal habits of youth, but even then school played but a small part in my life. It was an incident, an inconsiderable incident; a period of enforced repression which ended daily at four in the afternoon.

II

My boyhood must have been one of the idlest on record. Except in the last year of my Glasgow grammar school, I do not think that I ever consciously did any work. I sat far down in my classes, absorbing automatically the rudiments of grammar and mathematics, without conviction and with no shadow of a desire to excel. Now and then I shone, it is true, when I showed a surprising knowledge of things altogether outside the curriculum, for I was always reading, except in the Border holidays. Early in my teens I had read Scott, Dickens, Thackeray and a host of other story-tellers; all Shakespeare; a good deal of history, and many works of travel; essayists like Bacon and Addison, Hazlitt and Lamb, and a vast assortment of poetry, including Milton, Pope, Dante (in a translation), Wordsworth, Shelley, Keats and Tennyson. Matthew Arnold I knew almost by heart; Browning I still found too difficult except in patches. My taste was for solemn gnomic verse with a theological flavour; my special favourites were *Yesterday, To-day and Forever* by a former Bishop of Exeter, and the celebrated Mr. Robert Pollok's *Course of Time*; and my earliest poetic effort was not lyrical but epic, the first canto of a poem on Hell.

But all this was mere absorption, only half-conscious and quite uncritical. I found my first real intellectual interest in the Latin and Greek classics. This came to me when I was in my seventeenth year, just before I went to Glasgow University. For the next three years I was a most diligent student, mediaeval in my austerity. Things have changed now, but in my day a Scottish university still smacked of the Middle Ages. The undergraduates lived in lodgings in the city and most of them cultivated the Muses on a slender allowance of oatmeal. The session ran from October to April, and every morning I had to walk four miles to the eight o'clock class through every variety of the winter weather with which Glasgow fortifies her children. My road lay through the south side of the city, across the Clyde, and so to the slopes of Gilmorehill. Most of that road is as ugly as anything you can find in Scotland, but to me in the retrospect it was all a changing panorama of romance. There was the weather—fog like soup, drenching rains, winds that swirled down the cavernous streets, mornings that dawned bright and clear over snow. There was the sight of humanity going to work and the signs of awakening industry. There was the bridge with the river starred with strange lights, the lit shipping at the Broomielaw, and odours which even at their worst spoke of the sea. There was the occasional lift in the London train, which could be caught at a suburban station, and which for a few minutes brought one into the frowst of a third-class carriage full of sleepy travellers from the remote and unvisited realm of England. And at the end there were the gaunt walls of the college often seen in the glow of a West Highland sunrise.

As a student I was wholly obscure. I made few friends; I attended infrequently one or other of the numerous societies, but I never spoke in a debate; and I acquired the corporate spirit only at a rectorial election, when, though a professed Tory, I chose to support the Liberal candidate, Mr. Asquith, and almost came by my end at the hands of a red-haired savage, one Robert Horne, who has since been Chancellor of the Exchequer. My summers were spent in blessed idleness, fishing, tramping and bicycling up and down the Lowlands. But my winters were periods of beaver-like toil and

C

monkish seclusion. I returned home early each afternoon and thereafter was at my books until midnight.

After a brief dalliance with mathematics, my subject was classics. In Latin I was fairly proficient, thanks to my father's tuition, but my Greek was rudimentary, and I was fortunate to find in Gilbert Murray a great teacher. He was then a young man in his middle twenties and was known only by his Oxford reputation. To me his lectures were, in Wordsworth's phrase, like "kindlings of the morning." Men are by nature Greeks or Romans, Hellenists or Latinists. Murray was essentially a Greek; my own predilection has always been for Rome; but I owe it to him that I was able to understand something of the Greek spirit and still more to come under the spell of the classic discipline in letters and life. I laboured hard to make myself a good "pure" scholar; but I was not intended by Providence for a philologist; my slender attainments lay rather in classical literature, in history, and presently in philosophy. Always to direct me I had Murray's delicate critical sense, his imaginative insight into high matters, and his gentle and scrupulous humanism. In those years I read widely in the two literatures, covering much ground quite unfruitful for the schools. The other day I turned up an old paper on Claudian and was amazed at its futile erudition. I found that in another essay I had tried to analyse the mood of that wide-horizoned and fantastic sixth-century Ionia which made the background for Herodotus.

If Gilbert Murray was the principal influence in shaping my interests, another was the Border country, which I regarded as my proper home. In the old song of *Leader Haughs and Yarrow* Nicol Burne the Violer had given Tweeddale an aura of classical convention, and "Pan playing on his aiten reed" has never

ceased to be a denizen of its green valleys. There is a
graciousness there, a mellow habitable charm, unlike
the harsh Gothic of most of the Scots landscape. I got
it into my head that here was the appropriate setting
for pastoral, for the shepherds of Theocritus and Virgil,
for the lyrists of the Greek Anthology, and for Horace's
Sabine farm. I was wrong in fact; if you seek the true
classical landscape outside Italy and Greece you will
find it rather in the Cape Peninsula, in places like
the Paarl and Stellenbosch. But my fancy had its
uses, for I never read classical poetry with such gusto
as in my Border holidays, and it served as a link between
my gipsy childhood and the new world of scholarship
into which I was seeking entrance.

This preoccupation with the classics was the happiest
thing that could have befallen me. It gave me a standard
of values. To live for a time close to great minds is the
best kind of education. That is why the Oxford school
of classical "Greats" seems to me so fruitful, for it
compels a close study of one or two masters like Plato
and Thucydides. The classics enjoined humility. The
spectacle of such magnificence was a corrective to
youthful immodesty, and, like Dr. Johnson, I lived
"entirely without my own approbation." Again, they
corrected a young man's passion for rhetoric. This was
in the 'ninetics, when the Corinthian manner was more
in vogue than the Attic. Faulty though my own
practice has always been, I learned sound doctrine—
the virtue of a clean bare style, of simplicity, of a hard
substance and an austere pattern. Above all the
Calvinism of my boyhood was broadened, mellowed,
and also confirmed. For if the classics widened my
sense of the joy of life they also taught its littleness and
transience; if they exalted the dignity of human nature
they insisted upon its frailties and the *aidos* with which

the temporal must regard the eternal. I lost then any chance of being a rebel, for I became profoundly conscious of the dominion of unalterable law. Prometheus might be a fine fellow in his way, but Zeus was king of gods and men.

Indeed I cannot imagine a more precious viaticum than the classics of Greece and Rome, or a happier fate than that one's youth should be intertwined with their world of clear, mellow lights, gracious images and fruitful thoughts. They are especially valuable to those who believe that Time enshrines and does not destroy, and who do what I am attempting to do in these pages, and go back upon and interpret the past. No science or philosophy can give that colouring, for such provide a schematic, and not a living, breathing universe. And I do not think that the mastery of other literatures can give it in a like degree, for they do not furnish the same totality of life—a complete world recognisable as such, a humane world, yet one untouchable by decay and death—

> "based on the crystalline sea
> of truth and its eternity."

III

I came to philosophy quite naturally as a consequence of my youthful theological environment. Not that I ever had the itch of the metaphysician to make a rational cosmos of my own, for I did not feel the need for such a contraption. The cosmology of the elder Calvinism, with its anthropomorphism and its material penalties and rewards, I never consciously rejected. It simply faded out of the air, since it meant nothing to me. I remember that an ancient relative assured me that Sir Walter Scott, having neglected certain evangelical experiences, was no doubt in torment; the news gave me much satisfaction, for the prospect of such company removed for me any fear of the infernal regions; thenceforward, like Dante's Farinata degli Uberti, I "entertained great scorn for Hell." But the fundamentals of the Christian religion were so entwined with my nature that I never found occasion to question them. I wanted no philosophy to rationalise them, for they seemed to me completely rational. Philosophy was to me always an intellectual exercise, like mathematics, not the quest for a faith.

I had begun to read in the subject long before I took the philosophy classes at the University, my first love being Descartes, to whom I was introduced by our Tweeddale neighbour, Professor John Veitch, the last of the Schoolmen. Henry Jones was the Moral Philosophy professor at Glasgow, and with him I formed a life-long friendship, for a braver, wiser, kinder human being never lived. But the semi-religious Hegelianism then in vogue, first preached by Edward Caird and continued by Jones, did not greatly attract me, and I owed allegiance to no school. I read widely, with the consequence that when I went to Oxford I found that I had done most of the work for the final examination, and had leisure there to read more widely than ever.

Looking back, my industry fills me with awe. Before I left Glasgow I had read and analysed many of the English and Scottish philosophers, most of Kant, and a variety of lesser folk. At Oxford I read—with difficulty and imperfect comprehension—a large part of Hegel. I kept up this conscientious study right to the eve of the Great War. Then alas! I fell away, for I found, like Henry James, that history began to oust philosophy from my affections. Science, apart from what I picked up as a field-naturalist, was practically unknown to me, though I learned a certain amount of physics from my philosophical reading. That was the biggest gap in my education.

My interests, as I have said, lay not in the search for a creed, but in the study of the patterns which different thinkers made out of the universe. I had a tidy mind and liked to arrange things in compartments even when I did not take the arrangement too seriously. This meant that inevitably I missed much; *quidquid recipitur, recipitur ad modum recipientis*. My quest for truth, unlike Plato's, wholly "lacked the warmth of desire." It was a mental gymnastic, for I had neither the uneasiness nor the raptures of the true metaphysician. "Philosophy," Sir Isaac Newton once wrote, "is such an impertinently litigious lady that a man had as good be engaged in lawsuits as have to do with her." I loved the intricacies of argumentation. A proof is that while I am not conscious of having ever argued about religion, or about politics except professionally, I was always very ready to dispute about philosophy. I would have been puzzled to set down my views as to the nature of thought and reality, for they were constantly changing. I never considered it necessary to harmonise my conclusions in a system. Had I been a professed philosopher I should have been forced to crystallise my thought, but, as it was, I could afford to keep it, so to speak, in solution. *L'ineptie consiste à vouloir conclure.* I was of the opinion of the Scottish metaphysician that it is more important that a philosophy should be reasoned than that it should be true.

But two conclusions—or rather inclinations— emerged from my studies, and still abide with me.

Plato, not the system-maker but the poet, had a profound influence on my mind. Platonism was to me not a creed but a climate of opinion, the atmosphere in which my thoughts moved. Such an atmosphere is largely the consequence of temperament, and I think I was born with the same temperament as the Platonists of the early seventeenth century, who had what Walter Pater has called "a sensuous love of the unseen," or, to put it more exactly, who combined a passion for the unseen and the eternal with a delight in the seen and the temporal. *Dieu ne défend pas les routes fleuries quand elles servent à revenir à lui.* If men are either Platonists or Aristotelians then my category was certainly the first.

Again, my philosophical reading left me with certain intellectual habits—a dislike of grandiose mechanical systems, and a distrust of generalities. Having only one or two strong convictions, which might well be called prejudices, I was inclined to be critical of a superfluity of dogmas. Arthur Balfour's *Defence of Philosophic Doubt* and *Foundations of Belief*, which fell into my hands, increased this temperamental bias. I developed in most subjects, and notably in politics, a kind of relativism—a belief in degrees of truth and differing levels of reality—which made me judge systems by their historical influence and practical efficiency rather than by their logical perfections. I began to admire Carlyle's "swallowers of formulas." There were eternal truths, I decided, but not very many, and even these required frequent spring-cleanings. I became tolerant of most human moods, except intolerance. It was a point of view which I have since seen cause to modify, but it was perhaps a salutary one at that stage in my life.

IV

I have used the word politics, but at this stage I was no politician, being interested only to a small degree

in theories, and not at all in parties. In that complacent
old world before the South African War youth did not
easily feel the impact of national problems. Generally
speaking, I was of a conservative cast of mind, very
sensible of the past, approving renovation but not in-
novation. Lord Falkland's classic confession of faith
might have been mine—"When it is not necessary to
change it is necessary not to change."

High-flying political schemes seemed to me either
dangerous or slightly ridiculous—which was Dr.
Johnson's view. "So, sir," said Boswell, "you laugh
at schemes of political improvement?" "Why, sir,
most schemes of political improvement are very laugh-
able things." In those days my social conscience was
scarcely awake.

There was little reason why it should be. I was far
too absorbed in my studies to read the newspapers, and
I had no interest in the small beer of party controversy.
As for philanthropic sensibility in the face of poverty
and sickness, a minister's family had little time for such
a luxury. So far my life had been spent chiefly among
the poor—the fisher-folk and weavers of a Fife village,
one of the poorest quarters in the city. We were
engaged in a perpetual fight with destitution and suffering and had no leisure for theorising.

Again, I could never feel that emotional condescen-
sion with which the *âmes sensibles* approach the subject.
These see the pathological in any mode of existence
different from their own. I lived close to working-
class life and knew that it had its own humours and
compensations, and that it nourished many major
virtues like fortitude and charity. I respected the working classes so profoundly that, like William Morris, I
did not want to see them turned into middle classes,
as some of their patrons desired. My upbringing had

made any kind of class feeling impossible. I was one of the poor myself without a penny behind me, compelled to make my way in the world from nearly as bare a start as the lad from the plough-tail or the loom. I had had a better education, came of better stock and had better health than most—these were my sole advantages. But, except for the first, it did not seem to me that the politicians could do much about them.

My politics were largely based on my historical reading, which gave me a full crop of prejudices—prejudices of which I stood in a certain awe, as Hazlitt advised. I early discovered my heroes : Julius Caesar, St. Paul, Charlemagne, Henry of Navarre, Cromwell (of whom I acquired a surprisingly just appreciation), Montrose, Lincoln, Robert E. Lee. I disliked Brutus, Henry VIII, Napoleon (him intensely), most of the 1688 Whigs, all four Georges, and the whole tribe of French revolutionaries except Mirabeau. But I was a most patchy historian, and it was not until Oxford that I acquired a serious interest in historical science.

Meantime I was trying to teach myself to write. Having for years wallowed and floated in the ocean of letters I now tried to learn to swim. My attempts were chiefly flatulent little essays and homilies and limp short stories. My models were the people who specialised in style—Walter Pater and Stevenson principally ; but my uncle, my father's youngest brother, was a great lover of French literature, and under his guidance I became an earnest student of Flaubert and Maupassant. There was also Kipling, then a rising star in the firmament, but he interested me more because of his matter than his manner. The consequence of those diverse masters was that I developed a slightly meretricious and "precious" style, stiff-jointed, heavily brocaded, and loaded with philosophical terms. It took me years to supple it. But those imitative exercises did me good in the long run, for they taught me to be circumspect about structure and rhythm and fastidious about words. My performance, heaven knows, was faulty enough, but the intention was sound.

I wrote copiously, but I also read widely in English and French literature. Certain blind spots I discovered which alas! have remained blind. I had no taste for most of the minor Elizabethans or the Restoration dramatists. I thought the eighteenth-century novelists on the whole over-valued. Only a little of Shelley pleased me, and, though I revered Emily Brontë, I found it impossible to read Charlotte. While I revelled in Alexandre Dumas I could not rank him high. With Carlyle I was easily satiated. I think my chief admiration, so far as style was concerned, was for John Henry Newman and T. H. Huxley.

Stevenson at that time was a most potent influence over young men, especially Scottish university students. Here was one who, though much older than ourselves, was wonderfully young in heart. He had the same antecedents that we had, and he thrilled as we did to those antecedents—the lights and glooms of Scottish history; the mixed heritage we drew from Covenanter and Cavalier; that strange compost of contradictions, the Scottish character; the bleakness and the beauty of the Scottish landscape. He had tramped with a pack on Lowland and Highland roads, and had seen the dawn rise over the wet city streets, and had filled the midnight hours with argument, and had done all the things that we were doing. His hunger for life had not been less than ours. And then he had taught himself to write miraculously, and for those of us who were dabbling clumsily in letters his expertness was a salutary model, for it meant hard and conscientious labour. He spoke

our own language as a colleague and also as a mentor,
for he was a preacher at heart, as every young Scotsman
is, since we have all a craving to edify our fellows. As
a guide to northern youth in the 'nineties Stevenson
filled the bill completely. He was at once Scottish and
cosmopolitan, artist and adventurer, scholar and gipsy.
Above all he was a true companion. He took us by the
hand and shared in all our avocations. It was a profound
and over-mastering influence, and I think it was an
influence wholly benign.

With me it did not last. Presently his style and
manner began to mean less to me. He seemed to me
too much of a looker-on, a phrase-maker in life, and
I wanted robuster standards and more vital impulses.
His fastidiousness came to repel me. I remember some
years later reading the *Open letter to Dr. Hyde* on Father
Damien, and feeling that the great apostle of the lepers
would have had more in common with his vulgar
assailant than with his adjectival defender. Stevenson
seemed to me to have altogether too much artifice about
him, and I felt a suspicion of pose behind his optimism
and masculinity—the pose of an heroic invalidism, a
variant of the bedside manner (for there may be a bedside manner of the patient as well as of the doctor). It
was too self-conscious for greatness.

I have since returned to him with pleasure and revised
that verdict. The judgment of eighteen was juster than
the judgment of forty. I do not think that he was a
great master, but he was a master, for within certain
limits he ensued, and sometimes attained, perfection. I
am convinced that in each generation he will be rediscovered by youth—ordinary youth, not clever,
precocious, paradoxical young men, but the kind of
youth that happily we shall always have with us, those
whom Sir Walter Scott called "young people of bold

and active dispositions." That is a certain passport to immortality. Sophisticated middle age has its modes and changes, but the fashion of such youth is eternal.

V

My chief passion in those years was for the Border countryside, and my object in all my prentice writings was to reproduce its delicate charm, to catch the aroma of its gracious landscape and turbulent history and the idiom of its people. When I was absent from it I was homesick, my memory was full of it, my happiest days were associated with it, and some effluence from its ageless hills and waters laid a spell upon me which has never been broken. I found in its people what I most admired in human nature—realism coloured by poetry, a stalwart independence sweetened by courtesy, a shrewd kindly wisdom. I asked for nothing better than to spend my life by the Tweed.

But how was it to be managed? I considered sheep-farming, like my mother's brothers; but at the moment sheep were not prosperous, and in any case they needed capital. Then I thought of being a man of letters, with a home among the hills! but I remembered Sir Walter's saying that literature was a good staff but a bad crutch, and anyhow I did not fancy the business. It should be my hobby, not my profession. Meantime my interest in scholarship was daily growing, and it seemed to me that a Scottish professorship might offer the life I wanted. It became clear that I must somehow contrive to go to Oxford. If the worst came to the worst and other trades failed, I believed that I could always make a living as a hill-shepherd or a river-gillie.

CHAPTER III

OXFORD

I

AS children we lived much in the past, and, as commonly happens, we interpreted that past by the present, and also permitted bygone ages to colour our everyday lives. The history of Scotland, of which alone we had much knowledge, was to us not a legend but a living memory; we took violent sides in its disputes and attached ourselves vehemently to its protagonists. Like most Scottish families we believed ourselves to be gently born. A certain John Buchan, a younger son of the ancient Aberdeenshire house of Auchmacoy, came south in the beginning of the seventeenth century and was supposed to have founded our branch. There was a missing link in the chain, and an austere antiquary like my uncle would never admit that the descent had more than a high probability; but we children accepted it as proven fact, and rejoiced that through Auchmacoy we could count kin back to the days of William the Lion. So in the high story of Scotland we felt a proprietary interest. A Countess of Buchan (with whom we had no conceivable connection) had crowned Robert Bruce; an Earl of Buchan as Constable of France had avenged Joan of Arc; a Buchan of Auchmacoy had fallen at Flodden beside the King; another had led the Jacobite remnant after the death of Dundee.

Brooding over Scottish history made us intense patriots of the narrowest school. Against our little land

there had always stood England, vast, menacing and
cruel. We resented the doings of Edward I, Henry
VIII and Elizabeth as personal wrongs. The brutalities
of Cumberland after the 'Forty-five seemed to us un-
forgivable outrages which had happened yesterday.
We early decided that no Englishman could enter
Heaven, though, later, our delight in the doings of the
Elizabethan seamen forced us to make an exception of
the inhabitants of Devon. Even when we grew older
and the intolerance abated, England remained for us
a foreign place, not too friendly, to be suspected and
even dreaded. My interest in London, when I first
visited it, was not in its metropolitan wonders, but in
its connection with Scotland's history—that Simon
Lovat had died on Tower Hill, that Balmerino's head
had been stuck up on Temple Bar, and disguised
Jacobite spies had hid themselves in Soho. I had myself
one particular reason for this suspicion. As a child I
was always in terror of being compelled to earn my
bread as a clerk should my father die. This gloomy
fate I associated with some kind of English domicile,
probably a London suburb. The suburbs of the
metropolis, of which I knew nothing, became for me
a synonym for a dreadful life of commercial drudgery
without daylight or hope.

I looked forward, therefore, to visiting this sinister
and fascinating land with some foreboding. The thing
happened when I was seventeen, when, on a bicycle, I
crossed the bridge of Tweed at Coldstream and explored
a strip of Northumberland. I entered England with the
traveller's mingled sense of insecurity and distinction.
To my surprise I found it very like my own countryside. The people spoke with almost my own accent.
The bent and heather of the Cheviots were like my
domestic hills; the valley of Till was lusher perhaps

than that of my moorland waters, but the hill burns were in no way different. . . . The following year I paid my first visit to London to stay with a great-uncle. Incuriously I inspected the sights, but the place made little impression on me, though the scents and sounds of London in the autumn gave me a strong feeling of snugness and comfort. . . . Then a few months later I went up to Oxford to sit for a scholarship. This was my true first visit to England, when I came under the spell of its ancient magnificence and discovered a new loyalty.

It was, I remember, bitter winter weather. The Oxford streets, when I arrived late at night from the North, were deep in snow. My lodgings were in Exeter College, and I recall the blazing fires, a particularly succulent kind of sausage, and coffee such as I had never known in Scotland. I wrote my examination papers in Christ Church hall, that noblest of Tudor creations. I felt as if I had slipped through some chink in the veil of the past and become a mediaeval student. Most vividly I recollect walking in the late afternoon in Merton Street and Holywell and looking at snow-laden gables which had scarcely altered since the Middle Ages. In that hour Oxford claimed me, and her bonds have never been loosed.

II

Brasenose as the home of Walter Pater had a special fascination for me, and, though he had died in the spring before I sat for a scholarship, I was glad to go to a college where he had lectured on Plato, and which was full of his friends. My first impressions of Oxford were unhappy. The soft autumn air did not suit my health; the lectures which I attended seemed jejune and platitudinous, and the regime slack, after the strenuous life of Glasgow; I played no game well enough to acquire an absorbing interest in it. Above all, being a year older than my contemporaries, I felt that I had been pitchforked into a kindergarten. The revels of alcoholic children offended me, and, having an unfortunate gift of plain speech, I did not make myself popular among those emancipated schoolboys. I must have been at that time an intolerable prig. Consequently the friends I made at first were chiefly hard-working students like myself, or older men in other colleges. Also I was very poor. For two years I could not afford to dine in hall. My Oxford bills for the first year were little over £100, for my second year about £150. After that, what with scholarships, prizes and considerable emoluments from books and articles, I became rather rich for an undergraduate.

One advantage of my early seclusion, and of the fact that Brasenose was a small college situated in the heart of Oxford, was that I made friends throughout the University. Presently the political clubs, the Union, and Vincent's added to this circle, and I think that before I went down I had as catholic an acquaintance as any man of my time. I came to know well a few seniors who were either living in Oxford as dons, or came up often on visits—men like Hilaire Belloc and F. E. Smith, John Simon and Leo Amery. I had a large acquaintance among athletes and sportsmen, chiefly the rowing and rugby football groups, and thus I came to know my future partner in business, T. A. Nelson, the Oxford rugby captain, and a Scottish international. Among younger men who overlapped my time were Arthur Salter of Brasenose and Edward Wood (Lord Halifax) of Christ Church.

There were many of the older generation whose

OXFORD, 1899

friendship I enjoyed. First, in my own college, there
was the Principal, Dr. Heberden, whose slender figure
with its scholar's stoop seemed at first out of place in
the robust life of Brasenose. Slowly his gentle humanity
came to be understood, and when he died in 1922 the
College mourned for him as a close-knit family mourns
for its father. There was the chaplain, Dr. F. W.
Bussell, Walter Pater's chief friend, and the nearest
approach in my acquaintance to a mediaeval polymath.
He was my tutor, whom I delighted in surprising, for
from Nietzsche, whom I had just discovered, I would
quote extracts in my essays which were a little startling
to a clerk in holy orders. In Balliol there was the
Master, Edward Caird, who was always a little homesick, I think, for Scotland, as I realised at Sunday
breakfasts. There was J. A. Smith, who to philosophic
profundity added Gaelic scholarship ; there was Francis
Urquhart ("Sligger"), a happy boyish figure who
survived to be a link between post-War Oxford and
my own secure generation. At Trinity there was
R. W. Raper, silent and infinitely wise; at Magdalen
Herbert Warren, the President; and at Christ Church
the massive, bohemian figure of York Powell, and
John Phillimore, afterwards of Glasgow, one of the
best Latin scholars of our day. At Worcester there was
Dr. Daniel, the intimate of a host of literary men and
a connoisseur of fine printing; and at Jesus Sir John
Rhys, who nourished my new-found Celtic enthusiasm.
At All Souls there was Sir William Anson, the Warden,
lawyer and statesman; and W. P. Ker, with a face
"like an intelligent brick wall," who knew every
corner of Scotland, and whose flashes of silence were
more eloquent than speech. I had the privilege, too,
of knowing some of the bachelor Fellows of the old
regime, "characters" all, who kept the monastic flag

D

flying in despite of the new domesticated Oxford of the Parks. One, especially, I remember, who asked me to dinner at high table in my first year. For three courses he spoke not a word, while I plied him with nervous questions about the weather, the Boat-race, and what not. Then he turned on me his formidable face. "Young man," he said, "I would remind you of what Dr. Johnson said, that the art of conversation does not consist in unmeaning interrogatories." I was stricken with helpless laughter, in which he presently joined, and the ice was broken.

The charm of Oxford for me was less in the constellations than in the companionship of the ordinary man. Gradually I became one of what Mr. Pearsall Smith has called unkindly the "aborigines of Brasenose," and a happier fellowship no man could desire. I would pay my tribute to an ancient society for which I have acquired a devout loyalty—a loyalty shared by my brother (whose memorial is in the ante-chapel), and my eldest son. It was famous, then as now, as a sporting college, with a great record of exploits on the river and in the cricket and football fields. The scholars came mostly from grammar schools and the lesser public schools; the commoners largely from the country gentry of Lancashire and the North. It had not for some generations attained great academic success; indeed there was a wicked legend that a Brasenose man who achieved honours in the Schools had been put under the pump as a mark of public disapproval! I remember that I started an Ibsen society, which got on well enough until *Ghosts* was read aloud, upon which the members in disgust rejected the name of Ibsen and turned themselves into a dining club called the Crocodiles. Nevertheless there was no lack of intellectual vigour, and the College which gave Lord

Haig to the British army, and Lord Carnock, Lord Bradbury, Lord Askwith and Sir Arthur Salter to the public services, has little cause to be ashamed of its record. But its chief produce was the commoner, healthy, sane, adventurous, who, like Weir of Hermiston, had "no call to be bonny," but got through his day's work. It was a cross-section of all that was most vigorous in English society, and in distant parts of the Empire it proved its quality. The average Brasenose man was very close to English soil, and from him I learned something of the secret of the English character, that hardly communicable thing which even a Scotsman born in the same island understands only by slow degrees. There is nothing in the land more English than Brasenose.

My years at Oxford were, I think, one of those boundary periods, the meaning of which is missed at the time, but is plain in the retrospect. The place was still monastic, but the clamour of the outer world was at its gates, and it was on the verge of losing many of its idioms. Very ancient customs were still remembered; for example, it was only a few years before I went up that Brasenose men had to go out of college in pairs, a relic of the mediaeval town and gown troubles. Sartorially my time was beyond doubt a turning point. On Sundays a dark suit was still obligatory; on weekdays Brasenose inclined towards tailed coats of tweed and hunting waistcoats, and the headgear was a cap or a bowler; but before I went down the fashion had arrived from Winchester of flannel "bags" and any kind of jacket at all seasons, and the modern hatless era was dawning. It was the same with our speech, which had Early Victorian, if not Regency, traces. We still called a cigar a "weed" and used the word "blood" to denote whatever was dashing and high-coloured in raiment or behaviour. When I visited my brother a year after I went down, I found that this fashion had almost disappeared.

After the years of intellectual ferment in a Scottish university Oxford was for me a stabilising influence, but still more was it a mellowing of character through friendship. In my time there was no urgent political or religious question to divide people into militant fraternities. We sought not allies in a cause but friendships for their own sake. Our creed was Mr. Belloc's:

> "From quiet homes and first beginning
> Out to the undiscovered ends
> There's nothing worth the wear of winning
> But laughter and the love of friends."

That happy circle has long since been broken, for the South African War took heavy toll of it, and the World War completed the tragedy.

I lived a good deal in Balliol and my closest friends were of that college; indeed, I believe that I was the sole outsider who ever became an honorary member of its principal wine club. The Balliol generation of my time was, I think, the most remarkable in Oxford, only to be paralleled by the brilliant group, containing Charles Lister and the Grenfells, which flourished on the eve of the War. It was distinguished both for its scholars and its athletes, but it made no parade of its distinction, carrying its honours lightly as if they fell to it in the ordinary process of nature. It delighted unpedantically in things of the mind, but it had an engaging youthfulness, too, and was not above high-jinks and escapades.

In that circle there was no pose, unless it be a pose in youth to have no pose. The "grand manner" in the eighteenth-century sense was cultivated, which meant a deliberate lowering of key in professions, and a scrupulous avoidance of parade. A careless good-breeding, an agreeable worldliness were its characteristics. It was a very English end to strive for, and by no means a common one, for urbanity of mind is rarely the aim of youth. It implied, perhaps, an undue critical sense, and a failure in certain generous foibles. Some of us were men of the world too young; humour and balance were prized too highly; a touch of Gothic extravagance was needed to correct our over-mellow Hellenism. Such a circle does not breed Quixotes or reformers, and of few of us could it be said in the phrase of Villiers de l'Isle Adam, *il gardait au cœur les richesses stériles d'un grand nombre de rois oubliés.* I have known men like Hugh Dawnay and Francis Grenfell who would have ridden on a lost cause over the edge of the world. But our Oxford group was not of that kind; each of us would have rejoiced to ride over the world's edge, but it would have been not for a cause but for the fun of the riding.

Yet I would not have it thought that we were worldly-wise. We reserved our chief detestation for Worldly Wisemen. To think of a career and to be prudent in laying its foundations was in our eyes the unpardonable sin—a revolt no doubt against the Jowett tradition. It was well enough to be successful if success could be achieved unostentatiously and carried lightly, but there must be no appearance of seeking it. Again, while affectionate and rather gentle with each other, we wore a swashbuckling manner to the outer world. It was our business to be regardless of consequences, to be always looking for preposterous adventures and planning crazy feats, and to be most ready for a brush with constituted authority. All this, of course, was the ordinary high spirits of young men delighting in health and strength, which happily belong to the Oxford of every generation. The peculiar features of our circle were that this physical exuberance was found among men of real intellectual power, and that it implied no corresponding *abandon* in their intellectual life. In the world of action we were ripe for any venture; in the things of the mind we were critical and decorous, chary of enthusiasm—*revenants* from the Augustan age.

One habit we had which was derived from the earlier generation of Hubert Howard and Basil Blackwood, and which bore the mysterious name of "booms." In eighteenth-century Oxford they would have been called "schemes." It was a "boom" to canoe an immense distance on a short winter day, or to walk to the very limits of one's strength. The walk to London was a prosaic affair—I did it on a hot day on the eve of the Diamond Jubilee; more spectacular was the walk from Cambridge within twenty-four hours, a distance of over eighty miles, which was duly performed by some of us. One type of "boom" I remember vividly. Half a dozen of us on horseback would meet one morning at an appointed place, and each would ride a point-to-point course marked out on the map. We drew lots for our courses, which might lead us into back gardens and trackless woods, and compel us to swim rivers or canals, and sometimes brought us to the doors of the police court. In the evening we dined together and told our adventures. . . .

There was the Horace Club which we founded and which met in summer in the President's garden at Magdalen, when we supped on nuts and olives and fruits, drank what we made believe was Falernian, and read our poetical compositions. The club had outside members like Maurice Baring, and its published collection of verses is now, I believe, a collector's piece. . . .

And there were odder fraternities, like the White Rose Club, when we drank to the King over the Water without a notion of what we meant. I remember my surprise in 1915 in Flanders when I found that Prince Rupprecht of Bavaria, the commander opposite us, was the gentleman whom we had been wont to salute by telegram on his birthday as Prince Robert of Wales!

III

Father Knox, in the dedication which he never published to his *Spiritual Aeneid*, has told of the bright company which was scattered by the War. I hesitate to make such a survey for my own time, since it is all so long ago, and to-day most of the names would have little meaning. But one or two I may select from that old world where "the sun rose over Magdalen and set over Worcester."

Cuthbert Medd, who died in 1902 just as he was about to join me in South Africa, had in some ways the most powerful mind I have ever known in a young man, and Lord Rosebery was of my opinion. He was a Northumbrian and therefore in some sense a fellow-Borderer, and together we tramped over most of Scotland. Aubrey Herbert, gentle, whimsical, utterly courageous, lived to be a Member of Parliament and to have a fantastic record in various terrains of the War. He was taken prisoner in the retreat from Mons, when, armed with an alpenstock, he must have presented a figure like Don Quixote's; and, knowing Turkish, during a truce at Gallipoli he is said to have taken command of a Turkish unit and escorted it back to its trenches. To go tandem-driving with him at Oxford required fortitude, for he was very blind; to mountaineer with him deserved a Victoria Cross, for he was both blind and desperate. . . . Then there was always with us the stalwart figure of Hilaire Belloc, who preached exotic doctrines in his great gusty voice—a man full of gnarled wisdom and also of a youthfulness younger than ours—who warmed the air about him and whose kindliness and charity were of the early Christian pattern. He founded a so-called Republican Club, and it became necessary to correct its extravagance by starting a rival institution, the S.G.D.F.P., or the Society for Grinding Down the Faces of the Poor! Let me record my conviction that much of his output in letters is as likely to live as any work of our time; no man has attained more perfectly to the "piety of speech" of the seventeenth-century lyrists; no man has written purer and nobler prose in the great tradition.

Of two friends I must write more fully. The first is Raymond Asquith. There are some men whose brilliance in boyhood and early manhood dazzles their contemporaries and becomes a legend. It is not that they are precocious, for precocity rarely charms, but that for every sphere of life they have the proper complement of gifts, and finish each stage so that it remains behind them like a satisfying work of art. Sometimes the curtain drops suddenly, the daylight goes out of the picture, and the promise of youth dulls into a dreary middle-age of success, or, it may be, of failure and cynicism. But for the chosen few, like Raymond, there is no disillusionment. They march on into life with a boyish grace, and their high noon keeps all the freshness of the morning. Certainly to his cradle the good fairies brought every dower. They gave him great beauty of person; the gift of winning speech; a mind that mastered readily whatever it cared to master; poetry and the love of all beautiful things; a magic to

J.B., 1900

draw friends to him; a heart as tender as it was brave. One gift only was withheld from him—length of years.

The figure of Raymond in those days stands very clear in my memory, for he had always the complete detachment from the atmosphere which we call distinction. He wore generally an old shooting-coat of light grey tweed and grey flannel trousers; the laxest sumptuary law would have made havoc of his comfort. He had rather deep-set grey eyes, and his lips were parted as if at the beginning of a smile. He had a fine straight figure, and bore himself with a kind of easy stateliness. His manner was curiously self-possessed and urbane, but there was always in it something of a pleasant aloofness, as of one who was happy in society but did not give to it more than a fraction of himself.

He had come up from Winchester with a great reputation, and also, I think, a little tired. His scholarship was almost too ripe for his years, and he had already conquered so many worlds that he was little troubled with ordinary ambition. As the son of an eminent statesman he had seen much of distinguished people who to most of us were only awful names, so that he seemed all his time at Oxford to have one foot in the greater world. Not that he gave this impression by anything that he said or did; it was rather by his whole-hearted delight in Oxford and his lack of reverence for the standards that ruled outside it. He had the air of having seen enough of the outer world to judge it with detachment.

Even in those early years his great powers of mind were patent to all. I have never met anyone so endowed with diverse talents. In sheer intellectual strength he may have had his equals, and there were limits to his imaginative sympathies; but for manifold and multi-form gifts I have not known his like. He was a fine classical scholar, at once learned and precise; he was widely read in English literature; he wrote good poetry, Greek, Latin and English; he had the most delicate and luminous critical sense; he had an uncanny gift of exact phrase, whether in denunciation or in praise. His ordinary conversation was chiefly remarkable for its fantastic humour, but when he chose he was a master of manly good sense. As a letter-writer he was easily the best of us, but his epistles were dangerous things to leave lying about, for he had a most unbridled pen. He could not write a sentence without making it characteristic and imparting into it some delicate ribaldry.

As a speaker I never heard him in the political clubs; but in the Union he was easily the most finished debater of our time. It was a hey-day of Union oratory, for Hilaire Belloc, F. E. Smith and John Simon were our immediate predecessors and still took part in debates. He did not seem to seek to convince; smoothly, almost disdainfully, in his beautiful voice flowed his fastidious satire. There were no signs of careful preparation, and yet, had his speeches been printed verbatim, each sentence would have stood out as finely cut as in an essay of Stevenson's.

His politics were hereditary, not, I think, the result of any personal enthusiasm. He had a thoroughly conservative temperament, and loathed the worn counters of party warfare. Not greatly respecting many people, he had a profound respect for his father, and much resembled him, both in his style of speaking and in the quality of his mind. He would not condescend to cheap-jack argument, and he distrusted emotion in public life. He was like his father, too, in many traits of character—his loyalty, his hatred of intrigue, his contempt for advertisement, and his great courage. I do not think that at that time he had any strong political opinions (though many prejudices about political figures) except on the question of the Church. He detested clericalism, and like the Irishman at Donnybrook when he found its head anywhere he smote it. I only once saw him in the Union roused to a real show of feeling. The matter in debate was whether some work attacking the Oxford Movement should be cast out of the library. The book was admittedly trash, but those who opposed its rejection did so on the ground that the reason alleged was not its literary badness but its opinions, and that such censorship over thought was intolerable. I can remember Raymond speaking with a white face and an unwonted passion in his voice. He asked where such censorship would stop. There were books on the shelves, he said, by Roman writers which poured venom upon the greatest man that ever lived. Were these books to be expelled? "I assure you," he told the angry ranks of Keble and St. John's, "that the fair fame of Caesar is as dear to me as that of any dead priest can be to you."

I do not think he could ever have been called popular. He was immensely admired, but he did not lay himself out to acquire popularity, and in the ordinary man he inspired awe rather than liking. His courtesy was without warmth, he was apt to be intolerant of mediocrity, and he had no desire for facile acquaintanceships. Also—let it be admitted—there were times when he was almost inhuman. He would destroy some piece of honest sentiment with a jest, and he had no respect for the sacred places of dull men. There was always a touch of scorn in him for obvious emotion, obvious creeds, and all the accumulated lumber of prosaic humanity. That was a defect of his great qualities. He kept himself for his friends and refused to bother about

the world. But to such as were admitted to his friendship he would deny nothing. I have never known a
friend more considerate, and tender, and painstaking,
and unfalteringly loyal. It was the relation of all others
in life for which he had been born with a peculiar
genius.

I have said that he came up to Oxford with little
ambition, and he went down with less. He stood aloof
from worldly success, not from any transcendental
philosophy, but simply because the rewards of common
ambition seemed to him too trivial for a man's care.
He loved the things of the mind—good books, good
talk—for their own sake; he loved, above all, youth
and the company of his friends. To such a man it was
hard to leave Oxford, for it meant a break with youth
and the haunts of youth, and he had no zest for new
and commoner worlds. In looking over old letters
from him I find a constant lament that that chapter
must close.

No two friends were ever more unlike than he and
I. He chaffed me unmercifully about my Calvinism,
my love of rough moors in wild weather, my growing
preference for what he called the Gothic over the Greek
in life, my crude passion for romance. "You scoff at
the cult of Beauty," he once wrote to me, "in your
coarse Scotch way. I grind my teeth when I hear people
praise the machinery of Scotch education. Depend
upon it, my poor dear soul-starved pedlar, the English
public-school system is the only one which fits a man
for life and ruins him for eternity. And commendation
cannot go further than that, as you know well if you
had the honesty to acknowledge it."

There was one consequence of this lack of ambition
which the world may well regret. Except in his letters,
he scarcely used his great gift for literature. A few

poems are all that remain. One of these, an *Ode in Praise of Young Girls,* written shortly before the War, is to my mind the finest satirical poem of our day. He wrote many verses—he used to scatter them about his letters—but he rarely finished them. He and I once prepared a complete *Spectator,* a parody of that admirable journal. The three middle articles, I remember, were on *God, Bridge,* and *Harvest Bugs.* Raymond wrote the poem, a Tennysonian elegy, supposed to have been written by a well-known Oxford dignitary, *On a Viscount who died on the Morrow of a Bump Supper.*

When I went to South Africa in 1901 Raymond had just taken a first in "Greats," and was reading law for an All Souls' Fellowship. We maintained a regular correspondence, and the sight of his bold, beautiful handwriting was the pleasantest part of mail days in Johannesburg. He wrote pages of delightful political gossip, and unveracious accounts of the doings of our friends, and—very rarely—news of himself. Here are two extracts :

"Eighteenth-century methods worked well enough while we had a talented aristocracy, but we can't afford nowadays to limit our choice of Ministers to a few stuffy families, with ugly faces, bad manners, and a belief in the Nicene Creed. The day of the clever cad is at hand. I always felt it would come to this if we once let ourselves in for an Empire. If only Englishmen had known their Aeschylus a little better they wouldn't have bustled about the world appropriating things. A gentleman may make a large fortune, but only a cad can look after it. It would have been so much pleasanter to live in a small community who knew Greek and played games and

washed themselves. . . . I hear you think I oughtn't
to be up at Oxford a fifth year. You are probably
right, but, honestly, I haven't the ambition of a louse
and I don't see why I should pretend to it. There are
a few things and people at Oxford that I intend to
keep close to as long as I decently can, and I don't
care a damn about the rest. If one fell in love with
a woman or believed in the Newcastle Programme or
had no dress clothes it might be different. But the
world as I see it just now is a little barren of
motives. . . . I suppose I may have what is called a
spiritual awakening any day, and then I shall start to
lie and make money with the best of them. . . . The
law is a lean casuistical business and fills me with
disgust."

.   .   .   .   .

"The bleak futility of our public men on both
sides is a thing one never hoped to see outside the
neo-Celtic school of poetry. The general effect is
that of a flock of sheep playing blind man's buff in
the distance on a foggy day. Rosebery continues to
prance upon the moonbeam of efficiency and makes
speeches at every street corner; but he might just as
well call it the Absolute at once for all the meaning
it has to him or anyone else. No one has the least
idea what he wants to 'effect,' and beyond a mild
bias in favour of good government and himself as
Premier, nothing can be gleaned from his speeches. . . .
He has started a thing called the Liberal League,
which appears at present to consist of three persons—
himself, my father, and Grey—backed by a squad of
titled ladies, who believe that the snobbery of the
lower classes is greater than their greed. I trust that
may be so ; they say there is a good spot in everyone
if one knows where to find it. . . . As to law, I am

in the position of a Danaid incessantly pouring into the leaky sieve of my mind the damnable details of Praetorian Edicts and the Custom of Gavelkind. If they didn't run out at once I think I should be mad by now. God knew what He was about when He provided me with a bad memory, and I am not the one to withhold praise where it is due."

In 1902 I tried to induce Raymond to come and visit us in South Africa. Lord Milner also did his best, but nothing would make him leave England. "What have you to offer me?" he wrote. "Certainly not those who are clad in soft raiment (we saw them at the Coronation!), nor do I imagine that any voice cries in your desert in a way which tends to edification." He was now a Fellow of All Souls, and enjoying himself, as appeared from the pictures of delights which he drew to lure me home, and his hilarity about politics. "No two people seem to disagree about anything—except Rosebery and C. B.; and neither of them has anything you could call an opinion, except about each other; in which opinion, of course, they are both right." Then suddenly he was heard of in Egypt, and we found ourselves in the same continent. He thought meanly of the Nile, the monuments, the scenery ("about as picturesque as a spittoon"), everything except the climate. "The sunsets are wonderful, passing from palest green through every shade of yellow to deepest purple with a rapidity and precision which is more like Beerbohm Tree than the Almighty." He rejoiced to see a land where, he said, any kind of self-government was manifestly out of the question. At that time he was not enamoured of what he called "middle-Victorian shibboleths."

When I came back from South Africa at the end of

1903 I found that Raymond had cut loose from Oxford, and was already in London society the same distinguished and slightly detached figure which he had been at the University. He was reading for the Bar, and had plenty of leisure to enjoy life and see his friends. At that time I lived in the Temple with Harold Baker, and the three of us used to go for country walks of a Sunday and have periodical dinners at which we drank claret on the old scale. He had become even handsomer than before, and in London clothes he had a slightly ascetic look. Oxford was behind him, and he had set himself to make the best of his new life. He looked with a more kindly eye upon politics, for the Tariff Reform controversy had left him a strong Free Trader, and he began to speak a little for his party. But till he was settled in practice at the Bar he took neither law nor politics too seriously. He was not a whit more ambitious than at Oxford, and had still about him the suggestion of some urbane and debonair scholar-gipsy, who belonged to a different world from the rest of us. It was this air of aloofness which gave him his peculiar attraction to those who met him for the first time, and acquaintance did not stale that charm. There was in him all the fascination of the unexpected and unpredictable. His wit flowed as easily as a brook, and into curious eddies. He had a great talent for acute but surprising descriptions of people, especially those whom he did not love. His humour was oftenest the Aristophanic σκῶμμα παρὰ προσδοκίαν. I remember one instance. Someone, in one of the round games which were then popular, propounded a stupid riddle: "What is that which God never sees, kings rarely see, and we see every day?" The answer is "An equal." Raymond's answer was "A joke." In the autumn of 1903 John Morley's *Life of Gladstone* in three bulky volumes descended upon the world. I once heard Raymond asked the inevitable question—had he read them. "Often," he replied brightly.

Then he fell in love and married—in July 1907, the same month as my own wedding. He and I gave our final bachelor dinner together at the Savoy. Marriage did not, I think, wake his ambition, as he once prophesied it might, but it regularised his talents : canalised, as it were, a stream which had hitherto flowed at random. He settled down seriously to work at the Bar, with Parliament somewhere in the future. He succeeded, of course, up to a point. His father was now Prime Minister, and he was naturally briefed in important cases as a junior for or against the Crown. Of course, too, he did his work well, for he was incapable of doing anything badly. But I question if he would ever have made one of the resounding successes of advocacy. For one thing he did not care enough about it ; for another, he scorned the worldly wisdom which makes smooth the steps in a career. He had no gift of deference towards eminent solicitors or of reverence towards heavy-witted judges. He would probably have passed, if he had lived, through the stage of Treasury junior to a seat on the Bench, where his perfect lucidity of mind and precision of phrase would have made him an admirable judge—a second Bowen, perhaps, without Bowen's super-subtlety. But I do not think he would ever have won that commanding position at the English Bar which was due to his talents.

Politics were a different matter. Before the War he was adopted as Liberal candidate for Derby, and made a profound impression by his platform speeches. He had every advantage in the business—voice, language, manner, orderly thought, perfect nerve. The very fact that he sat loose to party creeds would have strengthened

B

his hands at a time when creeds were in transition. For, though he might scoff at dogmas, he had a great reverence for the problems behind them; and to these problems he brought a fresh mind and a sincere good will. His colleague at Derby, Mr. J. H. Thomas, believed, I know, most heartily in his future, and he won golden opinions among the Labour men with whom he came into contact. It was natural, for he was the spending type in life, the true aristocrat who prefers to give rather than to take, and makes no fetish of a narrow prudence. Democracy and aristocracy can co-exist, for oligarchy is their common enemy. I am very certain, too, that in Parliament he would have won instant fame. His manner of speaking was as perfectly fitted for the House of Commons as that of his father. I can imagine in some hour of high controversy Raymond's pale grace kindling like a fire.

.   .   .   .   .

The War did not produce a new Raymond; it only brought the real man to light, as the removal of Byzantine ornament may reveal the grave handiwork of a Pheidias. He disliked emotion, not because he felt lightly but because he felt deeply. He most sincerely loved his country, but he loved her too much to identify her with the pasteboard goddess of the music-halls and the hustings. War meant to him the shattering of every taste and interest, but he did not hesitate. It was no sudden sentimental fervour that swept him into the army, but the essential nature of one who had always been shy of rhetorical professions, but was very clear about the real thing. Austerely self-respecting, he had been used to hide his devotions under a mask of indifference, and would never reveal them except in deeds. Raymond, being of the spending type, when he gave did not count the cost, and of the many who did likewise few had so much to give.

He began his training in the Queen's Westminsters, from which after a few months he was transferred to the Grenadier Guards. There he was perfectly happy. He was among young men again—the same kind of light-hearted and high-spirited companionship in which he had delighted at Oxford. In London I think the young Guardsman had held him in some awe, and to his friends it seemed not the least surprising result of the War that it should have made Raymond a second-lieutenant in the Grenadiers. He himself used to say that it was an odd trick of Providence to send a "middle-aged and middle-class" man into the Guards. Yet he had never found a circle where he was so much at home, and his popularity was immediate and complete. He was an excellent battalion officer, and so much in love with his new life that he sometimes spoke of going on with the army as his profession. That, I think, he would not have done, for the army in peace time would have bored him; but in the mingled bondage and freedom of active service he was in his proper element.

For a few months he was a member of the Intelligence Staff at General Headquarters. It was just before I joined that section, and when I went there the memory of him was fresh among his colleagues. But he did not like it. He missed the close comradeship of his battalion, and he felt that it was too cushioned a job for an active man in time of war. So he went back to the Guards before the Somme battle began.

It is my grief that I never saw him during these months, and I was temporarily back in England on the day when he fell. In the great movement of 15th September the Guards Division advanced from Ginchy on Lesboeufs. Their front of attack was too narrow, their objectives were too far distant, and from the start their flanks were enfiladed. It was not till the second advance on the 25th that Lesboeufs was won. But on the 15th that fatal fire from the corner of Ginchy village brought death to many in the gallant Division, and among them was Raymond Asquith. In his letters he had often lamented the loss of others, but his friends knew that he had neither fear nor care for himself.

Our roll of honour is long, but it holds no nobler figure. He will stand to those of us who are left as an incarnation of the spirit of the land he loved. "Eld shall not make a mock of that dear head." He loved his youth, and his youth has become eternal. Debonair and brilliant and brave, he is now part of that immortal England which knows not age or weariness or defeat.

The other is Auberon Thomas Herbert, commonly known as Bron. I have met a fair number of gipsies in my life, often in most unfitting professions. Sometimes fate was kind to them and gave them scope for vagrancy; pencilled scrawls with odd outlandish post-marks were all we heard of them; and once in a blue moon they would turn up with brown faces and far-regarding eyes to tantalise us homekeepers with visions of the unattainable. Oftener their gipsyhood was repressed, and only the old fret in spring told where their thoughts lay. But I have never known a more whole-hearted, hard-bitten nomad than Bron. Nomad, indeed, is not the word, for he did not crave travel and change; a Hampshire meadow gave him all that he wanted. But he was a gipsy to the core of his being, a creature of the wayside camp, wood-smoke and the smell of earth. Some very ancient forbear was reborn in him; as in his cousin Julian Grenfell, who wrote of himself as one "who every year has an increasing desire to live in a blanket under a bush, and will soon get bored with the bush and the blanket."

At Oxford he was the link of his Balliol set with the world of sport, for his perfect physique made him a great athlete, and he rowed for his last two years in the University boat. But Bron had uncommonly little of the ordinary sportsman about him, being, as I have said, a gipsy. Far better than the ritual of games he loved his own private adventures in by-ways of the country-side. He had an astonishing knowledge of birds and beasts and all wild things. Most of his friends were fine scholars, but he did not essay the thorny path of academic honours, having better things to think about. We were all lovers of poetry and contemners of music. Bron loved poetry, but he had also a passion for music. I once induced him to make a speech in the Union; but after an excellent beginning he grew bored and stopped to yawn in the middle of a sentence. For politics he cared not at all. He was most pleasant to look at, and most gentle and courteous in manner, but his petulant mouth and great wondering eyes gave him a changeling air, as of one a little puzzled by life. He was like some wild thing tamed and habituated to a garden, but still remembering "the bright speed it had in its high mountain cradle."

On the outbreak of war in 1899 he was off at once to South Africa, taking the first chance he got, which was that of *Times* correspondent. There he was abundantly happy. He was not specially interested in military affairs, but he loved the spacious land and the adventurous life. His letters to me at the time were one long chant of praise. "When I think of the dull things I was doing last year," he wrote, "I am simply staggered at the luck that has brought me here." Presently, advancing too far forward in an action (for those were

the days when the trade of war correspondent was
still an adventure), he got a rifle bullet in his foot. The
wound was badly mismanaged, and when he came back
to England his leg had to be amputated below the knee.

To a man of his tastes such a loss might well have
been crippling. To Bron it simply did not matter at
all. He behaved as if nothing had happened, and went
on with the life he loved. It cannot have been an easy
job, but he never showed the strain of it. He was just
as fine a sportsman as before, and his high spirits were,
if anything, more infectious. During the later stages of
his convalescence I used to stay with him at his uncle's
house of Panshanger, and catch trout with the dry-fly
in the Mimram. He was a wonderful fisherman, but
that gentle art was only one of his accomplishments.
Soon he was scampering about in the New Forest, and
hunting, and playing tennis, and stalking on some of
the roughest hills in Scotland. He must have had bad
hours, but he held his head high to the world and his
friends. He was not going to be depressed even for a
moment by a small thing like the loss of a leg.

His uncle, the last Lord Cowper, died in the summer
of 1905, and Bron became Lord Lucas and the owner
of several great houses. He got them off his hands as
fast as he could, for the only place he really cared for
was his home at Picket Post in the New Forest. A
lesser man might have been oppressed by his possessions,
but Bron was too unworldly to feel any oppression.
They mattered nothing in his scheme of life. For he
was still the gipsy, careless of a sedentary world, and
with all the belongings he needed in his wallet.

Then there befell him the most fantastic fate. In
1906 a Liberal Government came into power, and Bron,
as one of the few Liberal peers, was marked down for
preferment. He became Mr. Haldane's private secretary

at the War Office. In 1908 he was Under-Secretary for War, and rebutting in the House of Lords Lord Roberts' plea for national service. He was not a good speaker, but his boyish charm and gallantry pleased people, and even his opponents wished him well. In 1911 he was for a short time Under-Secretary for the Colonies. That same year he went as Parliamentary Secretary to the Board of Agriculture, where he was a real success, for he was a true countryman, knowing at first hand what most politicians are only told. In 1914 he entered the Cabinet as President of the Board of Agriculture, and held the office till the formation of the Coalition in May 1915, when he most thankfully laid it down.

Was there ever an odder destiny for a gipsy than to be a Cabinet Minister in spite of himself at thirty-eight? No man could have wanted it less. He did his work well—the agricultural part extraordinarily well—but his heart was never in it. He had no ambition, and the long round of conferences, deputations, unmeaning speeches, idle debates, was wholly distasteful. He disliked London, shunned ordinary society, and was happy only in the company of his friends. At a ball, when by any rare chance he attended one, he had the air of a hunted stag. To see him at a party was to get some idea of how Marius looked among the ruins of Carthage. But at Picket or in Scotland, shooting, hunting, fishing, or bird-watching, he was the old Bron again, with the old zest and simplicity. When I met him in London in those days I used to think that he looked more puzzled than ever. He seemed to find the world rather tarnished and dusty, and to be longing for a clearer air.

When he left the Cabinet in 1915 he found what he had been seeking. Though he was many years over the age, he managed to join the Royal Flying Corps and trained for his pilot's certificate. Here his wonderful

eye and nerve stood him in good stead, and presently
he became a most competent pilot. He was sent out
to Egypt, whence stories came back to us of strange
adventures—crashing in the desert many miles from
help, and such like. He was back in England in the
spring of 1916, engaged in instructing recruits, and
more than once came very near death. But Bron had
risked his neck all his days, and his friends hoped that
his standing luck might carry him through.

In May of that year to my surprise I found him at
a party—almost the last given by Count Benckendorff
at the Russian Embassy. He asked me if I thought that
the old political game would ever start again. "If it
does," he said, "it will start without me." He was a
picture of weatherbeaten health, but I noticed that his
eyes were different. They had become more deeply
set, as happens to airmen, and also they had lost their
puzzled look. He had found something for which he
had long been seeking. Up in the clouds he had come
to his own and discovered the secret of life. He never
spoke of it, for he was as shy and elusive in these things
as a young girl, but it could be read in his eyes.

It had always been his desire to serve on the Western
Front, and he went there half-way through the battle
of the Somme. I am glad to think that I saw something
of him during his last weeks on earth. His camp was
beside the road from Amiens to Doullens: his friend
Maurice Baring was at the R.F.C. Headquarters, and
I was at General Headquarters at Beauquesne; so we
were all three only a few miles from each other. The
concluding days of October and the first week of
November were full of strong gales from the south-
west, which gravely hampered our flying, for our
machines drifted too far over the enemy lines, and had
to fight their way back slowly against a head wind. It

was an eery season on the bleak Picardy downs, scourged and winnowed by blasts, with the noise of the guns from the front line coming fitfully in the pauses like the swell of breakers on a coast. One evening, I remember, I rode over to have tea with Bron, when the west was crimson with sunset and above me huge clouds were scudding before the gale. They were for the most part ragged and tawny, like wild horses, but before them went a white horse, the leader of the unearthly cavalry. It seemed to me that I was looking at a ride of Valkyries, the Shield Maids of Odin hasting eastward to the battle front to choose the dead for Valhalla.

Two days later Maurice came to me and told me that Bron was missing. The chances were about equal that he was a prisoner, and for some time we dared to hope. Then, early in December, we heard that he was dead. When our troops advanced to victory in the autumn of 1918 they found his grave.

There could be no sorrow in such a death, though for his friends an undying regret. The homely English countryside, the return of spring, the sports which he loved are the emptier for his absence. Maurice Baring has written of this in his beautiful elegy.

> "So when the Spring of the world shall shrive our stain
> After the winter of war,
> When the poor world awakes to peace once more,
> After such night of ravage and of rain,
> You shall not come again.
> You shall not come to taste the old Spring weather,
> To gallop through the soft untrampled heather,
> To bathe and bake your body on the grass.
> We shall be there. Alas!
> But not with you. When Spring shall wake the earth,
> And quicken the scarred fields to the new birth,
> Our grief shall grow. For what can Spring renew
> More fiercely for us than the need of you?"

But Bron had been gathered into these things, for he belonged to them. He was not quite of this world; or, rather, he was of an earlier, fairer world that our civilisation has overlaid. He lived close to the kindly earth, and then he discovered the kindlier air, and that pure exultant joy of living which he had always sought. "In the hot fit of life"—the words are Stevenson's— "a-tiptoe on the highest point of being, he passes at a bound on to the other side. The noise of the mallet and chisel is scarcely quenched, the trumpets are hardly done blowing, when, trailing with him clouds of glory, the happy-starred, full-blooded spirit shoots into the spiritual land." But he had never been very far from it. Death to him was less a setting forth than a returning.

IV

On foot, on a bicycle, or on horseback I explored Oxfordshire far afield, from the Chilterns in the east to the Cotswolds, from the Berkshire downs to Edge Hill field, and many a desperate rush I had to get back to college before midnight. A man is only truly intimate with the countryside which he has known as a child, for then he lived very near the ground, and knew the smell of the soil and the small humble plants and the things that live at the roots of the grasses. He explored it on all-fours, whereas he strides or gallops over later landscapes. I have a host of memories of places which have strongly captured my fancy, and sometimes my affection—in Europe, in the Virginian and New England hills, above all in South Africa and in Canada. But I have never "taken sasine" of them as I did of the Tweedside glens and in a lesser degree of the Oxfordshire valleys. For with the first I had the intimacy of childhood, and with the second of youth.

No one can understand Oxford unless he knows the Oxford countryside. Half her beauty lies in her setting. Cambridge, which has many special lovelinesses, is a city of the plains, and over what she calls her hills one is apt to walk without noticing them. But Oxford has a cincture of green uplands and a multitude of little valleys. It is only from her adjacent heights that her charms can be comprised into one picture and the true background found to her towers. Her history, too, or much of it, was moulded by her environs. Oxfordshire was a famous place when there were no human dwellings on the spit of gravel between the Cherwell and the Isis. The Romans built their villas on these uplands long before the Double Ford was discovered. The city, as it developed, drew much from its neighbourhood and gave back much in return, and the records of the two are closely interwoven.

A view from one of Oxford's hills shows at a glance how her importance came about. The site at the Double Ford was an inspiration, for it was the meeting-place of the great routes of southern England. If we take our stand, say, on the Elsfield ridge, we can reconstruct the past. Here from Saxon times was a clearing, but for the Middle Ages we must see the rest of the landscape as a great mat of forest with the only bare patches the tops of the Berkshire downs and the far Cotswold, and with a much bigger Isis and Cherwell making bands of light among the narrow meadows.

The key is the Isis itself, for from very early days the valley of the Thames was a main route for traffic between London and the west. The slow-flowing river, with weirs from the start, and with locks after Henry VIII, was the cheapest and easiest way for merchandise to the towns and abbeys of the valley, and, with a short portage, to the Severn and Wales. Up it

London wares travelled in slow barges, and down it came the wool and stone of Cotswold, the produce of the farms, and the craftsmen's work from the religious houses. At Oxford this trunk route was cut by a road from south to north, from Southampton and the ports to the Midlands. Oxford, walled and castled, with the mighty house of Oseney at her western gates, would have been a place of importance though she had never known a collegiate foundation, for apart from her merchants was she not the chosen resort of royalty, the centre of a famous monastic life, and a place of strategic value in any inland war?

With the coming of the university the converging roads acquired a new meaning and discovered a new type of traveller. Turbulent, disputatious lads journeyed along them from all quarters to cluster round the lamp of learning. From our viewpoint on the hill we can see how they came. Over the Berkshire ridges they flocked from the southern shires, and some of them from beyond the Channel. From London they came by what was one of the oldest highroads in the land, that from the capital to Worcester (the road by which Shakespeare must have often travelled), leaving it at Wheatley for the final stage over Shotover. From the west they had the road through Cotswold, by which the pack-trains of the wool-staplers travelled, descending upon Oxford either by Woodstock or by Eynsham and the Botley causeway. From the north they also followed the skirts of Cotswold, for the valleys were too marshy. To all such pilgrims the first sight of Oxford must have come with a shock of delighted surprise; it is wonderful enough to see your goal on a far hill-top and travel with it in sight for hours or days, but it is more wonderful to come on it suddenly when you have wearily topped the last ridge. In those days Oxford was close and compact, with no sprawling faubourgs, for her ancient stones rose sharply from green meadows—such a view can still be got to-day from the Elsfield hill. The first glimpse of the spire of St. Mary's and the tall tower of Oseney—the third greatest in the land—as seen from Shotover or Boar's Hill or over the Campsfield moor, must to many a foot-sore pilgrim have come like the vision of John in Patmos.

From this hill we can reconstruct another great moment in history, when Oxford and her countryside were linked in one dream—the Civil War and the Siege. Charles held west England, his opponents London and the east, and the ridge on which we stand, running north to the Brill upland and lying half-way between Cotswold and the Chilterns, was a strategic point in the campaign, for it must be occupied before the city could be surrounded. So for two years there was a great marching and counter-marching here. Boarstall castle towards Brill was defended for the King. Islip bridge and the fords of Cherwell were vital points; Parliament had its artillery park in the Elsfield clearing, and all the adjacent towns were drawn into the orbit of war. The last act was played at the foot of this hill, in the manor house of Marston, when Fairfax and Rupert agreed the terms of Oxford's surrender.

So much for the history of the city. It is a long tale half-forgotten. But the memory of it makes the Oxford country as haunted a place as any in our land. From Roman centurion to Norman baron, from churchman to cavalier, much of the drama of England was staged here. These things have passed, but there remain the rural loveliness and the

> "bright and intricate device
> Of days and seasons."

Time has brought its wrongs. Boar's Hill and Cumnor, which I remember as downs and cornfields, are now dotted with villas; Cowley is an industrial town, and an eruption of red brick has spread far along the Woodstock, Banbury and Iffley roads. But much of Oxfordshire is as unspoilt as in the Middle Ages, and some of it is lonelier to-day than then.

The hills remain, though two of them are a little marred. Wytham is still a sanctuary, and the tableland of Shotover has been preserved. The Elsfield ridge is unspoilt. Further afield there is nothing to complain of. The hill-top of Brill, from which the eye may cover half the southern midlands, is less urban to-day than at the beginning of last century, when it threatened to become a spa and a rival of Bath. The Ilsley downs are still thymy sheep-walks. The hillocks of the Bicester country have not been touched by man. The long slopes of Cotswold, which rise slowly from Woodstock and Ditchley and Witney to end in the scarp above the Severn, are still a pastoral upland, hiding in their nooks the loveliest of English villages. Oxford remains a lowland city, but with gates opening on all sides into the hills.

The forests have for the most part given place to tillage and pasture, though the self-sown saplings in the meadows are a reminder of the old days of oak and ash and thorn. Stowood is now only a patch, but the newer woods, which are called the Quarters, and which stretch along the southern side of Otmoor, enable us to picture how Oxfordshire must have looked in earlier times. The one great forest remnant is Wychwood, between the Evenlode and the Windrush, several thousand acres of unspoilt coppice and glade. But though the forests have mostly gone, much of Oxford-shire remains forest country. There are still forest

crafts among the people and much of the wild life is
the same. Wherever it is permitted, bracken resumes
its old dominion. Were the hand of man withdrawn
the shire would soon go back to primeval woodland.

The key to the Oxford topography is the valleys,
for they are the natural divisions. First there is the
"stripling Thames," which above Godstow becomes a
different stream from the sophisticated lower river. It
twines through its meadows like a brook in a missal,
always within sight of uplands. If a man wants to
recover the Middle Ages let him go there on a summer
day when the grass is high, and he will see and hear
nothing which was not there five hundred years ago
when the monks of Eynsham caught their Friday's
trout. Of the tributaries two are wholly lowland, the
little Thame which threads the vale of Aylesbury, and
the Cherwell which rises far up in the Midlands. But
the latter has an affluent which traverses one of the
wildest patches of south England, for the Ray, which
enters it at Islip, flows through the great marsh of
Otmoor. Otmoor is divided by rough hedges, but it
is undrained, and perhaps undrainable. In a wet winter
it is one vast lagoon; in summer it is a waste of lush
grass, and its few mud tracks are pitted and ribbed like
the *seracs* of a glacier. Once it was the preserve of the
Seven Towns of Otmoor which pastured their geese
on it, and there were riots early in last century when it
was enclosed. Now the Royal Air Force has a bombing-
station there, and by day it is apt to be a noisy place,
but at night and in wild weather it recovers its loneliness.
To ride or walk there in an autumn twilight is to find
oneself in a place as remote from man as Barra or
Knoydart.

But it is the little valleys which are the glory of the
Oxford countryside—those of Coln and Leach, Wind-

rush and Evenlode. The first two are in Gloucestershire, but the latter two are Oxford's avenues into Cotswold. There we have a landscape which is still unravished. The names of the streams are in themselves a melody, and the valleys wind into the recesses of the hills so softly that they combine upland austerity with lowland graces. What *The Scholar Gipsy* and *Thyrsis* have done for Oxford's immediate environs Mr. Belloc's *Dedicatory Ode* does for those magical little streams.

> "A lovely river, all alone,
>   She lingers in the hills and holds
> A hundred little towns of stone,
>   Forgotten in the western wolds."

And there are slender affluents of both—the Dickler, the Glyme, and the Dorn—which a man may trace happily to their source during a long summer's day.

To those bred in the Scottish Borders the Oxford landscape has always had a peculiar charm. It laid its spell on Walter Scott, as *Kenilworth* and *Woodstock* witness, and on Andrew Lang, and ever since my undergraduate days I have felt it. The reason, I think, is that it recalls my native countryside, but with an entrancing difference. It is pastoral, but it has no "pastoral melancholy." It is haunted, but only by idyllic things. The shallows of the Windrush are never the "wan water" of Yarrow. It is a country wholly and exquisitely fitted for the gentler uses of life.

V

Oxford enabled me to discover Scotland. Before I came up I had explored a great part of the Lowlands with the prosaic purpose of catching trout; but apart from my own Borders, the land, though I was steeped in its history, made no special appeal. Scottish litera-

ture, except the ballads and Sir Walter Scott, was
scarcely known to me, and I had read very little of
Robert Burns. But now as a temporary exile I
acquired all the characteristics of the Scot abroad. I
became a fervent admirer of Burns and a lover of
Dunbar and the other poets of the Golden Age. I
cultivated a sentiment for all things Scottish and brought
the Highlands and the Isles into the orbit of my interest.
A quarter of my blood was Highland and in that I
developed a new pride, for it was a time when people
talked of the "Celtic twilight," and Mr. Yeats had just
published his *Wind Among the Reeds*. Oxford was full
of Scotsmen of every type—studious Scots, orgiastic
Scots, rhetorical Scots who talked in the Union,
robustious Scots from the football teams. The result
was a new Caledonian Club. An earlier institution had
been suppressed some years before by the University
authorities after a carnival of special disorder. Some of
us reconstituted it on an austere basis. It was limited to
members with a proven Scots descent on both sides for
at least three generations; an English club in the
University, which adopted the same principle, could
only find two who passed the test conditions! · We
specialised in vintage clarets and dined in a uniform of
green and purple, intended to represent the thistle in
flower. *Semel insanivimus omnes*.

But the real Scotland for me was discovered in my
spring walking tours and my summer holidays. I had
been a miserable headachy little boy, but at the age of
five I had a serious carriage accident, when my skull
was fractured, and I lay for the better part of a year in
bed. I arose a new child, and throughout all my youth
I was as hardy as a seal; indeed, apart from dysentery
and a slight malaria in South Africa, I scarcely had an
ailment until the War. I was lean and tough in body,

F

accustomed to sleep out of doors in any weather, including December frosts, and, though never an athlete, capable of a good deal of physical endurance. Once I walked sixty-three miles on end in the Galloway hills. It was my custom in the long vacations to bury myself in the moorlands, taking up my quarters in a shepherd's cottage. There I rose early, worked for five or six hours, and then went fishing until the summer midnight. I throve on a diet of oatmeal, mutton and strong tea, and, with the habit to which I have already referred of linking philosophy with terrestrial objects, the works of Aristotle are for ever bound up for me with the smell of peat reek and certain stretches of granite and heather.

The chief episodes were the spring walking tours. Each year after much planning I would tramp with a friend or two on a circuit north of Tweed. We covered the Cheviots from Liddesdale to the sea, and footed it over most of Argyll and Lochaber. Those expeditions have given me memories of which time has not dimmed the rapture. There would be wild days among wet or snowy hills, or on moorland roads in the teeth of a hailstorm, and nights in inns before roaring fires, when, replete and content, we talked the rhetoric of youth. And there would be blue days beside western sea-lochs when oyster-catchers piped on the shingle and curlews wailed on the bent, and April evenings when the far mountains were etched in violet against a saffron sky. After those escapades it was always a little hard to adjust oneself to Oxford; the call of a more strenuous world seemed to have broken in on our academic peace.

I was little use at games, but about this time I took to field sports. About fishing I already knew a good deal, and now I discovered the charm of the dry-fly, to which

I was introduced on some college water on the Wind-rush. In the spring tours I began mountaineering, on the Buachaille Etive Mhor, and the Glencoe peaks, and the north-east face of Ben Nevis. I took to shooting also, especially rough shooting, for I never cared much for a battue of pheasants or a grouse drive; my prefer-ence was for some place like the delectable island of Colonsay where in a day it was possible to get a dozen varieties of game. At that time the Mecca of sport for us was the house of Ardwall in Kirkcudbrightshire, the home of Lord Ardwall, the last of the great "characters" on the Scottish Bench and a figure who might have stepped out of a Raeburn canvas. There between the hills and the sea a party of us forgathered each autumn. Those were royal days when we rode and walked and shot all over Galloway as far as the Dungeon of Buchan, and returned in the small hours of the morning to prodigious feasts. Looking back it is hard to see how we escaped with our lives, for we would hunt the hare on horseback with greyhounds among the briars and bogs and boulders of a Galloway moor, and swim our horses over the estuary of the Fleet at high tide. We almost came to believe that our necks were spared for the judicial end which Lord Ardwall always predicted.

VI

It was a secure and comfortable world, that close of Victoria's reign before the disillusion and change of the South African War. Peace brooded over the land and we should not have believed a prophet had he told us that most of our group would fall in battle. We were hardly aware of the problems of the State or its demands upon our services, and the University Volun-teers had a hard time keeping up their strength. It was the day when Mr. Chamberlain was preaching a new gospel of empire, and Lord Milner beginning his difficult course in South Africa, but we were scarcely conscious of their efforts, except to laugh at Raymond Asquith's parodies of Kipling. There were political clubs—like the Conservative Canning and Chatham, and the Liberal Palmerston and Russell; but they were chiefly pretexts for annual dinners, when statesmen came up to speak to audiences which were interested in their persons but apathetic about their policies. I called myself a Tory and belonged to the Canning, but that club at two successive meetings, after drinking Church and King, had by a large majority disestablished the Church and nationalised the land of England; and it had adventurous members who belonged also to the Fabian Society. Raymond Asquith and I at the Union usually spoke on the same side on foreign affairs and always carried our motion. When we troubled our heads about politics we debated questions by the cold light of reason, oblivious of party fervours. There were, of course, busy partisans who pulled wires and spoke at by-elections, but they were not highly regarded. The statesmen who visited us did not greatly impress me, with one exception. I met Sir Wilfrid Laurier at an All Souls luncheon, and began an acquaintance which in later years I highly valued.

After the War I came to live near Oxford and have had the chance ever since of studying the young entries. How shall I compare them with my own generation? Upon them has fallen the shadow of economic disaster, so that Oxford cannot seem an end in itself as it seemed to us, but only a means of finding a niche in the world. Moreover, transport facilities have made the place less of a sanctuary which devised its own life, and more of a London suburb. The modern undergraduates are what

we should have called "banausic," with a strict utili-
tarian outlook. For their virtues : they are more
temperate and frugal than we were, less snobbish about
athletics, more industrious, better sons to their parents,
and, I am inclined to think, better mannered. For their
defects : they lack our disinterested curiosity about the
things of the mind, and in the broad sense they are less
well-educated. Their average man lacks our average
man's general culture. They tend to fall into grooves
and exclusive cliques. The Union, for example, is a
resort only of earnest politicians, chiefly of the left wing,
and its debating quality seems to me to have declined,
as has its catholicity of membership ; in my time everybody belonged to it and more than one rowing Blue
was president.

But the spirit of physical adventure, I believe, is more
alive to-day than ever. A few years ago I made a list
of how some of my son's contemporaries were spending
the long vacation and found the following : as deck-
hand in a Hull trawler in the White Sea ; working at
the Canadian harvest ; as purser in a South American
liner ; helping Welsh miners to cultivate the land ;
trading old rifles in the Arctic for walrus ivory ! It is
as though they felt they were living in a hard and
dangerous world and were resolved there should be no
experience they could not face. And one characteristic
they have in which we were sadly lacking. They feel
their responsibility to the State. Politics have become
for them a serious personal duty. Youth is inclined to
political extremes, and it is small wonder that the causes
which most appeal to them are the grandiloquent
world-reconstructions ; but the reason, I think, is not
only the rhetorical turn of youth, but the fact that such
causes require sacrifices and an austere discipline. Since
most Englishmen over thirty are inclined to com-

promise, it is right that some Englishmen under thirty should redress the balance by extravagance.

During my four years at Oxford I read hard and finished with a considerable stock of miscellaneous knowledge. That mattered little, but the trend which my mind acquired mattered much. Generally speaking, I accepted the brand of idealism which was then fashionable, that derived from Thomas Hill Green, and expounded in my day by F. H. Bradley, and H. H. Joachim. More and more I became sceptical of dogmas, looking upon them as questions rather than answers. Philosophy did not give us solutions, but it taught us to ask the right questions, about which we could cheerfully go on disputing until the dawn put our candles out. The limited outlook of my early youth had broadened. Formerly I had regarded life as a pilgrimage along a strait and steep path on which the pilgrim must keep his eyes fixed. I prided myself on a certain moral austerity, but now I came to realise that there was a good deal of self-interest in that outlook, like the Puritan who saw in his creed not only the road to Heaven but the way to worldly success. I began to be attracted by the environs as well as by the road, and I became more charitable in my judgment of things and men.

I had some of my Gothic corners smoothed away, but I still had a good many angles, and there remained a large spice of the Shorter Catechist in my make-up. Just as my walks were not random contemplative saunters, but attempts to get somewhere, so a worthy life seemed to me to be a series of efforts to conquer intractable matter, to achieve something difficult and perhaps dangerous. Much as I detested Napoleon, I was for him, as against Thackeray in his "Ballad of the Drum":

"Come fill me one more glass of wine
And give the silly fools their will."

Even a perverse career of action seemed to me better than a tippling of ale in the shade, for that way lay the cockney suburbanism which was my secret terror. Again, while I was very conscious of man's littleness in face of the eternal, I believed profoundly in his high destiny. Human beings were compounded of both heavenly and hellish elements, with infinite possibilities of sorrow and joy. In consequence I had an acute sense of sin, and a strong hatred of whatever debased human nature. The conception of mankind, current in some quarters, as a herd of guzzling, lecherous little mammals seemed to me the last impiety.

Had I wished it, I could have stayed on and taught philosophy. But at the end of my fourth year I had come to feel that I was not sufficiently devoted to any branch of learning to give up my life to it, either as don or professor. I wanted a stiffer job, one with greater hazards in it, and I was not averse to one which offered bigger material rewards. The supreme advantage of Oxford to me was that it enabled me to discover what talents I had and what I really wanted to do. Horizons had extended and revealed a surprising number of things which woke my curiosity. I wanted to explore the wider stages of life. Besides, I had become attached to the study of law, and under the inspiration of a great scholar, the late A. H. J. Greenidge, had taken a lively interest in the most arid details of the Greek and Roman legal systems.

So I decided that my profession should be the Bar.

CHAPTER IV

LONDON INTERLUDE

I WENT to London at the beginning of 1900, in the darkest period of the South African War. At the outbreak of that war (after walking for hours one night on the Embankment) I decided that it was not my duty to volunteer for service, and presently I had almost forgotten public affairs in the excitement of a new profession.

To pass from Oxford, where one was in a modest way a personage, to the utter insignificance of a unit among metropolitan millions, was a harsh and wholesome experience. In my early weeks at Brasenose I had been lonely—I remember how the odour of tea sharpened my homesickness!—but my first weeks in London were a worse solitude. On my frequent visits to keep my terms at the Bar I had found the place friendly and gay. Now it was flat, dingy and inhospitable. It seemed to have an engrossing life of its own which had no link with my former worlds. My first rooms were in Brick Court, the ugliest part of the Temple; they were small and new, reached by a staircase of lavatory bricks, and with no prospect but chimney-pots. Later I moved to pleasant chambers in Temple Gardens, where I had a view of the river, and at night in winter could hear overhead the calling of wild birds in their flight upstream.

In a month my loneliness had gone, and I had become an ardent student of the Law. I spent some months in an office in Bedford Row with a firm of solicitors who had a large agency business, and learned there the minor details of practice. Then I went to read with John Andrew Hamilton, the future Lord Sumner, and was his last pupil before he took silk. That was a privilege for which I shall always be grateful, for it gave me the friendship of a great lawyer, who, in the evenings when the Courts had risen, would discourse cynically and most brilliantly on men and affairs. Then I passed to the chambers of the junior counsel to the Inland Revenue, who, as Sir Sydney Rowlatt, was to have a distinguished career on the Bench. From Rowlatt I learned many lessons, chief of which was that scholarship was as valuable in law as in other things. He taught me to look always for principles, and if necessary to search far back in legal history. Moreover, he stripped the subject of pedantry and dullness; he had the same boyish zest in tracking out a legal conundrum as in sailing his little yacht in the gusty Channel.

The consequence was that I became an enthusiast for the law. In those days the Bar examinations were trivial, and I succeeded in being ploughed once in my finals through treating the thing too cavalierly. But I toiled prodigiously at my own kind of study. I read the law reports avidly. I discovered an antiquary's zeal in tracing the origins of legal doctrine. My favourite light reading was the lives of lawyers. I developed a special admiration for Mansfield, and, finding that the life of the great Chief Justice had never been written, I set myself to remedy the lack. To this day I possess three stout volumes in which I have analysed and classified every one of his decisions. I had no ambition at the time except legal success, and politics I thought of only as a step to that goal. It seemed to me that the position of a judge was the most honourable, dignified and independent of any—ease without idleness, an absorbing intellectual pursuit in which daily one became more of a master. My view was that of *Weir of Hermiston* : "To be wholly devoted to some intellectual exercise is to have succeeded in life ; and perhaps only in law and the higher mathematics may this devotion be maintained, suffice to itself without reaction, and find continual rewards without excitement." Moreover, another side of me loved the appurtenances of it all—the Inns of Court with their stately dining-halls and their long histories, the ritual of the Bar and Bench, the habits of mind and the ways of speech of the profession, the sense that here was the hoar-ancient intimately linked to modern uses.

It was a pleasant apprenticeship, for I had not the nervous strain of a busy lawyer who has to struggle with obtuse juries and captious judges. I had the mental interest of determining the precise significance of words, using what sailors call cross-bearings, elucidating shades of meaning and *nuances* of atmosphere—the interest of a mathematical proof, or a chess conundrum, or an elaborate piece of classical music. I had the historical interest of tracing doctrines back to their dim beginnings. I had the more human interest of watching the play of able minds and of seeing life vividly from a special angle. I am convinced that an education in the humanities should be supplemented and corrected by a training either in law or in some exact science. Besides, it admits one to a great and loyal brotherhood. Once a lawyer always a lawyer. Though I soon ceased to practise, for years I read the law reports first in the morning paper, and fragments of legal jargon still tend to intrude themselves in my literary style.

If I was an industrious apprentice I was also a happy one. The spell of London wove itself around me. Fleet Street and the City had still a Dickens flavour, and Holywell Street had not been destroyed. In the daytime, with my fellow solicitor's-clerk, I penetrated into queer alleys and offices which in appearance were unchanged since Mr. Pickwick's day. On foggy evenings I would dine beside a tavern fire on the kind of fare which Mr. Weller affected. Behind all the dirt and gloom there was a wonderful cosiness, and every street corner was peopled by ghosts from literature and history. I acquired a passion for snugness, which I fancy is commoner in youth than is generally supposed. A young man, a little awed by the novelty of everything, is eager to find his own secure niche. At any rate I, who had begun by regarding life as a strenuous pilgrimage, and at Oxford had come to interest myself in the environs of the road, was now absorbed by the wayside gardens and inclined to dally at the inns.

I had lost any wish ever to leave England, for it seemed to me that I could not exhaust the delights of my own country. I had never desired possessions, regarding them as a clog rather than a blessing, but now I toyed with the idea of a house of my own with a good library, and especially of a Scots moorland dwelling to which I could retire for the legal vacations. Unconsciously I was "ranging" myself and acquiring the habit of mind of that suburbanite who had once been my dread. The gipsy impulse which had dominated my boyhood seemed to have vanished. I saw without regret my path marked out for me, a straight and decorous highroad. My love of country life had not diminished, but I was content with a trim, habitable countryside. Andrew Lang and I shared a rod on a little dry-fly trout stream in Hertfordshire, where I spent many pleasant Saturdays, and he used to laugh at my new-found enthusiasm for lowland waters, as he jeered at my absorption in law. He thought it a sad descent from the Borderer and erstwhile Jacobite.

Another proof of the new mood was the attachment I acquired to the eighteenth century. Before, my favourite century had been the seventeenth with occasional leanings to the sixteenth, and the age of Anne and the Georges had interested me only in their connection with the Jacobite risings. Now I found a supreme attraction in the "teacup times," a consequence, no doubt, of my new profession, for they were a happy season for lawyers. They were also the era when urban life in England came to its flower, and I was rapidly becoming a Cit. The taste was shared by my friends, and we wrote to each other in the manner of Horace Walpole. The affectation must have sat ill on me, for I was not born with much devotion to the bric-à-brac of life. I had become a close student of eighteenth-century memoirs, and the fad had one good result, for it made me a devotee of Edmund Burke. Also it led me to appreciate many pleasant things on which I had hitherto cast a lack-lustre eye. Dr. Johnson's is a sound philosophy: "Life is barren enough surely with all her trappings; let us be therefore cautious of how we strip her."

London at the turn of the century had not yet lost her Georgian air. Her ruling society was aristocratic till Queen Victoria's death and preserved the modes and rites of an aristocracy. Her great houses had not disappeared or become blocks of flats. In the summer she was a true city of pleasure, every window-box gay with flowers, her streets full of splendid equipages, the Park a showground for fine horses and handsome men and women. The ritual went far down, for frock-coats and top-hats were the common wear not only for the West End, but about the Law Courts and in the City. On Sunday afternoons we dutifully paid a round of calls. Conversation was not the casual thing it has now become, but was something of an art, in which competence conferred prestige. Also clubs were still in their hey-day, their waiting lists were lengthy, and membership of the right ones was a stage in a career. I could belong, of course, to none of the famous institutions; my clubs were young men's clubs, where I met my university friends. One was the Cocoa Tree in St. James's Street, a place with a long and dubious history, of which the bronze cocoa-tree in the smoking-room, stuffed with ancient packs of cards, was a reminder. At that time its membership was almost confined to young men from Oxford and Cambridge. I belonged also to the Bachelors', then situated at the foot of Hamilton Place, a pleasant resort for idle youth, from whose bay-windows one could watch the tide of fashion flowing between Hyde Park and Piccadilly.

Now I made my first real entry into the society of my elders. Youth and age were not segregated then as they tend to be to-day, and a young man had the chance of meeting and talking with his seniors and betters—an excellent thing, for to mix with abler men than yourself is to learn humility. It was an era of big dinner parties, where there was far too much to eat, but where the men sat long at table and there was plenty of good talk. Those dinners must have been a heavy imposition on tired folk with feeble digestions, but they were fascinating things for the eupeptic newcomer. I had the opportunity of meeting people whose careers stretched, it seemed to me, far back into history—Lord Rowton, who talked to me of Disraeli; judges like Lord Halsbury, who remembered the days before the Judicature Acts; elder statesmen like Lord Goschen on one side and Lord Rosebery on the other. With Canon Ainger, who was then Master of the Temple, I dined nearly every week. I frankly enjoyed dining out. For a minnow like myself there was the chance of meeting new and agreeable minnows, and the pleasure of gazing with awe up the table where at the hostess's side was some veritable triton.

Then there were the week-ends, when for the first time I saw the inside of great English dwellings, my visits having been hitherto confined to modest Scottish country houses. I must have been an unsatisfactory week-end guest, for after long confinement in London the sight of the countryside intoxicated me, and I would disappear early on the Sunday morning and return late at night, sometimes—to the disgust of my hostess—taking with me some guest whose company was more desired than my own.

Looking back, that time seems to me unbelievably secure and self-satisfied. The world was friendly and well-bred, as I remember it, without the vulgarity and the worship of wealth which appeared with the new century. Its strength was its steadiness of nerve, its foible its complacence—both soon to be rudely shattered. Public affairs were pretty much left to the professionals, and except among them there was no strong interest in politics. The South African War affected only those who had kin in the fighting ranks. I supplemented my income by articles in the *Spectator*, of which I came to be a sort of assistant-editor. Usually I wrote on foreign affairs, sometimes on legal points, but I cannot remember having a strong interest in any of my subjects. My kind colleagues were in the same case. Both St. Loe Strachey and Meredith Townsend were by nature prophets and propagandists, but the first had to content himself with amateur military criticism, and the second with apocalyptic murmurings about the Far East. Nowhere on the surface, as I remember the time, could one discern any strong movement of popular emotion or thought.

Then one day early in the August of 1901 I was suddenly jolted out of my comfortable rut, for I accepted the invitation of Lord Milner, who was home on leave, to go with him to South Africa.

CHAPTER V

FURTH FORTUNE

IT was a change with a vengeance. Hitherto I had
lived among books and in a society where books were
a major interest. My approach to practical life had been
from the side of theory. My colleagues had been people
with the same background as myself. Now my duties
were to be concerned with things for which my education had in no way prepared me, and my daily associates
were to be for the most part drawn from worlds of
which I had no experience. But in my new vocation I
had two advantages. My Oxford circle had had a
notable culture, but we did not make too much of it.
We cherished it as a private delight, and did not
exaggerate its value. We were modest people, anxious
to learn, and disposed perhaps to be over-humble in face
of an unbookish world. Again, educated society had
not absorbed my time, for I had spent long parts of
each year among shepherds, gillies, keepers, fishermen,
poachers, and other men of their hands, and had a great
liking for such company.

I had never been out of Britain—indeed I had never
wanted to. In London I had slipped into a sort of
spiritual middle-age. Now, at the age of twenty-five,
youth came back to me like a spring tide, and every day
on the voyage to the Cape saw me growing younger.
As soon as we had passed the Bay of Biscay I seemed to
be in a new world, with new scents, new sounds, new
sights. I was intoxicated with novelties of which
hitherto I had only had glimpses in books. The blue
days in tropical waters were a revelation of bodily and

mental ease. I recovered the same exhilaration which long ago, as a boy on the Fife coast, I had got from the summer sea. This mood continued until the morning when I looked out of a port-hole and saw Table Mountain rising into the clouds; it was not broken by a week's jolting in a slow train through the Karroo and the dusty Free State; its exhilaration even survived the decanting of a very homesick youth in an unlovely Johannesburg Street at what I suppose to have been the most comfortless hotel in the world.

I

I had only met Lord Milner once before, but the name had been long familiar to me, for at Oxford men spoke it reverentially. He had won every kind of academic honour and had impressed Jowett as the ablest man of his time. He had risen fast in the public service in Egypt and Whitehall; had gone to South Africa with the goodwill of all parties; had there become the most controversial figure in the Empire, applauded by many as the strong man in a crisis, bitterly criticised by others as bearing the chief responsibility of the war. Here was Plato's philosopher-turned-king, a scholar who in his middle forties had made history.

The first impression I had was that there were very few signs of the scholar, except in the fastidious rationalism of his thought. In his speaking and writing he had none of the literary graces, except order and lucidity. Though deeply versed in the classics I never knew him quote Latin or Greek. A small, well-thumbed library accompanied him about the world, but he seemed to read little, and he had no taste for new books. Mr. Asquith overflowed with literary interests and was always reading; Lord Cromer,

G

who had more or less educated himself, loved dearly a learned reference; even Lord Curzon could unbend joyfully and talk books. But I do not remember that Milner ever showed a craving for literature or for any of the arts, any more than for games and sports. One of the finest scholars of·his age, he had put away his scholarship on a high shelf.

I believe that this was done deliberately. Early in life he became aware that he had a limited stock of vitality, bodily and mental. He could do some things superbly, but not many at the same time. He had none of the overflowing, boisterous facility of certain types. He had received—chiefly from Arnold Toynbee—an inspiration which centred all his interests on the service of the State. He had the instincts of a radical reformer joined to a close-textured intellect which reformers rarely possess. He had a vision of the Good Life spread in a wide commonalty; and when his imagination apprehended the Empire his field of vision was marvellously enlarged. So at the outset of his career he dedicated himself to a cause, putting things like leisure, domestic happiness and money-making behind him. In Bacon's phrase he espoused the State. On the intellectual side he found that which wholly satisfied him in the problems of administration, when he confronted them as Goschen's secretary, and in Egypt and at Somerset House. He had a mind remarkable both for its scope and its mastery over details—the most powerful administrative intelligence, I think, which Britain has produced in our day. If I may compare him with others, he was as infallible as Cromer in detecting the centre of gravity in a situation, as brilliant as Alfred Beit in bringing order out of tangled finances, and he had Curzon's power of keeping a big organisation steadily at work. He was no fanatic—his intellect was too supreme for that, but in the noblest sense of the word he was an enthusiast.

He narrowed his interests of set purpose, and this absorption meant a certain rigidity. He had cut himself off from some of the emollients of life. Consequently the perfect administrator was a less perfect diplomatist. When I went to South Africa I was aware that he had been much criticised for what happened before the outbreak of war, but that subject did not concern me. My business was with the future, not with the past, about which I did not trouble to form an opinion. To-day, after more than a quarter of a century's friendship, I can see that Milner was bound to have certain limits in negotiation. He was not very good at envisaging a world wholly different from his own, and his world and Kruger's at no point intersected. There was a gnarled magnificence in the old Transvaal President, but he saw only a snuffy, mendacious savage. It was the fashion among his critics to believe that a little geniality on Milner's part, something of the hail-fellow, masonic-lodge atmosphere, would have brought the Bloemfontein conference to a successful conclusion. Such a view seems to me to do justice neither to Kruger nor to Milner, men deeply in earnest who were striving for things wholly incompatible, an Old Testament patriarchal regime and a modern democracy. I doubt if a compromise was ever possible, though a delay might have been contrived which would have given a chance to the more liberal elements in the Transvaal, like Joubert and Louis Botha. Anyhow I am certain that Milner was the last man for the task. He detested lies, and diplomacy demands something less than the plain truth. He was nothing of the countryman, and could not understand the tortuosities of the peasant mind. His spiritual integrity made it difficult for him, when he had studied a problem, to temporise about the solution which he thought inevitable. Such a course seemed to him to involve some intellectual cowardice, some dereliction of duty, and to duty he had a Roman faithfulness.

It is easy to see that he could never have been a popular leader. He profoundly distrusted rhetoric. He had no means of getting his personality across to masses of people, and, even if he had had the means, that personality could never have attracted the multitude; it was insufficiently coloured, too austere, too subtle. Gold must have some alloy in it before it can become coinage in circulation. But as an administrator he had no equal. In South Africa in a year or two he had rebuilt the land from its foundations and given it the apparatus of civilisation. The impress of his strong hand is still on its institutions. In the Great War, from 1916 to 1918, he was the executant of the War Cabinet who separated the sense from the nonsense in the deliberations of that body, and was responsible for its chief practical achievements. To him were largely due the fruitful things which emerged from the struggle, the new status of the Dominions and the notable advances in British social policy. Sometimes he was overruled, and he has been credited with schemes to which he was strongly opposed. In South Africa, for example, he differed about some of the more contentious measures dictated by military policy. In 1918 he advocated a liberal attitude towards the conquered Powers and protested in vain against certain extravagances of Versailles.

In what precisely lay his administrative genius? I can only give the impressions of a humble fellow-worker. In the first place he had in a high degree what Cavour called the *tact des choses possibles*. The drawback to a completely rational mind is that it is apt to assume that what is flawless in logic is therefore practicable. Milner never made that mistake; he knew too well the stubborn illogicality of facts. But he seemed to have an instinct for what was possible, an extra sense which must have been due to nature and not to experience, for he had not direct knowledge of very many walks in life. How often he would study a scheme of mine with knitted brows, and lay it down with a smile. "Very pretty; but it won't work!"

Next I should put the orderliness of his mind and his capacious memory. He could control any number of wires at once, for he had all the terminals in his hand. Things, too, were kept in their proper perspective; recollection did not amplify some and lessen others, for his mind did not make pictures, but did what Napoleon recommended, and saw facts in their true proportions as if through a telescope. Hence it was not necessary for him to concentrate on one matter rather than on another; he could keep a score steadily moving under his hand. For finance he had a peculiar genius. Figures to him were real counters of thought, and a balance sheet as lucid as a page of print. A good accountant no doubt has this gift, but Milner supplemented it with a rarer endowment, the power of divining the item on which everything hung. He could do what the lumberman does in a log-jam, and pick out the key log which, once moved, sets the rest going. He was thorough, too, scamping no detail, and not easily satisfied. I have gone over with him trivial contracts in connection with land settlement to which he gave all the diligence of a conveyancing counsel.

But his greatest administrative gift was his courage. He had what the French know as *courage de tête*, the boldness to trust his reason. When he had satisfied himself about a particular course—and he took long to satisfy—his mind seemed to lock down on it, and after that there was no going back. Doubts were done with, faced and resolved; he moved with the confident freedom of a force of nature. It was a dangerous gift for a statesman in a democracy where policy to the end must often be kept fluid, but, for the maker of a new country or the restorer of a broken one, it was an endowment beyond price.

For the better part of three years I had the privilege of watching this strong mind at work. But a higher privilege was that I was brought into close touch with a great character. Milner was the most selfless man I have ever known. He thought of his work and his cause, much of his colleagues, never of himself. He simply was not interested in what attracts common ambition. He could not be bribed, for there was nothing on the globe wherewith to bribe him; or deterred by personal criticism, for he cared not at all for fame; and it would have been as easy to bully the solar system, since he did not know the meaning of fear. He was a solitary man; but his loneliness never made him aloof and chilly, and in his manner there was always a gentle, considerate courtesy. I have worked with him often when he was desperately tired, but I never remember an impatient or querulous word. He was a stern judge of himself, but lenient to other people. Once I was involved in an unpleasant and rather dangerous business, for which I was not to blame, but the burden of which I was compelled to shoulder. I consulted Milner and he gave me the advice which he would have given himself, to go through with it whatever happened; it was the highest compliment I have ever been paid. For the humble and unfortunate he had infinite charity, and out of small resources he

was always helping lame dogs. Often he got little
gratitude, and when I would remonstrate he had the
same answer: "The man's miserable, and misery has
no manners."

II

Milner's friends were his own college contemporaries
and the young men whom he gathered round him.
In those days we were a very young company, which
Johannesburg, not unkindly, labelled the "Kindergarten." Our *doyen* was Patrick Duncan, who had
been brought out from Somerset House to take charge
of the Transvaal's finances. Milner himself and his
personal staff lived in a red-brick villa, called Sunnyside,
in the suburbs. His military secretary was Major
William Lambton of the Coldstream Guards, and his
aides-de-camp were Lord Brooke (afterwards Lord
Warwick) and Lord Henry Seymour. Among the
secretaries were Geoffrey Dawson, Lord Basil Blackwood, Hugh Wyndham and Gerard Craig Sellar.
There was also a group who had special tasks assigned
to them; it included Lionel Curtis, R. H. Brand,
Lionel Hichens and Philip Kerr. Hugh Wyndham and
I shared a staff cottage at the gate of Sunnyside, but most
of my time was spent ranging the country from the
Cape to the Limpopo.

It was a pleasant and most varied company, wonderfully well agreed, for, having a great deal to do, we did
not get in each other's way. Loyalty to Milner and
his creed was a strong cement which endured long
after our South African service ended, since the *Round
Table* coterie in England continued the Kindergarten.
When I look back upon that companionship my feelings
are like those in Thackeray's *Bouillabaisse* ballad and
Praed's poem on his Eton contemporaries, for since

those days "the world hath wagged apace." Lionel
Curtis, having arranged the affairs of South Africa,
India, China and Ireland, is a philosopher on the banks
of the Cherwell; Lionel Hichens is head of a great
shipbuilding firm, and Robert Brand an illustrious
London banker; Philip Kerr is Lord Lothian, a political
thinker of international repute, and now British
Ambassador at Washington; Patrick Duncan is the
present Governor-General of South Africa; Geoffrey
Dawson has for many years controlled the *Times*.

Most are dead. Billy Lambton (whom I held in
affectionate awe, for he used to take me riding before
breakfast and expound my shortcomings) commanded
the 4th Division at the battle of the Somme and shortly
afterwards had a riding accident which made him a
cripple for life. Henry Seymour had a distinguished
War record, finishing as a brigadier-general, commanded his own regiment, the Grenadier Guards, and
died in 1939. Guy Brooke, after adventures in many
parts of the globe, had a Canadian brigade in the War
and died in the first decade of peace. Gerard Sellar
succeeded to great wealth, and his Highland home,
Ardtornish, was the meeting place for all of us till his
sudden death in 1929. With him something very rare
and fine, generosity without limit and the kindliest,
most whimsical humour, was lost to the world.

Of Basil Blackwood I had heard much at Oxford,
but he was so often out of England on hunting trips
and other ventures that I had never met him until I
found him in South Africa. He was precisely such a
figure as I had expected from his reputation. I remember him as he first appeared in that ugly office in
Johannesburg, where we occupied adjacent rooms.
Slight in build, with a beautifully shaped head and soft,
dark, sleepy eyes, everything about him—voice,

manner, frame—was fine and delicate. His air was full
of a quiet cheerfulness, with a suggestion of devil-
ment in the background as if he were only playing
at decorum. I can see him with his dog Gyp, walking
with his light foot on the dusty red roads; or cantering
among the blue gums, for he was never long out of
the saddle. With his pointed face and neat black
moustache he had the air of a Spanish hidalgo, and
there was always about him a certain silken foreign
grace. Once I saw the hidalgo capering down the
road on an elegant mule; but a mule's shoulders are
precarious things, and the next I knew was that rider
and saddle had gone over the beast's head into the dust.

It was Basil who introduced the fantastic element
that kept us from the usual ennui of a staff. His serene
good temper was unshakable, and I do not think he
was ever bored in his life. He had the expectant mood
and was always waiting for adventure to turn up. In
his official work he had some difficulty in restraining
his propensity to make fun of things. He drafted
despatches for Milner to sign, and I remember one which
began: "With reference to my able despatch of such
and such a date,"—an opening which, had it been sent
in that form, would have startled the Colonial Office.

He was always drawing in that brilliant manner he
had discovered for himself, for he had never been
taught by anybody. I recollect hundreds of sketches,
some of which I possess, admirable in wit and bold
draftsmanship. He used to illustrate despatches for
our private edification. One contained the informa-
tion that "The Land Board is empowered to make
advances to settlers." Basil drew a picture of a gross and
sentimental Land Board making advances to a coy
settler. He and I projected a Child's History of South
Africa, for which he was to do the drawings and I the

verses. The work had perforce to stop, having become too scandalous. My rhymes were bad enough, but Basil's pictures of Dingaan's Day and of some of the semitic kings of the Rand were an outrage.

Most of us returned from South Africa to our different professions, but Basil scorned his proper trade of the law, and preferred a life of interest to a career of success. The truth is he was not the kind of man who falls easily into a groove. He was too versatile, too much in love with the coloured aspects of life, and too careless of worldly wisdom. For one calling, indeed, he had the highest talent. Not for nothing was he the son of Lord Dufferin, Viceroy and Ambassador. He had an hereditary instinct for administration and diplomacy, and his gift of winning popularity, his charm of manner, his fine sense of atmosphere, his imagination and his very real love of his fellow-creatures would have made him the perfect colonial governor. He should have begun at the top, for he was better fitted for that than for any intermediate stage.

In one thing he was wholly successful. He was the most cherished and welcome of friends. Whenever he appeared he brought warmth and colour into the air. It is difficult to describe the fascination of his company because it depended on so many subtle things —a peculiar grace and gentleness of manner; a perpetual expectation, as if the world were enormously bigger and more interesting than people thought; a spice, too, of devil-may-careness, which made havoc of weary partition walls. He was an incomparable letter-writer, the best I have ever known save Raymond Asquith and T. E. Lawrence, and he had the extra advantage of being able to illustrate his epistles.

To him the first hint of war was like the first waft of scent to a pack of hounds. He was off like an arrow

on the old search for adventure. He began by being
attached to the 9th Lancers, and in October 1914 was
badly wounded at Messines. After some time in
Ireland he received a commission in the Grenadiers,
and went to France early in 1917. In July of that year
the British armies were beginning to get into position
for the Third Battle of Ypres, and all along the front
there was a succession of raids on the enemy lines. On
the night of the 3rd Basil led one of these forays and
did not return. It was of a piece with the anomalies
of the War that a man of such varied powers and rich
experience should fall at the age of forty-six as a
second-lieutenant.

The phrase "Elizabethan," too casually applied, can
be used with truth of Basil. He was of the same breed
as the slender gallants who singed the beard of the King
of Spain and, like Essex, tossed their plumed hats into
the sea in joy of the enterprise, or who sold their
swords to whatever cause had daylight and honour in
it. His like had left their bones in farther spaces than
any race on earth, and from their unchartered wander-
ings our empire was born. He did not seek to do things
so much as to see them, to be among them and to live
in the atmosphere of wonder and gay achievement.
He was not like Bron Lucas, a gipsy, for he was a
creature of civilisation, but of another civilisation than
ours. If spirits return into human shape perhaps his
once belonged to a young grandee of the Lisbon court
who stormed with Albuquerque the citadels of the
Indies and died in the quest for Prester John. He had
the streak of Ariel in him, and his fancy had always
wings. "For to admire and for to see" was his motto.
In a pedestrian world he held to the old cavalier grace,
and wherever romance called he followed with careless
gallantry.

III

My nominal post was that of assistant private secretary, but, apart from drafting a certain number of despatches, I had none of the ordinary secretarial duties. In that strenuous time it was a case of all hands to the pump, and I was given a series of emergency tasks which were intended to prepare the ground for a normal administration. Since the War had smashed the old machine it meant starting at the beginning and dealing in bold improvisations. Not many young men with an academic past are given such a chance of grappling with the raw facts of life. Mistakes were many, for the road was largely unmapped and we had to proceed by trial and error. But the worst blunder would have been supineness, and we were not supine.

My first job was to take over on behalf of the civilian government the concentration camps for women and children established by the army. These at the start, in spite of the best intentions, were no better than lazar-houses, for to bring into close contact people accustomed to living far apart was to invite epidemics. When we took charge the worst was over, and in our period of administration we turned them into health resorts, with the assistance of officers seconded from the Indian Medical service and a committee of English ladies under Dame Millicent Fawcett. The camps gave us a chance, too, of laying the foundations of a new system of elementary education. It was a queer job for a young man, whose notions of hygiene to begin with were of the sketchiest, and to whom infantile diseases were as much a mystery as hyper-space. The word of a bachelor carried no weight with the Boer mothers, so, in order to speak with authority, I had to invent a wife and a numerous progeny.

Next, with the end of the war in sight, we had to prepare for the repatriation of the Boer inhabitants from the commandos, the concentration camps, and the prisoner-of-war camps overseas. This was a heavy business, and it had to be done at racing speed. Since so much of the land was devastated, huts and tents and building material had to be provided in vast quantities; transport, too; horses and mules and cattle; seeds and every kind of agricultural implement; as well as rations for many months. We had the help of people with an intimate knowledge of the country, and the task was duly accomplished, though at a high cost owing to the necessity for speed. I have always considered repatriation a really creditable achievement. We had no luck, for the first year of peace saw a serious drought. Nevertheless, within a year from the treaty of Vereeniging burgher families to the extent of nearly a quarter of a million souls had been settled on their farms and equipped with the means of livelihood.

Simultaneously with this work I was instructed to prepare schemes of land settlement for newcomers, and the nucleus of a department of scientific agriculture. The hope of breaking down the racial barrier between town and country was always very near to Milner's heart. He wanted to see the Dutch share in the urban industries, and men of British stock farming beside the Boers on the veld. For settlement we had a considerable amount of crown land, and we bought more in places where new farming methods could be tried. We looked forward to an era of mining prosperity, when the overspill from the cities would go to the land, and we also hoped to place in farms many soldiers from Britain and the Dominions who had fallen under the spell of South Africa. As for agriculture, it was clear that we must have the best advice that science could offer. The existing quality of stock was poor, and the whole country was plagued by pests and honeycombed with disease. We needed first-class experts to advise us in every branch of husbandry.

So before I had been many months in the country I had the problem of the land fairly on my shoulders, and had to spend much of my time on the road. Long before the War ended I was travelling far and wide, often in areas where fighting was going on, and I was fairly often in difficulties. I have ridden many miles faster than I cared, to avoid losing my breeches to a commando whose clothing had given out. As soon as peace came an agricultural department was started and we engaged experts from all over the world at high salaries—to the disgust of certain sections in Johannesburg, who regarded as misspent all public monies which did not go to the mines. For some reason or other I was selected as the scapegoat by these critics, and even the farmers, whom we were trying to benefit, were suspicious. Yet I believe—and I have Louis Botha's word for it—that no part of Milner's reconstruction so amply justified itself as his agricultural policy. But our hopes of land settlement were disappointed. There came lean years in the mining industry which spoilt the market for farm produce; we had underrated, too, the difficulties of South African farming when higher standards were aimed at than the simple pastoralism of the veld. My chief interest was in co-operative settlements, which would have sold and bought in bulk and had their own factories to work up their products, but I found that the men of our race are not easily induced to co-operate.

Those were wonderful years for me, years of bodily

and mental activity, of zeal and hope not yet dashed by failure. I learned perforce a little about a great many things and a good deal about one or two things. Having always been something of a farmer I plunged happily into a dozen new kinds of farming. I had to be in some degree a jack-of-all-trades—transport-rider, seedsman, stockman, horsecoper, merchant, lawyer, not to speak of diplomatist. By and by we had proper departments with chiefs and staffs, but at first it was almost a one-man show, and I tried to avoid worrying Milner more than I could help. I trust that my work was of some benefit to the country; it was beyond doubt of enormous benefit to myself. For I came to know and value a great variety of human beings, and to know and love one of the most fascinating lands on earth.

IV

My first group of new friends came from the British army, of which hitherto I had known nothing. I made the acquaintance of some of the High Command, who were to be famous figures in the Great War, but my knowledge was chiefly of junior officers and the rank and file. In this way I learned something of that wonderful brotherhood, the old regular army, which came to an end at First Ypres. Many of the troops had been in India and they opened up for me a new world of experience. It was now that I acquired an interest in military history and the art of war which has never left me. "Shop," the talk of an expert on his own subject, has always seemed to me the best kind of conversation, and my appetite for military "shop" was prodigious.

Also I first came in touch with the men of the Dominions—South Africans of the various irregular corps, Canadians, Australians and New Zealanders. Batches of them were seconded to assist me in various jobs, and I had their company in many starlit bivouacs. At Oxford we had had a few colonials, but they were soon absorbed into the atmosphere of the place and seemed to lose their idiom. I had regarded the Dominions patronisingly as distant settlements of our people who were making a creditable effort under difficulties to carry on the British tradition. Now I realised that Britain had at least as much to learn from them as they had from Britain. I found something new to me, something in their outlook at once imaginative and realistic which I had never met before. They were an audacious folk, very ready, if need be, to throw rule and convention overboard, and often I was saved by their sagacious lawlessness. Yet in a sense they were stiffer traditionalists than the British. They combined a passionate devotion to their own countries with the vision of a great brotherhood based on race and a common culture, a vision none the less real because they rarely tried to put it into words. I began to see that the Empire, which had hitherto been only a phrase to me, might be a potent and beneficent force in the world.

The civilian population of Johannesburg was the whipping-boy of the anti-government press and politicians. It scarcely deserved this malign pre-eminence. Those of British stock were the ordinary mercantile community to be found in any English city, worthy people, many of whom had fought gallantly in regiments like the Imperial Light Horse. Some of them, like Percy FitzPatrick, George Farrar and Abe Bailey, were far-sighted and patriotic citizens. There was a big cosmopolitan admixture, inevitable in a mining centre, which had its proportion of riff-raff, but also its able and honest element. Johannesburg, both on its good and bad side, was like any new urban growth in the British Empire or the United States, where individual wealth has come before a civic tradition could be established. But it had one unique feature which has never been repeated—the overshadowing influence of a great personality.

I had met Cecil Rhodes several times in England. He knew that he was dying, and he did not want to die. He asked me my age. "You will see it all," he said bitterly, "and I won't, for I am going out." He gave me various pieces of advice. One was to beware of the vain man. "You can make your book with roguery," he said, "but vanity is incalculable—it will always let you down." He died at his cottage near Cape Town during my first months in Africa, and his funeral in the Matoppo hills and the publication of his will were events which for the moment switched our attention away from the War. He impressed me greatly—the sense he gave one of huge but crippled power, the reedy voice and the banal words in which he tried to express ideas which represented for him a whole world of incoherent poetry. I did not know him well enough to like him or dislike him, but I felt him as one feels the imminence of a thunderstorm. But I did not realise the greatness of his personality until I had been some time in the country. Then I found that in all sorts of people—simple farmers and transport-riders, commonplace business men, Jewish financiers who otherwise would have had no thought but for their bank accounts, even trivial, intriguing politicians—he had kindled some spark of his own idealism. He had made them take long views. Common as their minds might be, some window had been opened which gave them a prospect. They had acquired at least a fragment of a soul. If it

H

be not genius thus to brood over a land and have this power over the human spirit, then I do not understand the meaning of the word.

Very slowly I came to know something of the Dutch. While the War lasted, of course, I saw nothing of them except a few National Scouts. The army was in the habit of praising the Boer at the expense of the uitlander; he was a good fighter and a sportsman with the virtues of a squirearchy, and not the get-rich-quick offscourings of European capitals. This attitude was so manifestly unfair that in my revolt against it I was in danger of acquiring an anti-Dutch prejudice. At Vereeniging I saw the Boer generals, lean men browned by sun and wind, whose ragged clothes seemed to enhance their dignity. It was my privilege later to know some of them well; Louis Botha, built on lines of a primitive simplicity and wise with an elemental wisdom; Smuts, the acute legal intelligence and the philosophic mind who saw the problems of the day in the light of eternal principles—the two statesmen who between them made the early grant of responsible government to the new colonies a success, when otherwise it might have been a fiasco. De la Rey had a face which I have never seen equalled for antique patriarchal dignity. He offered to take me on his staff in the next war, which in his view was to be fought by the British and Dutch against the Jews; it would have been a real Armageddon, for among the Jews I think he classed all foreigners except Americans!

After Vereeniging in my repatriation and land settlement work I lived much among the country Boers. I had little love for the slick Afrikander of the towns, but for the veld farmer I acquired a sincere liking and respect. He had many of the traits of my Lowland Scots, keen at a bargain and prepared to imperil his immortal soul for a threepenny bit, but ready to squander pounds in hospitality. When I spent the night at a farm and at family worship listened to Dutch psalms sung to familiar Scottish psalm-tunes, I might have fancied myself in Tweedsmuir. I knew all types : progressives who were pioneers in dry farming ; the old *takhaar* of the back-veld who was a remnant of a vanished world ; and I think I must have met the last of the great Boer hunters, whose lives were spent far beyond the edge of civilisation and to whom the War signified nothing.[1] I was a Scot, a Presbyterian, and a countryman, and therefore was half-way to being a kinsman.

It happened that I met some of my friends again. In the Great War I was much with the South African Infantry Brigade, and at the request of General Smuts I wrote its history. That brigade was a superb fighting unit ; three times it was annihilated, and each time— at Delville Wood, at Marrières Wood and on the Lys —its sacrifice saved the British Front. About one-third of its members were Dutch and most of them had fought against Britain ; some indeed had been in revolt against the peace terms and had long refused the oath of allegiance. Now they were fighting with complete conviction beside their old antagonists. History has seen many fine stocks brought within the pale of our Empire, but none stronger and finer than this one which turned defeat into victory and led captivity captive.

V

But it is the land itself which holds my memory. Wordsworth had long been my favourite poet.

---

[1] In Peter Pienaar, a character who appears in several of my romances, I have tried to draw the picture of one of those heroes.

This was partly on intellectual grounds, for he seemed to me to rank very high in the hierarchy of literature, and partly because he was the authentic voice of my own Borderland. His mild pantheism suited a landscape instinct with human traditions and wholly fitted for human life. His Nature was Natura Benigna, austere, with moments of an awful sublimity, but not inimical to the hopes and habits of men—a half-tame, habitable world built on the human scale, interpenetrated with human history, and readily taking the colour of human dreams. But, as Mr. Aldous Huxley has pointed out in one of his essays, there is also Natura Maligna, where the Wordsworthian philosophy means nothing. Mr. Huxley's instance is the cruel, obscene superabundance of a tropical forest. I have had the same feeling of malevolence in a place like the delta of the Mackenzie, where the river pours its billions of tons of foul water through bottomless mires scummed with coarse vegetation; or on a mountain range like the Alaskan, which is not passive like the Alps under man's efforts, but seems to react savagely against him.

In South Africa one does not feel the malevolence of Nature, not even in the Limpopo or Zambesi swamps or the Kalahari desert, so much as its utter aloofness from human life. Snug little homes may be carved out of the wilds, but a thousand of them have no effect upon the wilds, which are waiting to swallow them up as soon as our efforts slacken. A hundred Johannesburgs would not change the country's character. It seems not to take the impress of man. Its history—and South Africa has a long history—the story of the ancient earth-dwellers, of the great Bantu migrations, of generations of adventurers from the Sabaeans to the Chartered Company, is as evanescent as a cloud shadow. You will find it in the books, but

somehow it is not in the atmosphere and never will be.
There is nothing cruel in the blue days and starry
nights, the tempests and droughts and summer heats,
but there is something eternally aloof.

> "Lo! for there among the flowers and grasses
>   Only the mightier movement sounds and passes;
>   Only winds and rivers,
>   Life and death."

It was a refreshment to be in a world so superbly
impersonal, so divinely inhuman, and I found
Wordsworth irrelevant. Indeed, I discovered that
I did not want any sort of literature, with one curious
exception. This was Euripides. I had never greatly
cared for him, but for some obscure reason I took to
reading him on the veld.

The country is like an inverted pie-dish, a high tableland sloping steeply to the ocean on south and east, less
steeply to the Zambesi in the north. Its selvedge of
coast land is temperate in the south, and as it sweeps
north becomes sandy desert or tropical flats. The pie-
dish contains every variety of landscape. In the Cape
peninsula you have the classic graces of Italy, stony,
sun-baked hills rising from orchards and vineyards and
water-meadows. On the high veld you have grey-
green plains, which carry the eye to an immense
distance. The mountain rim from the Drakensberg to
the Rhodesian scarp breaks down in wild kloofs and
pinnacles to the bushveld; and the streams, which
begin as strings of pools on the veld, are transformed
first into torrents and then into sluggish tropical rivers.
That is the general configuration, but there are a
thousand hidden nooks which recall to every traveller
his own home, for it is the most versatile of lands. Yet
there is a certain subtle unity in the landscape, something indefinable which we know to be South African.

This has much to do with the climate, which I take to be the best in the world, not because there are no discomforts—for there are many—but because no climate that I know produces so keen a sense of well-being. One could go supperless to bed in the rain on the bare veld, and awake whistling from pure light-heartedness. Whoever has once drunk Vaal water, says the proverb, will always return, and for certain the old enchantress lays a spell which is ill to loose. The scent of a dung fire or wood smoke or mimosa, the creak of a wagon axle, a mule coughing in the dust, and a dozen other little things are still to me as evocative of memories as the "smell of the wattles in Lichten-burg" was to Mr. Kipling's Australian.

There was little of the country which I did not see, from the Cape peninsula, where from shining seas the staircase of the hills climbs to the many-coloured Karroo, to the dull green forests of the Zambesi. But it was the northern plateau which I explored intensively: the castled summits of Mont aux Sources and Basutoland, where the streams descend in sheer veils of lawn to Natal; the scarp whence one looks into the Swaziland and Zululand glens, and, further north, across a hundred miles of bush to the dim outline of the Lebombo; the ridges which huddle behind Lydenburg into the sunset; the lake country of Ermelo; the endless spaces of the high veld; the Zoutpansberg and other ranges of the north, honeycombed with caves and secret waters; the Limpopo running its fantastic course from its springs on the edge of the Rand through high veld and bushveld to the lush flats of Mozambique. I used every kind of transport—Cape cart, mule wagon, horses of all kinds from half-broken Argentines and Texans to handy little Boer ponies—anything Remounts provided, for in those days we could not be particular. Often I had company, but often I had lonely rides and solitary bivouacs. There is something to be said for leaving youth a good deal alone that it may discover itself.

Two pictures I have always carried to cheer me in dismal places. One is of a baking noon on the high veld, the sky a merciless blue, the brown earth shimmering in a heat haze. I am looking into a wide hollow where a red road like a scar descends and disappears over the next ridge. In the bottom there is a white farm with a clump of gum trees, a blue dam, and blue water-furrows threading a patch of bright green alfalfa. An outspan fire is sending up spirals of milky blue smoke. A hawk is hovering far above, but there are no sounds except the drone of insects, and very far off the jar of an ungreased axle. The air is hot but not heavy, pungent and aromatic. I have never had such a sense of brooding primeval peace, as from that sun-drenched bowl brimming with essential light.

The other picture is the Wood Bush in the North Transvaal which lies between Pietersburg and the eastern flats. You climb to it through bare foothills where the only vegetation is the wait-a-bit thorn, and then suddenly you cross a ridge and enter a garden. The woods of big timber trees are as shapely as the copses in a park laid out by a landscape-gardener. The land between them is rich meadow, with, instead of buttercups and daisies, the white arum lily and the tall blue agapanthus. In each cup is a stream of clear grey-blue water, swirling in pools and rapids like a Highland salmon river. These unite to form the Bruderstroom which, after hurling itself over the plateau's edge, becomes a feeder of the Olifants. Here is a true lodge in the wilderness, with on the one side the stony Pietersburg uplands, and on the other the malarial bushveld. The contrast makes a profound impression, since the Wood Bush itself is the extreme of richness and beauty. The winds blow as clean as in mid-ocean, soil and vegetation are as wholesome as an English down. I have entered the place from different sides—by the precipitous road up the Bruderstroom, by the Pietersburg highway, from the north along the scarp, and once from the bushveld by a tributary glen where my Afrikaner pony had to do some rock-climbing; and on each occasion I seemed to be crossing the borders of a *temenos*, a place enchanted and consecrate. I resolved to go back in my old age, build a dwelling, and leave my bones there.

VI

In South Africa I recovered an experience which I had not known since my childhood, moments, even hours, of intense exhilaration, when one seemed to be a happy part of a friendly universe. The cause, no doubt, was largely physical, for my long treks made me very fit in body; but not wholly, for I have had the same experiences much later in life when my health was far from perfect. They came usually in the early morning or at sunset. I seemed to acquire a wonderful clearness of mind and to find harmony in discords and unity in diversity, but to find these things not as conclusions of thought, but in a sudden revelation, as in poetry or music. For a little, beauty peeped from the most unlikely wrappings and everything had a secret purpose of joy. It was the mood for poetry had I been anything of a poet.

> "I was all ear
> And took in strains that might create a soul
> Under the ribs of death."

Looking back I find my South African memories studded with those high moments. One especially stands out. I had been ploughing all day in the black dust of the Lichtenburg roads, and had come very late to a place called the Eye of Malmani—Malmani Oog— the spring of a river which presently loses itself in the sands of the Kalahari. We watered our horses and went supperless to bed. Next morning I bathed in one of the Malmani pools—and icy cold it was—and then basked in the early sunshine while breakfast was cooking. The water made a pleasant music, and near by was a covert of willows filled with singing birds. Then and there came on me the hour of revelation, when, though savagely hungry, I forgot about breakfast. Scents, sights and sounds blended into a harmony so perfect that it transcended human expression, even human thought. It was like a glimpse of the peace of eternity.

There are no more comfortable words in the language than Peace and Joy, which Richard Hooker has conjoined in a famous sentence. Peace is that state in which fear of any kind is unknown. But Joy is a positive thing; in Joy one does not only feel secure, but something goes out from oneself to the universe, a warm possessive effluence of love. There may be Peace without Joy, and Joy without Peace, but the two combined make Happiness. It was Happiness that I knew in those rare moments. The world was a place of inexhaustible beauty, but still more it was the husk of something infinite, ineffable and immortal, in very truth the garment of God.

I had one experience in South Africa which has since been twice repeated. We all know the sensation of doing something or seeing something which is strangely familiar, as if we had done or seen it before. The usual explanation is that we have had the experience in our dreams. My version is slightly different. I find myself in some scene which I cannot have visited before, and which yet is perfectly familiar; I know that it was the stage of an action in which I once took part, and am about to take part again; I await developments with an almost unbearable sense of anticipation. And then nothing happens; something appears which breaks the spell. . . .

I was in the bushveld going from one native village to another by a road which was just passable, and which followed a sedgy stream. I was walking ahead, and my mules and boys were about two hundred yards behind. Suddenly I found myself in a glade where the brook opened into a wide clear pool. The place was a little amphitheatre; on my left was a thicket of wild bananas, with beyond them a big baobab, and on my right a clump of tall stinkwood trees laced together with creepers. The floor was red earth with tufts of coarse grass, and on the edge of the pool was a mat of ferns. . . . I stopped in my tracks, for I had been here before. Something had happened to me here, and was about to happen again; something had come out of the banana thicket. I knew the place as well as I knew my own doorstep. I was not exactly frightened, only curious and excited, and I stood waiting with my heart in my mouth. And then the spell broke, for my mules clattered up behind me.

Twice since I have had the same feeling. Just before the War I was staying at a house on a sea-loch in the West Highlands. I was about to stalk a distant beat of the forest which could only be reached by sea, so it was arranged that after dinner I should go down to the yacht and sleep there so as to be ready to start very early next morning. A boatman ferried me out to the yacht. I had dressed for dinner in a kilt, and suddenly in the midst of the shadowy loch I got a glimpse of my shoe-buckles protruding from beneath my ulster. . . . I was switched back two centuries. I had been here before on these moonlit waters in this circle of dark mountains. I had been rowed out to a ship by a boatman who muffled his strokes, for danger was everywhere. Something fateful awaited me when I got aboard that hull which loomed above the heathery islet. . . . I sat with my hands clenched in suspense. I leaped at the ship's ladder as if I had been a castaway. . . . But nothing happened; only the skipper was waiting to offer me a whisky-and-soda !

The third occasion was during my first year of office as Lord High Commissioner in Edinburgh. I had gone out to read in the garden of Holyroodhouse and had chosen a spot close to a shrubbery, where one looked over a piece of unshorn lawn to the old pile. It was a balmy May morning, with the air blowing free from the Firth and great cloud galleons cruising in the sky. The grass in front of me was starred with daisies, and a little further on were blossoming fruit trees, and then the *tourelles* of the most ancient part of the Palace. There seemed to be a flight of white doves somewhere near, but they may have been seagulls from Mussel-burgh. . . . I lifted my eyes from my book and was suddenly transported to another age. I was in France at some château of Touraine. I was looking at the marguerites and apple blossom of which Ronsard sang. Once this stage had been set for high drama in which I had had a share, and now it was set again. In a moment I should be summoned. . . . But alas ! it was only an aide-de-camp come to remind me that seventy provosts and bailies were invited to luncheon !

VII

I learned a good deal in South Africa, and the chief lesson was that I had still much to learn about the material world and about human nature. I was given a glimpse into many fascinating tracts of experience which I longed to explore. I discovered that there was a fine practical wisdom which owed nothing to books and academies. My taste in letters was winnowed and purged, for the spirit of the veld is an austere thing. I learned to be at home in societies utterly alien to my own kind of upbringing.

Above all I ceased to be an individualist and became a citizen. I acquired a political faith. Those were the days when a vision of what the Empire might be made dawned upon certain minds with almost the force of a revelation. To-day the word is sadly tarnished. Its mislikers have managed to identify it with uglinesses like corrugated-iron roofs and raw townships, or, worse still, with a callous racial arrogance. Its dreams, once so bright, have been so pawed by unctuous hands that their glory has departed. Phrases which held a world of idealism and poetry have been spoilt by their use in bad verse and in after-dinner perorations. Even that which is generally accepted has become a platitude. Something like the sober, merchandising Jacobean colonial policy has replaced the high Elizabethan dreams. But in those days things were different. It was an inspiration for youth to realise the magnitude of its material heritage, and to think how it might be turned to spiritual issues. Milner, like most imperialists of that day, believed in imperial federation. So did I at the start; but before I left South Africa I had come to distrust any large scheme of formal organisation. I had begun to accept the doctrine which Sir Wilfrid

Laurier was later to expound; that the Dominions were not ready for such a union and must be allowed full freedom to follow their own destinies. But on the main question I was more than a convert, I was a fanatic.

I dreamed of a world-wide brotherhood with the background of a common race and creed, consecrated to the service of peace; Britain enriching the rest out of her culture and traditions, and the spirit of the Dominions like a strong wind freshening the stuffiness of the old lands. I saw in the Empire a means of giving to the congested masses at home open country instead of a blind alley. I saw hope for a new afflatus in art and literature and thought. Our creed was not based on antagonism to any other people. It was humanitarian and international; we believed that we were laying the basis of a federation of the world. As for the native races under our rule, we had a high conscientiousness; Milner and Rhodes had a far-sighted native policy. The "white man's burden" is now an almost meaningless phrase; then it involved a new philosophy of politics, and an ethical standard, serious and surely not ignoble.

The result was that my notion of a career was radically changed. I thought no more of being a dignified judge with a taste for letters, or a figure in British politics. I wanted some administrative task, some share in the making of this splendid commonwealth. I hoped to spend most of my life out of Britain. I had no desire to be a pro-consul or any kind of grandee. I would have been content with any job however thankless, in any quarter however remote, if I had a chance of making a corner of the desert blossom and the solitary place glad.

CHAPTER VI

THE MIDDLE YEARS

I

THE years from 1903 to 1914, a truce for Britain between two campaigns, are for the historian the germinal period of the Great War, but to some of those who lived through them they seemed rather an empty patch—*confusae sonus urbis et inlaetabile murmur.*

I had looked forward in South Africa to spending the next decade in foreign service. When I returned to England late in 1903 it was in the expectation of going soon to Egypt, where Lord Cromer had selected me for an important financial post; but the home authorities declined to ratify his choice, no doubt rightly, on the ground of my youth and inexperience. So I was compelled to go back to the Bar, where, with much restlessness and distaste, I continued for the next three years. Though I hoped daily for an appointment abroad, I realised that I must behave as if the Law were to be my life's profession. I went back to Rowlatt's chambers, had an occasional brief of my own, and "noted" cases for the Attorney-General, my old friend Sir Robert Finlay.

But my chief work was the preparation of a law book. I asked Lord Haldane's advice and he suggested a study of that intricate and evasive topic, the liability to the British tax of income earned abroad. So I published in 1905 a monograph on the taxation of foreign income, which for many years was the only work on the subject, and which I am proud to think that great man, F. W. Maitland, pronounced a work-manlike performance. When the Balfour Government fell and the Attorney-General went out of office, I had a year of private practice, in which, because of my book and my South African connections, I made a fair income. But I found it a dull job, for I rarely had the chance of going into court, and in any case the business of waiting to be hired compared unfavourably with the steady rhythm of administrative work. So, when it became clear that there was no immediate hope of service abroad, I seized a chance which offered and went into business. I left the Bar with sincere regret. There is no more honourable and expert profession, none in which the sinews of the mind are kept in better trim, as there is no more loyal and kindly fraternity. And I believe that there are few callings in which success is more certain for anyone with reasonable talents and the requisite industry and patience.

Those years were not the pleasantest in my life. South Africa had completely unsettled me. I did not want to make money or a reputation at home; I wanted a particular kind of work which was denied me. I had lost my former catholicity of interests. I had no longer any impulse to write. I was distressed by British politics, for it seemed to me that both the great parties were blind to the true meaning of empire. London had ceased to have its old glamour. The eighteenth-century flavour, which entranced me on coming down from Oxford, had wholly departed, leaving a dull mercantile modern place, very different from the strenuous, coloured land I had left. I sat in my semi-underground chambers in Middle Temple Lane, feeling as if I were in Plato's Cave, conversant not with mankind but with their shadows. Something, too, seemed to have happened to London society. I had now acquired a large circle of acquaintances, and had become an habitual diner-out, but it was in a society with little charm for me. The historic etiquette was breaking down; in every walk money seemed to count for more; there was a vulgar display of wealth, and a *rastaquouère* craze for luxury. I began to have an ugly fear that the Empire might decay at the heart.

But I had my consolations. The first was new friends, and of these the chief was Richard Haldane, then enjoying a huge practice at the Bar and much prestige in Liberal circles. Some time earlier I had got to know what was left of that pleasant esoteric group which their critics called the "Souls," and through them I met Haldane. With him, besides, I had many Scottish connections. We both came of Presbyterian stock, and we had both a strong interest in philosophy. As a young lawyer I revered a counsel who had cast his shoe over the House of Lords and made the Judicial Committee his wash-pot. We were both hardy walkers. In his younger days at the Bar, Haldane, after a busy week, would take a Saturday evening train to Brighton and tramp the fifty-odd miles to London on the Sunday. But what chiefly attracted me to him was his loyalty to Milner. Milner thought him the ablest man in public life, abler even than Arthur Balfour, and alone of his former Liberal allies Haldane stood by him on every count.

How can I hope to reproduce my old friend for those who did not know him, or knew only his public form? To the ordinary man he was a reputation rather than a person. His large smooth face, with the kindly wrinkles round the eyes, suggested a benevolent sphinx; his manner of speech was that of an oracle declaiming wisdom from some cloudy tripod, an impression enhanced by his small toneless voice. His appearance was that of some bland ecclesiastic of the Middle Ages, as if his true vocation were not legal or judicial, but priestly. One could picture him at midnight conclaves in an archiepiscopal palace, or splitting hairs at some high Church Council. There is a story that in his early days in London he was present at a dinner in an evangelical household, at which two famous American preachers were the principal guests. Before leaving, the evangelists spoke to each of the company privately on spiritual affairs. When they reached Haldane and saw his smile they left him alone. "No need, dear brother," they said, "to ask how it is with *your* soul."

His personality was so unlike those of other public men that he became the centre of myth. The impression got abroad that his methods were of a subtlety which was almost devious. It was wholly false. He was a practical man, and was always prepared "by indirections to find directions out," but he was eminently single-minded and sincere. As a friend said of him, you could hear him "tramping up the back stairs." What he had in a full degree was the gift of persuasion, the power of wearing down opposition by sheer patience and reasonableness; and he had also that chief of diplomatic talents, the ability to read an opponent's mind and shape his argument accordingly. His old affection for Germany made him slow to give up hope of peace, but it never blinded him, and he probably understood the German spirit better than any man in Britain.

This persuasiveness made him a tremendous figure at the Bar. He was a learned lawyer, but there were many legal pundits. Where he differed from his rivals was in his power of getting back to principles and presenting his argument as an inevitable deduction from

I

any sane conception of the universe. To differ from him seemed to be denying the existence of God. He could dignify the most prosaic case by giving it a philosophic background. This was no mere forensic trick; it was the consequence of sincere conviction, of a habit of mind which saw everything in organic relations.

It made him a most formidable advocate, especially in questions of constitutional law, but now and then it led to disaster. The Scottish Church case was an example. The point there was whether the United Free Church could alter certain ecclesiastical and doctrinal tenets without forfeiting endowments which had been given while these tenets were held in their unchanged form. Haldane led for that Church, and his argument fell into two parts—one historical and the other philosophical. The historical argument was simply that a Scottish Church, looking at the historical growth and the traditional conception of a Kirk in Scotland, must be assumed to have the right to change its tenets within certain broad limits and to retain its endowments, unless the instruments creating such endowments contained specific words to the contrary. To that argument I believe there was no answer, and had it been really pressed the Court could not have resisted it. But Haldane was not an historian, and he concentrated on the philosophical argument based on the familiar Hegelian formulas—that identity exists through change and difference, that a thing is itself only because it is also in some sense its opposite, and so forth. It was a remarkable piece of dialectic, but it was an impossible argument to present to a court of justice, and it had the most disastrous effect upon various members of the House of Lords. One, I remember, became fatally confused between the philosophic term "antinomy" and the metal "anti-mony." Lord Halsbury's masculine intelligence dealt harshly with Haldane's metaphysics, and the Court—wrongly, I think—decided against the United Free Church.

His gift of philosophical synthesis and of adequate language in which to expound it had, of course, its very real dangers. He had great speculative ability, and his Gifford Lectures, *The Pathway to Reality*, composed while walking between his flat and the Law Courts and delivered extempore, are a wonderful instance of a popular philosophical exposition in clear and graceful language. But I used to feel that his facility tended to blunt the edge of his mind. A man who has been nourished on German metaphysics should make a point of expressing his thoughts in plain workaday English, for the technical terms of German philosophy seem to have a kind of hypnotic power; they create a world remote from common reality where reconcilia-tions and syntheses flow as smoothly and with as little meaning as in an opiate dream. I remember that once, while staying with him at Cloan, a Scottish professor and I consulted him about a difficult passage in Hegel's *Phenomenology*, and received a fluent explanation which apparently satisfied him, but which seemed to us to leave the difficulty untouched. In later years he became deeply interested in those questions where metaphysics, physics and mathematics have a common frontier, but experts in such matters have told me that he never quite grasped the points at issue, though he was always ready to expound them. There were moments when his impressive words seemed to mean nothing in particular. I once accompanied him through his constituency of East Lothian when he was defending Milner's policy, including Chinese labour on the Rand. I came out of the hall with two old farmers. "Was he for it or against it?" one asked. Said the other, "I'm damned if I ken." Also his brand of Hegelianism inclined him to be a little too optimistic about the friendliness of the universe. He was apt to ante-date the higher unity in which contraries were to be reconciled.

There was another side to him, not often found in a philosopher. He had a genius for practical work, for construction and administration. Britain never had a greater War Minister, for he made the army which triumphed in 1918, though the mischances of politics did not permit him to direct it in the campaigns. This is now universally acknowledged, and the best authority, Lord Haig, has paid his work a tribute which I do not think any civilian War Minister in history ever received before from a Commander-in-Chief. But his labours also in the cause of national education should not be forgotten. There is no subject on which it is so easy for the mind to ossify and generous ideals to end in stale platitudes. Haldane was never the slave of a dogma, and could look at a question freshly on its merits. It was this matter more than any other which alienated him from the traditional parties, who seemed to him to lack imagination and to be slavishly bound to formulas. He was never a socialist in the Marxian sense, but on the question of education the Labour party seemed to him more open-minded than the others, and readier to kindle to a new vision.

His positive work belongs to history. So long as his friends live the man himself will be held in affectionate memory, for it would not be easy to overrate his essential goodness. He lived most fully the creed which he preached. Whoever sought his advice was given the full benefit of his great powers of mind. There was nothing slipshod in his benevolence. He

loved humanity and loved the State, not as an abstraction but as a community of lovable and fallible human
beings. He had a religion in the deepest sense. I think
he was one of the least worldly men I have ever known,
almost as unworldly as Milner. He enjoyed the various
comforts vouchsafed to us in this melancholy vale—
good food, good wine, good talk; he was devoted to
his friends and happy in their society; but he always
seemed to me to sit loose to the things of Time. When
friends failed him he had no reproaches. He bore
unjust attacks and popular distrust with a noble magnanimity. He lived his life as one who had a continuing
vision of the unseen.

Another of my consolations was mountaineering.
In South Africa I had scrambled among the kloofs of
the Drakensberg and the ranges of the Northern
Transvaal, and, long before, I had climbed in the
Highlands, but it was not until 1904 that I paid my first
visit to the Alps. There I did a number of the usual
courses, my chief resorts being Chamonix and Zermatt,
and in 1906 I became a member of the Alpine Club.
But my favourite ground was the Scots hills, especially
Skye and the Coolins. In them it was still possible to
make first ascents, and I came to know every crack and
cranny from Garbsheinn to Sgurr-nan-Gillian. It was
my ambition to be the first to traverse the whole
range in a summer's day, but I put off the enterprise
too long and others got in before me.

We have many confessions of faith from those who
have lifted their eyes to the hills. I like best Mr.
Belloc's in his *Path to Rome*. "Up there, the sky above
and below them, part of the sky, but part of us, the
great peaks made communion between that homing,
creeping part of me which loves vineyards and dances

and a slow movement among pastures, and that other part which is only properly at home in Heaven." The wittiest thing ever said about mountaineering, I think, was by George Meredith, that "every step is a debate between what you are and what you might become." For myself, it brought me again into touch with the wild nature with which I had lived intimately in South Africa. My other sport, fishing, did not do that in the same degree; it was essentially a "slow movement among pastures," even when it was pursued in March on the Helmsdale among scurries of snow. Just as sailing a small boat brings one close to the sea, so mountaineering lays one alongside the bones of mother earth. One meets her on equal terms and matches one's skill and endurance against something which has no care for human life. There is also the joy of technical accomplishment. I never took kindly to snow and ice work but I found a strong fascination in rock climbing, whether on the granite slabs of the Chamonix *aiguilles*, or the sheer fissured precipices of the Dolomites, or the gabbro of the Coolins. A long rock climb is a series of problems each one different from the rest, which have to be solved by ingenuity of mind and versatility of body. I was fortunate to have the opposite of vertigo, for I found a physical comfort in looking down from great heights. Bodily fitness is essential, for there are always courses which you must have the strength to complete or court disaster. In any mountaineering holiday there are miserable days when the muscles are being got into order by training walks; but when these are over I know no physical well-being so perfect as that enjoyed by the mountaineer.

Then there are the moments of illumination. On a snow mountain there is the miserable getting up in the small hours, coffee in a bleak dining-room by the

light of a single candle, a long stumble through dark
pine woods and over dusky alpine pastures, a slow
ascent among the crevasses of the glacier, and then—
the second breakfast high up on a snow ridge when
the world seems to heave itself out of night into day.
Or on a rock mountain, when, after hours spent
hugging the framework of the earth in cracks and
chimneys, one comes out at the top to a spacious sunlit universe. I always felt the drama of the transition
most sharply in Skye when, after a course among
difficult chimneys or over faces with exiguous holds,
one reached the ridge and saw the Minch, incredibly
far below, stretching its bright waters to the sunset and
the ultimate isles. Such moments gave me the impression of somehow being outside the world in the ether
to which clouds and birds belong, of being very nearly
pure spirit—until hunger reminded me that I had still
a body.

I never had an accident mountaineering, or anything
like one, though I often got into trouble, and once or
twice came so near the limits of my strength that the
mountains seemed to be leaping like the Scriptural
rams. But I had one experience which I shall not soon
forget. It was in 1910 in the Bavarian Wettersteinge-
birge above Partenkirchen. There is a small rock peak
in the neighbourhood called the Alpspitze which I set
out to climb about 2 a.m. one June morning, with, as
my companion, a young forester called Sebastian. We
duly reached the summit, and about 9 a.m., after breakfast at a little mountain inn, began our walk of six
miles or so to the valley. It was a brilliant summer day
with a promise of great heat, but our road lay through
pleasant shady pine woods and flowery meadows. I
noticed that my companion had fallen silent, and,
glancing at him, was amazed to see that his face was

dead-white, that sweat stood in beads on his forehead, and that his eyes were staring ahead as if he were in an agony of fear, as if terror were all around me so that he dared not look one way rather than another. Suddenly he began to run, and I ran too, some power not myself constraining me. Terror had seized me also, but I did not know what I dreaded; it was like the epidemic of giggling which overcomes children who have no wish to laugh. We ran—we ran like demented bacchanals, tearing down the glades, leaping rocks, bursting through thickets, colliding with trees, sometimes colliding with each other, and all the time we never uttered a sound. At last we fetched up beside the much-frequented valley highway, where we lay for a time utterly exhausted. For the rest of the road home we did not speak; we did not even dare to look at each other.

What was the cause? I suppose it was Panic. Sebastian had seen the goat-foot god, or something of the kind—he was forest born, and Bavarian peasants are very near primeval things—and he had made me feel his terror. I have never had any similar experience, but a friend of mine had something like it in Norway. He was alone, climbing in the Jotunheim, and suddenly in a wild upland glen the terror of space and solitude came upon him. He ran for dear life, crossed a considerable range of mountains, and at last reached a saeter. There was no one in the place, but there were cattle, and he found sanctuary in a byre, where he nuzzled his face into the neck of a most astonished cow!

II

In the autumn of 1906 my unsettled years came happily to an end, for I became engaged to Susan

SUSAN CHARLOTTE GROSVENOR

Grosvenor, and we were married in the following July. I had no longer any craving for a solitary life at some extremity of the Empire, for England was once more for me an enchanted land, and London a magical city. I think that, in spite of my many friends and interests, I had been suffering from loneliness, since my family were four hundred miles away. Now I acquired a vast new relationship—Grosvenors, Wellesleys, Stuart-Wortleys, Lytteltons, Talbots—and above all I found the perfect comrade. I have been happy in many things, but all my other good fortune has been as dust in the balance compared with the blessing of an incomparable wife.

Just before my marriage I changed my profession, and at the invitation of my Oxford friend, Thomas Arthur Nelson, became a partner in his publishing firm, one of the oldest in Britain, which had its headquarters and its printing works in Edinburgh, and branches in London, New York and throughout the Empire.

It is not easy to draw on a little canvas the man whose nature is large and central and human, without cranks or oddities. The very simplicity and wholesomeness of such souls defy an easy summary, for they are as spacious in their effect as daylight or summer. Often we remember friends by a gesture, or a trick of expression, or by a favourite phrase, or some nicety of manner. These were trivial things in our friendship, but they spring first to the mind in the act of recollection. But with Tommie Nelson I do not find myself thinking of such idiosyncrasies. I can recall many mannerisms of his, but it is only by an effort of thought, for they do not run to meet the memory. His presence warmed and lit up so big a region of life that in thinking of him one is overwhelmed by the multitude of things that he made better by simply existing among them,

If you remove a fire from a hearth, you will remember the look, not so much of the blaze itself, as of the whole room in its pleasant glow.

At Oxford he and I were exactly contemporary. He was in some ways the most conspicuous figure of our academic generation, as president of Vincent's, a rugby "Blue" and an "Internationalist," and I think that, if at any time of our four years' residence a poll had been taken for the most popular man in the University, he would have headed it. When I joined his firm in the autumn of 1906 I found that he had changed very little, except that his hair was slightly grizzled. He always looked fit, with a clear brown skin and the untroubled eyes of a boy. I never saw him haggard except at the Front. He was an adept in all Scottish sports—a good shot with gun and rifle, a bold rider to hounds, and a fisherman of the first order. He was a fine sportsman, not merely because he did everything well and with immense gusto, but because he had in his bones a love of wild life and adventure and contest. He was very serious too. He looked upon all classes of men with friendliness and understanding, and some response was won from the most angular. For all his abounding zest he had a rather grave, reflecting mind, natural in one who kept so fine a mental balance; and as time went on this seriousness increased. Yet he was very shy of talking about his creed, for he had a horror of anything like rhetoric and grandiosity. He could never forget what Carlyle has put into famous words: "It is a sad but sure truth that every time you speak of a fine purpose, especially if with eloquence and to the admiration of by-standers, there is the less chance of your ever making a fact of it in your own poor life."

For ten years I was associated with him in business, and I cannot imagine a happier companionship. But,

looking back, I can see that I was never quite at ease
about him. I felt that he was fitted for greater things
than anything I could foresee. About some people one
has that consciousness of powers too big for their
environment. A life of great domestic happiness,
innumerable friends, a world enlivened and comforted
by his presence—it would have seemed enough for
most people, but it seemed too little for Tommie. . . .
Then came the War and the old life passed away in
a night.

At first I saw nothing of him and we did not meet
until the autumn of 1916, during the later stages of the
battle of the Somme. He was having a trying time,
with a number of observation posts to look after, and
no kind of home anywhere. He was happier when, in
early 1917, he entered the Tank service. When I used
to visit Hugh Elles's mess at Bermicourt I found that
he had recovered his youth. But that youth was near
its close, for in the last day of the battle of Arras he was
killed instantaneously by a long-distance shell. I had
to do a good deal of searching before I found and
identified his grave.

His death made a bigger hole in the life of Scotland
than that of any other man of his years. *Heu! quanto
minus est cum reliquis versari quam tui meminisse.* He was
a rare being because he was so superbly normal, so
wholly in tune with ordinary humanity, and therefore
fitted to help in the "difficult but not desperate life of
man." In the case of others we might regret the
premature loss to the world of some peculiar talent;
with Tommie we mourned especially the loss of a
talent for living worthily and helping others to do
likewise. It is the kind of loss least easy to forget, and
yet one which soon comes to be contemplated without
pain, for he had succeeded most fully in life.

III

In business I found that I had a reasonable amount of leisure, for my firm was well organised and I had able colleagues. We were a progressive concern, and in our standardised Edinburgh factories we began the publication of cheap books in many tongues. On the eve of the War we must have been one of the largest businesses of the kind in the world, issuing cheap editions of every kind of literature, not only in English, but in French, German, Magyar and Spanish, and being about to start in Russian. I had opportunities for European travel, and, when our children were young, my wife and I visited the Balkans and Constantinople, Spain, Portugal, the Canaries and the Azores; we had a wonderful yachting trip in the Aegean and along the Dalmatian coast; we went to Norway to fish; and we had part of a summer in the Bavarian highlands. But most of our holidays were spent in Scotland.

On my marriage I gave up mountaineering as scarcely a married man's game. I still fished whenever and wherever I got the chance, and I discovered a new sport in deer-stalking. About that time I ceased to shoot with a gun, for my love of birds was so great that I disliked killing them. I had never been much of a gun shot at my best, like the Ancient Mariner, "stopping one of three," but I was fairly good on my day with a rifle. Stalking supplied the hunting element, and also took me to the high tops as much as in my old climbing days. In my time I have stalked in over twenty deer forests, and I have always had a clear view of how the game should be played. I liked best those forests in which long experience gave me some knowledge of the ground, so that I was not the slave of the stalker. I was a professed scavenger, and shot only for the sake of the forest. I wanted to kill freaks like hummels and switch-horns and old back-going beasts that would perish in the next winter. I would gladly stalk a young royal, but when I got my sights behind his shoulder I would take off my cap to him and go home—a habit popular with owners but not so popular with stalkers and gillies. Then I was in terror of wounding, and in the days of my pride, when I could trust myself, I generally took neck shots, which meant a dead kill or a clean miss. I only once wounded a stag, and after a sleepless night I got him the following day.

Stalking gave me a host of pleasures. In the first place, like Duncan Ban Macintyre, I loved the dun deer and was never tired of watching them and studying their ways. Those beautiful wild things were my chief link with the natural world. This love of the deer is common among stalkers and gillies, but in my experience it is rare among the "gentlemen," who are too apt to regard them like the targets on a rifle range. Hence the talk in a lodge smoking-room in the evening is apt to be a dreary business: the steepness of the hills is cursed, weather and wind anathematised, and the shot, the least important part, described in weary detail. Such sportsmen recapitulate their dull experiences until they grow old and die, like the shade of Orion which Odysseus saw in Hades chasing the wraiths of the beasts which he once hunted on the hills.

Then there was the technical interest of the stalk, of which the shot is only the conventional finale. The red deer is by nature a woodland animal, but in Scotland he inhabits mountains which are for the most part treeless, and he has had to develop a new technique of defence. Living under conditions which are more or less artificial, he has become far more wary than, say, the African kudu or the Canadian wapiti. His sense of smell and hearing are acute; but his eyesight is indifferent, for though he can see things far off he is not clever at recognising them. I found endless interest in devising new ways of circumventing him, devices which every professional stalker knows, but which he does not usually communicate to his "gentlemen." For example, if you are looking down on a glen with stags in the bottom and the wind is wrong, it is often possible to have your scent carried by the wind so that it ricochets off the opposite wall of the glen, and, coming up behind the stags, makes them move towards you. Camouflage, too, is important. I always believed in breaking up my costume, for, whatever the forest, its colour will not be uniform, and I would wear, say, a checked jacket, grey flannel knickerbockers and grey-blue stockings. The ground often consists of a ribbon of turf bounded by heather and shingle, and by crawling along the border-line between the green and the rough, keeping half of the body in each, if the wind is right it is possible to get within shot, though you are in full view of the deer.

I enjoyed greatly the company of the gillies, whether Highland or Lowland—and some of the best were Lowlanders. From them I heard many tales of the ancient world of the hills. The old type of gillie is fast disappearing—the type with a beard like Moses and little English, who always lit the dottle in a foul pipe before starting on a steep ascent. The new kind of gillie, who has usually served in the War, can point out a stag with the precision of an artillery observer. The old type used to labour heavily. "D'ye see yon white stone?"—"I see a million white stones." "Ah, but d'ye see another?" But he had often wonderful phrases. "Gang quiet, sir," I remember one telling me.

"Gang as if ye was something growing." Gaelic, un-fortunately, was the true key to their world, and I used to lament that I had no Gaelic, having, like my father before me, tried in vain to learn the tongue. For that you must have had a Gaelic-speaking nurse.

But especially I rejoiced in the companionship ot the hills. I have stalked in every kind of forest—the *machairs* of the Isles, the great round shoulders of the Cairngorms, the splintered peaks of Torridon and Glencoe and Dalness, which are almost mountaineer-ing ground, the varied rock and bent of the Black Mount. What I liked best was to get to the heights early in the morning—and early in the season when the stags feed high—and spend the day exploring the corries from above. The sport had not the sustained tension of mountaineering; indeed, much of its charm lay in the long spells of idle waiting, one's nose in thyme or heather, when the mind was gathered into the mountain peace. The high moments were the start in the freshness of morning, when the dew was on the birches, and one had the first spy from a hillock in the glen; the sunny hours on the tops when cloud shadows patterned the corries; the return in the even-ing in a flaming sunset with—or without—a lumpish hill pony carrying a stag. Such a day could not be blank even if one never saw a shootable beast, or missed him when seen, for, as Sir Walter Scott said of himself when he watched Tom Purdie at work, "one's fancy could be running its ain riggs in another world."

IV

I found another way of using my leisure. In the spring of 1911 I became the Conservative candidate for the counties of Peebles and Selkirk, a constituency which then stretched from within a dozen miles of Edinburgh to within twenty miles of the Border.

My motives were mixed. I had always felt that it was a citizen's duty to find some form of public service, but I had no strong parliamentary ambitions. Nor was there any special cause at the moment which I felt impelled to plead. While I believed in party government and in party loyalty, I never attained to the happy partisan zeal of many of my friends, being painfully aware of my own and my party's defects, and uneasily conscious of the merits of my opponent. Like Montaigne I could forgive "neither the commendable qualities of my adversaries nor the reproachful of those I followed." I was apt to fall into the mood which Macaulay attributes to Halifax:

> "His place was on the debatable ground between the hostile divisions of the community and he never wandered far beyond the frontier of either. The party to which he at any moment belonged was the party which, at that moment, he liked least, because it was the party of which he had, at that moment, the nearest view. He was therefore always severe upon his violent associates and was always in friendly relations with his moderate opponents. Every faction in the day of its insolent and vindictive triumph incurred his censure; and every faction, when vanquished and persecuted, found in him a protector."

My political experience at the time was nil, and my views were shallow and ill-informed—inclinations rather than principles. I believed profoundly in the possibilities of the Empire as a guardian of world peace, and as a factor in the solution of all our domestic problems, but I no longer accepted imperial federation, and I had little confidence in Mr. Chamberlain's tariff policy. For socialism I had the distrust that I felt for all absolute creeds, and Marxism, to which I had given some attention, seemed to me to have an insecure speculative basis and to be purblind as a reading of history. On the other hand I wanted the community to use its communal strength when the facts justified it, and I believed in the progressive socialisation of the State, provided the freedom of the personality were assured. I had more sympathy with socialism than with orthodox liberalism, which I thought a barren strife about dogmas that at that time had only an antiquarian interest. But I was a Tory in the sense that I disliked change unless the need for it was amply proved, and that I desired to preserve continuity with the past and keep whatever of the old foundations were sound. As I used to put it in a fisherman's simile, if your back cast is poor your forward cast will be a mess.

So I went into politics with a queer assortment of interests. I hoped to see the Empire developed on the right lines; the Dominions enabled to grow into self-conscious nations; emigration undertaken as a reasoned policy, fully planned at each end, and not as a mere overspill of population. Then I wanted something done about resettling the land of Scotland. Since my boyhood I had seen land slipping out of cultivation into pasture, and glens where once a dozen hearths smoked now inhabited only by a shepherd and his dog. For the rest I was critical of the details of Mr. Asquith's policy, but approved its purpose—old-age pensions, health and unemployment insurance, and most of the famous 1910 Budget. In the quarrel with the House of Lords I was on the Government's side. By 1914 I had come to differ violently from them on the matter of Ulster, for though a federal home-ruler, after the fashion of

K

my friend, F. S. Oliver, their blundering in the treatment of Ulster roused some ancient Covenanting devil in my blood.

I came of a Liberal family, most of my friends were Liberals, I agreed with nine-tenths of the party's creed. Indeed, I think that my political faith was always liberalism—or rather "liberality," as Gilbert Murray has interpreted the word. But when I stood for Parliament it had to be the other side.

Now that the once omnipotent Liberal party has so declined, it is hard to realise how formidable it was in 1911—especially in Scotland. Its dogmas were so completely taken for granted that their presentation partook less of argument than of a tribal incantation. Mr. Gladstone had given it an aura of earnest morality, so that its platforms were also pulpits and its harangues had the weight of sermons. Its members seemed to assume that their opponents must be lacking either in morals or mind. The Tories were the "stupid" party; Liberals alone understood and sympathised with the poor; a working man who was not a Liberal was inaccessible to reason, or morally corrupt, or intimidated by laird or employer. I remember a lady summing up the attitude thus: Tories may think they are better born, but Liberals know that they are born better.

All this was a little trying to the natural man, and he longed to breach the complacency. It had small justification. In the old bad days of the early nineteenth century the Whigs were probably more intellectually alive than the Tories; but the situation had wholly changed. A youth in Scotland who called himself a Tory was almost certain to be thinking about politics, and not merely cherishing a family loyalty. I got together a fine group of young men, and we refused no challenge, but argued any question anywhere with anyone; my public meetings frequently ended in a discussion at a street corner or in a public-house. That brave band is now scattered; many of them fell in the War; some are now ornaments of the Labour party. We were crude enough, but at any rate we tried to get down to realities, on which our opponents for the most part maintained a conspiracy of silence. Their strength lay partly in what remained of Mr. Gladstone's Sinaitic authority, and partly in a stubborn, almost feudal, conservatism. Their sires and grandsires had been Liberal, and it would be treason to desert the standard. It was a moral question; not reason but loyalty was at issue. I had innumerable Liberal friends, who would speed me from the door with "I'd dae onything for ye but vote for ye."

It was hard to fight against this family compact. But we steadily made way, and we certainly gave the place a fairly thorough political education. For example, I find that I once discoursed for an hour and a half on the taxation of land values and had a keen discussion afterwards. I brought eminent speakers into the constituency, such as F. E. Smith, Lord Robert Cecil, Sir Robert Finlay, Alfred Lyttelton and Robert Horne, and that was a delicate business, for in many matters I differed from my party. In 1914 my energy declined. I began to feel that the ordinary matters of debate were falling out of the picture as I saw creeping towards us the shadow of war.

Old electioneering tactics can interest nobody, and they never greatly interested me. What made my work as a candidate a delight was the people I moved among. I did not want to be just any kind of Member of Parliament; I wanted to represent my own folk of the Border. I have written of them in an earlier chapter that they had the qualities I most admired in human nature; realism coloured by poetry, a stalwart independence sweetened by courtesy, a shrewd kindly wisdom. To the first quality the ballads bear witness, to the second the history of Scotland. As examples of the third let me tell two stories.

Mr. Gladstone once paid a visit to a Tweedside country, and in the afternoon went out for a walk and came to a gate which gave upon the glen. It was late in November, a snowstorm was threatening, and the sheep, as is their custom, were drawing out from the burn-side to the barer hill where drifts could not lie. An old shepherd was leaning on the gate, and to him Mr. Gladstone spoke in his high manner. "Are not sheep the most foolish of all animals? Here is a storm pending, and instead of remaining in shelter they are courting the fury of the blast. If I were a sheep I should remain in the hollows." To which the shepherd replied: "Sir, if ye were a sheep ye'd have mair sense."

The second belongs to my own candidature. Heckling in the Borders is carried, I think, to a higher pitch of art than anywhere else in Britain. It is pursued for the pure love of the game, and I have known a candidate heckled to a standstill by his own supporters. Mr. Lloyd George's Insurance Act had just been introduced, and at a meeting at remote Ettrickhead the speaker was defending it on the ground that it was a practical application of the Sermon on the Mount. A long-legged shepherd rose to question him, and the following dialogue ensued:

"Ye believe in the Bible, sir?"

"With all my heart."

"And ye consider that this Insurance Act is in keepin' with the Bible?"

"I do."

"Is it true that under the Act there's a maternity benefit, and that a woman gets the benefit whether she's married or no?"

"That is right."

"D'ye approve of that?"

"With all my heart."

"Well, sir, how d'ye explain this? The Bible says the wages of sin is death and the Act says thirty shillin's."

For three years my wife and I spent most of our leisure in getting acquainted with my possible constituents. We visited twice every hamlet, farm and cottage in the two shires. That involved lengthy journeys in wintry weather, but it meant also halcyon summer days in the long glens of Tweed and Ettrick and Yarrow. It was not canvassing, for I rarely mentioned politics. Since I spoke their own tongue and knew most men by their Christian names, those visits gave me a chance of entering into the pastoral life of the uplands, as Sir Walter Scott entered into it in his quest for ballads. I learned many things that do not come usually within the orbit of a politician. I cannot tell how my friends regarded me in that capacity, but I think that they came to consider me as one of themselves with whom they need not stand on ceremony. Once at a lamb fair a shepherd paid me what I believe was a sincere though left-handed compliment. "We've gotten the richt sort of candidate in you this time," he said. "Your predecessor was an awfu' nice man, but he was far ower much of a gentleman and far ower honest!"

V

During those years I moved among a good many social groups. I had friends in commerce and finance, in the army and navy and civil service, in most branches of science and scholarship, and especially in the law and politics. But as a writer it was my misfortune to be too little in the society of writers. This was partly due to my preoccupation with other interests. My upbringing never gave me the chance of the pleasant bohemianism associated with the writer's craft. As a publisher I came to know many authors, English and French, but it was only a nodding acquaintance. I must confess, too, I fear, that I rarely found a man of letters who interested me as much as members of other callings. A writer must inevitably keep the best of himself for his own secret creative world. I had no appetite for studio talk. I never knew the enthusiasm which is given by membership of a coterie designed to preach some new gospel in art. My taste was for things old and shabby and unpopular, and I regarded with scepticism whatever was acclaimed as the Spirit of the Age. I was born to be always out of fashion.

Also I felt—no doubt wrongly—that the author in social life was rarely the natural creature that God intended. His public form inclined to be an innocent pose forced on him by his admirers—robustious, cynical, forward-looking, elfin, wistful—something, anyhow, that could not be sustained without artifice. A man who as a longshoreman or a mason would have been a pleasant companionable fellow, became as a writer as restless as a grasshopper and apt, like the grasshopper, to be a burden.

Andrew Lang was a close friend, and after his death Henry Newbolt, but these friendships were based on other things than literature. With G. K. Chesterton and Hilaire Belloc and Maurice Baring I never differed —except in opinion. I was fascinated by Rudyard Kipling's devouring interest in every detail of the human comedy, the way in which in conversation he used to raven the heart out of a subject. I knew Thomas Hardy fairly well and revered his wonderful old age "like a Lapland night," and what T. E. Lawrence called "his unbelievable dignity and ripeness of spirit." Stephen Reynolds, who wrote *A Poor Man's House*, and who chose to live as a Devon fisherman, was an intimate friend.

Of the greatest figures I saw most of Henry James. Would that I had seen more of him, for I loved the man, and revelled in the idioms of his wonderful talk, which Mr. Percy Lubbock has admirably described—"his grandiose courtesy, his luxuriant phraseology, his relish for some extravagantly colloquial term embedded in a Ciceronian period, his humour at once so majestic and so burly." I have two vivid memories of him. Once I had to act as host in a relative's country house where he was a guest. A New Englander knows something about Madeira and the house had a wonderful cellar of that wine, so at the end of dinner I called his attention to what he was about to drink, promising him a new experience. He sipped his glass, and his large benign face remained impassive while he gave his verdict. I wish I could remember his epithets; they were a masterpiece of the intricate, evasive and non-committal, and yet of an exquisite politeness. Then I tasted the wine and found it swipes. It was the old story of a dishonest butler who was selling the famous vintages and replacing them by cheap stuff from a neighbouring public-house. The other occasion was when an aunt of my wife's, who was the widow of Byron's grandson, asked Henry James and myself to examine her archives in order to reach some conclusion on the merits of the quarrel between Byron and his wife. She thought that those particular papers might be destroyed by some successor and she wanted a statement of their contents deposited in the British Museum. So, during a summer week-end, Henry James and I waded through masses of ancient indecency, and duly wrote an opinion. The thing nearly made me sick, but my colleague never turned a hair. His only words for some special vileness were "singular"— "most curious"—"nauseating, perhaps, but how quite inexpressibly significant."

The people I saw most of were the politicians. The pre-War years witnessed the end of a fashion which had continued since the 1688 Revolution, and which made politics the chief interest of the educated classes. To-day, when they are the uneasy preoccupation of everybody, it is hard to recapture the precise atmosphere of that decade when to many they were still a game ruled by all kinds of social and family etiquettes. Controversy was not so sharp as to prevent the different sides mixing pleasantly, and I still remember the surprise of old-fashioned people when in 1913 the Parliament Act and the Ulster question led to breaches of private friendship. There was a good deal to be said for the fashion, since Britain's traditional policy is always compromise. Its drawback was that it handicapped fresh and sincere thinking on public affairs. The Government party, with the exception of a few rebels, was content to stand in the ancient ways; Mr. Lloyd George's social experiments were rather the development of an old, than the inception of a new, creed, and his much-criticised finance was cuts off the standard joints. The Opposition confined itself to opposing, though a few younger men, like Mark Sykes and Aubrey Herbert, stood for something more than a negation. One turned to the new Labour party to find people who were trying to strike out new paths—and rarely found them.

Politics in the circles in which I dwelt were an absorbing topic, at least the small change of politics. A by-election woke a spate of gossip; a general election had the sporting interest of a struggle between counties for the cricket championship. The bitterness caused by Mr. Lloyd George's platform manners has been much exaggerated; I have heard aged Tories describe him as "varminty" with unwilling admiration in their voices. The assumption seemed to be that the fundamentals of politics were fixed and much the same as they had always been, and that disputes were only about pace and emphasis. To many they were a drawing-room game, almost a drawing-room comedy. In certain circles there was, of course, discussion about principles and theories, and the traditional creeds were always being analysed and defined. But they remained the traditional creeds. The social and economic fabric was assumed to be what it had been at the close of the nineteenth century, with a few novel elements which could easily be adjusted. There was little consciousness that new facts were emerging in all quarters, social, political, economic, religious, which required a new interpretation, that all our problems needed a fresh analysis, and that the most venerated principles must be rethought and restated. The world was undergoing chemical combinations in which no element was left unchanged. The constituents of society were being altered, both in proportion and quality. The old economics were going out of date since they were deductions from a state of things which had ceased to be. Current beliefs in every department were imperceptibly changing, and what was true of Britain was not less true of the world at large.

The imperception of the nation was reflected in the Government. That Government contained, I think, as high an average of ability as was ever found in a British Cabinet. Its members were admirably fitted to carry on; they were not so well fitted to foresee and originate. Haldane was different, but he was absorbed in his department, and Mr. Churchill, too, had definitely become a specialist. Two men, Edward Grey and Asquith, set the tone of the administration. Both were in the great tradition of our public life. Grey had some of the qualities of the Lord Althorp of the first Reform Bill, and as Foreign Secretary something of the patient sagacity of Lord Salisbury. Half a century earlier he would have been a very great Foreign Minister, but he was a man of an era, and that era had passed. The position of Britain in Europe had radically changed, and the old business of wise compromise and nice adjustment was out of date. New, strange, inconsequent forces were at work to upset the old balances. He felt these forces but he did not understand them—perhaps no man did. When the crisis came he was in my belief as adequate to it as was possible for any British statesman cast in his mould. What was needed was a different mould, something like the desperate boldness of Cromwell or Chatham.

The Prime Minister, Mr. Asquith, had in his character every traditional virtue—dignity, honour, courage, and a fine selflessness. In temperament he was equable and generous. He was a most competent head of a traditional Government and a brilliant leader of a traditional party. But he was firmly set in the old ways, and the master of an *expertise* which was fast losing its meaning. Like his colleagues he was immensely intelligent, but he was impercipient. New facts made little impression on his capacious but insensitive mind. His Irish policy ignored the changed situation both in the south and north of Ireland, and was a score of years out of date.

He had no serious philosophy to meet the new phenomena in the world of labour and in the national economy. He was most at home in the cause which had always engaged his party, the furtherance of political freedom, but it was a cause which had become for the moment of lesser importance. He was a man of wide knowledge and many intellectual interests, but he was essentially the Balliol type of the 'seventies, rational, sceptical, a devotee of a liberty which he left half-comprehended, as a Schoolman left the mysteries of his Church. Whatever ran counter to his bland libertarianism seemed an impiety. I remember, when the audacities of Lytton Strachey's Victorian studies were delighting the world, suggesting to Mr. Asquith that the time was ripe for a return match. It was easy, I said, to make fun of the household of faith, but I thought that just as much fun could be made out of the other side, even with the most respectful and accurate presentation. I suggested a book to be called *Three Saints of Rationalism* on the lines of *Eminent Victorians*, and proposed for the chapters John Stuart Mill, Herbert Spencer and John Morley. He was really shocked, as shocked as a High Churchman would be who was invited to consider the comic side of the Oxford Movement.

Let me take three figures of the time who were not impercipient. I did not know Ramsay Macdonald intimately until after the War, and I was not greatly impressed by the ordinary Labour intellectual, who seemed to be threshing and rethreshing the thin crops of Fabianism and Marxism. But I knew Philip Snowden, to whom I was introduced by Charles Masterman, who married my wife's cousin. I have rarely met a man whose character was so four-square and compact, so wholly without loose fringes. He was like one of his own stony, grey Yorkshire moors, grim at first sight, but hiding in its folds nooks of a rare beauty. The austere face could break into the kindliest and tenderest of smiles. He had a corrosive irony in handling opponents, but he was bitter only about creeds, never about human beings.

His faith, I think, was more radicalism than any form of socialism, for he fought shy of theories and was never happy with abstractions. To his radicalism he joined something of the old nonconformist missionary fire. He knew the life of the poor at first hand, and laboured to better it, but he had no sentimentality about the transcendent virtues of the working classes, and would talk to them as firmly as to their masters. In discussion I have never known a more candid mind. He put all his cards on the table, and had none of the intellectual vanity which worships a false consistency. He realised the new forces which had come into being and faced them with perfect courage. For at the back of all he had a kind of rugged, ultimate optimism. He deeply loved his country and reverenced his countrymen, and believed that there was no problem which Englishmen could not solve if only they were true to themselves and to sound reason. It was this fine union of candour and optimism about human nature—at least English human nature—which endeared him to a man like Arthur Balfour, otherwise so different in mind and antecedents.

Lord Rosebery was also a realist who recognised that the old world was passing away. I had met him occasionally ever since my Oxford days, and in the years immediately preceding the War we used to forgather every autumn at his moorland house of Rosebery and walk the green confines of Lothian and Tweeddale. I have written elsewhere[1] of his career in politics and

[1] In "Proceedings of the British Academy," reprinted in Men and Deeds, 1935.

letters, which had by that time virtually come to an end. He had lost nearly all the aristocratic radicalism which had made him Mr. Gladstone's chief lieutenant in Scotland, and had adopted something very like old-fashioned Toryism, with occasional outbursts against individual Tories. His creed was based largely on Burke, and, like Burke, he distrusted anything in the nature of plebiscitary democracy. He disliked the new type of demagogic statesman. He regarded the *entente* with France as a menace which must end in a European War. Like Philip Snowden he believed in his countrymen, but unlike him he had also an enthusiasm for the Empire, about which he knew a great deal and Snowden nothing. But he had none of the latter's stalwart optimism about human nature, for his cosseted life had limited his knowledge of it. In our talks he was deeply pessimistic. Britain, he held, was on a razor edge internationally, and in domestic affairs was losing her former dignity and discipline. Had he written letters they would have been as devastating forecasts of calamity as those of Henry Adams—him of *The Education*. It was a melancholy experience for me after the War—I visited him almost every month—to see this former Prime Minister of Britain crushed by bodily weakness, sorrowing over the departing world and contemptuous of the new. It was sadly reminiscent of the old age of Chateaubriand. I went for a drive with him, I remember, at the Durdans on an April day in 1929, just before starting out for the elections in Scotland. I had never seen Surrey more green and flowery, but he was unconscious of the spring glories and was sunk in sad and silent meditations. When news of his death came a fortnight later I could not regret that my old friend was free of his bondage.

If it be a statesman's first duty to see facts clearly and to make the proper deductions from them, then I think that Arthur Balfour was the greatest public figure of that time. He was the only man in public life for whom I felt a disciple's loyalty. When he retired from the leadership of the Conservative party in 1911 the glamour went out of politics for me, and my feeling was that of the current parody of the Prayer Book: "Lord have mercy upon us and incline our hearts to Bonar Law."

A statesman should not be judged by his policy alone, since much of that may be the work of others; to get at the real man we must have cross-bearings from different angles. One key to the understanding of Arthur Balfour was his conversation. Unhesitatingly I should put him down as the best talker I have ever known, one whose talk was not a brilliant monologue or a string of epigrams, but a communal effort which quickened and elevated the whole discussion and brought out the best of other people. He would take the hesitating remark of a shy man and discover in it unexpected possibilities, would probe it and expand it until its author felt that he had really made some contribution to human wisdom. In the last year of the War he permitted me to take American visitors occasionally to lunch with him in Carlton Gardens, and I remember with what admiration I watched him feel his way with the guests, seize on some chance word and make it the pivot of speculations until the speaker was not only encouraged to give his best but that best was infinitely enlarged by his host's contribution. Such guests would leave walking on air, feeling no special obligation to Arthur Balfour—that was his cunning—but convinced that they were bigger men than they had thought.

In conversation, as in parliamentary debate, he had
a delicate courtesy, which was without a suspicion of
patronage. Hence he had friends of every type and
of all parties, and the only grumblers were the small
fry who considered that a leader should chain his soul
to party headquarters. The personalities of our friends
shift and change as they are lighted up differently by
a change of circumstance; but Arthur Balfour seemed
independent of his environment; the lighting changed,
but the light seemed to be in himself as in an opal or a
star-sapphire. There was nothing slack-lipped in his
geniality. He could be a stern critic of incompetence
and make devastating comments; as, for instance, his
remark about a certain politician that if he had a little
more brains he would be half-witted. Also he had
strict moral standards. In the graver matters of conduct
people were surprised to find that this urbane man of
the world had a stiff knuckle of puritanism, the stiffer
because it was so completely intelligent.

Another angle of approach was his prose, which to my
mind must rank in its dry purity with the best of our
time—the prose most in consonance with the peculiar
qualities of our English speech. It has an easy colloquial
pitch, which hardens now and then into a delicate
eighteenth-century formalism. Above all it is notable
for its exquisite logic, rare in these high-coloured days, a
logic which interpenetrates the sequence of sentences,
the choice of illustrations and the selection of epithets.
Its clarity is crystalline not watery, and it offers perfect
aptness and coherence in place of flowers and tears.

From his prose style and his talk one could gather
something about Arthur Balfour. A strong critical
mind and a fastidious taste; but also a reverence for
the plain man and the plain man's modes of thought.
The argument in his writings is usually directed against

the pedant with his specious generalities. He believes in and reverences the human reason, but that reason is not the contorted visionary thing of the metaphysician; it is common sense, the ordinary consciousness, a wise appreciation of the working rules of human society— the free play of the intellect, but an intellect which can understand the intractable subject matter it works with. Just as Rosebery was a seventeenth-century type, so there was much of the eighteenth century in Balfour, for he had its aversion to too roseate dreams about humanity, but also its profound consciousness of homely worth and homely wisdom. His enthusiasm, slow to kindle, was for what was practicable, for the business of carrying on the work of the world, and his hero was the man who was willing to take a hand.

He had few of the attributes of a popular leader since he was unrhetorical and fastidious and hated all that was showy and glossy, and his mental processes were often too subtle for popular comprehension. Yet he was a great party leader because of his overwhelming power in debate, and a moral elevation of which the nation became increasingly aware.

His character will be a puzzle to future historians, and it sometimes puzzled even his friends, since it united so many assumed contradictories. For example, he combined a real earnestness and a thorough-going scepticism. We find it in his philosophy. He approaches the world of simple faiths with reverence, and will never heedlessly disturb them, since he not only sees their practical value but shares in their spiritual appeal. He is sceptical chiefly of conventional scepticism. He has none of the poetry and the sudden high visions of the great system-makers; he is never *exalté*, his metaphors are never grandiose, he builds no cloud cities. But he does provide a rational basis for belief, and, speculatively, he

clears the air and defines the problems which he leaves
for later and more fortunate philosophers to solve.
Nor is his exposition without emotional fervour, and
sometimes his austere style can kindle into eloquence.
Take this from *The Religion of Humanity*. I could
quote better examples of his prose, but none more
typical of his essential faith.

"The 'religion of humanity' seems specially fitted
to meet the tastes of that comparatively small and
prosperous class, who are unwilling to leave the dry
bones of Agnosticism wholly unclothed with any
living tissue of religious emotion, and who are at the
same time fortunate enough to be able to persuade
themselves that they are contributing, or may con-
tribute, by their individual efforts to the attainment
of some great ideal for mankind. But what has it to
say to the more obscure multitude who are absorbed,
and well-nigh overwhelmed, in the constant struggle
with daily needs and narrow cares; who have but
little leisure or inclination to consider the precise role
they are called on to play in the great drama of
'humanity,' and who might in any case be puzzled
to discover its interest or its importance? Can it
assure them that there is no human being so insignificant as not to be of infinite worth in the eyes
of Him who created the Heavens, or so feeble but
that his actions may have consequences of infinite
moment long after this material system shall have
crumbled into nothingness? Does it offer con-
solation to those who are in grief, hope to those who
are bereaved, strength to the weak, forgiveness to
the sinful, rest to those who are weary and heavy
laden? If not, then, whatever be its merits, it is no
rival to Christianity. It cannot penetrate and vivify

L

the inmost life of ordinary humanity. There is in it no nourishment for ordinary human souls, no comfort for ordinary human sorrow, no help for ordinary human weakness. Not less than the crudest irreligion does it leave us men divorced from all communion with God, face to face with the unthinking energies of nature which gave us birth, and into which, if supernatural religion indeed be a dream, we must after a few fruitless struggles be again dissolved."

Still another rare combination was his pessimism and optimism. He had none of the Victorian belief in progress. He saw no golden age in the future, and he doubted the existence of any in the past. Hope and dream, he seemed to say, but if you are wise do not look for too much; this world is a bridge to pass over, not to build upon. But at the same time he revered the fortitude of human nature, the courage with which men stumbled up the steep ascent of life. It was the business of a leader, he thought, not so much to put quality into his following as to elicit it, since the quality was already there. Above all he trusted his countrymen. After the battle of Jutland he held that they were stout-hearted enough to hear the plain truth. He revised the doctrine of the Empire so as to shift the emphasis from constitutional bonds to human loyalties. But the most remarkable union of opposites was his devotion to what was old and his aliveness to what was new. He had the eighteenth-century sense of living in a world which was not made yesterday and emphatically would not be remade to-morrow, and he saw the long descent of the most novel problems. Like Burke, he would not destroy what many generations had built merely because some of the plasterwork was shaky. At the same time he was wholly in tune with his age and aware of every *nuance* of the modern world. He would never admit that there was any merit in a thing merely because it was new, but he gave it a judicial examination. We see this spirit in his philosophy. In his essay on "Berkeley" he observes that it is essential for a philosopher to possess "the instinct which tells him where, along the line of contemporary speculation, that point is to be found from which the next advance may best be made." This instinct he had in a remarkable degree, and his channel of thought, which when he produced his first book was a backwater, became presently, under the guidance of Bergson and others, the fashionable stream. He saw deeper into labour problems than most of the Labour leaders. He was a far more prescient economist than either the practical business men or the academic expositors. He early saw the inevitable development of the Empire, and it was his hand in 1926 that wrote its new charter.

So unique a combination of qualities rarely combined made him a major force in public life, whether in or out of office. As I have said, he had none of the gifts which attract an easy popularity. He had his shortcomings too. Sometimes he used his powers on behalf of an obscurantism which was not his true creed. But he was a very great servant of the State and a great human being. To many there was something chilly in his aloofness from the passions of the market-place, something not quite human. Could he suffer and rejoice like an ordinary creature? Assuredly he could. I have seen him in old age show the light-heartedness of a boy, and he could mourn long and deeply, though silently, for the loss of friends. As the phrase goes, he "maximised" life, getting and giving of the best, and on his death-bed he looked forward to the end calmly and hopefully as the gateway to an ampler world.

CHAPTER VII

INTER ARMA

I

THE outbreak of War in 1914 found me a sick man. A combination of family anxieties and public activities had played havoc with my digestion, and the remedy was either a major operation or a long spell of rest. I was thirty-nine and consequently well over the age for enlistment, and in any case no recruiting office would accept me. So I went to bed for the better part of three miserable months, while every day brought news of the deaths of my friends. In the spring of 1915 I was convalescent and was able to act as *Times* correspondent at the Front until after the battle of Loos. Then I was annexed for a short season by the Foreign Office. In 1916 I was at last commissioned as an officer in the Intelligence Corps, and was in France until the early part of 1917, when I was recalled to a post under the War Cabinet. I obtained leave to have the necessary operation, and thereafter was engaged in intelligence work at home until the Armistice.

Such was my undistinguished record of service. That it was so meagre may be partly set down to my health. Compared with most men I had but a small share in the dangers of campaigning, but I had a full measure of its discomforts, since for the four years of war, and for some time afterwards, I was almost continuously unwell. The battle of the Somme was one long nightmare, when ill weather and fatigue had to be endured by a body which was nearly always in pain and was steadily declining in strength. My time in

164

France was purgatorial, for though I had few of the hardships of the actual trenches, lengthy journeys in the drizzling autumn and winter of 1916, damp billets, and irregular meals reduced me to such a state of physical wretchedness that even to-day a kind of nausea seizes me when some smell recalls the festering odour of the front line, made up of incinerators, latrines and mud. When I was brought home I had more in the way of bodily comforts, but excessive busyness soon undid the good effects of the operation, and all my work was a struggle against the collar.

The attitude of the detached observer was always difficult for me. To achieve any peace of mind I had to have some share, however small, in the business itself. The years of war were like a trough into which I found myself flung, in company with several million others. Life seemed to stand uneasily still, and in no direction was there any prospect. Much of my pleasure in the past had been due to the gift of reacting quickly to stimuli, and regarding each new day as a new creation. But now there were no stimuli, only a leaden routine of duties. The science of war had always been one of my hobbies, but it was hard for a minor cog to find interest in the operations of a huge impersonal machine which seemed to move with little intelligent purpose.

At first my ailments hid the world from me. By and by they also became a matter of routine, a background against which other objects stood out, and I could observe things and people. These ailments did me one service; they blunted my feeling about the sufferings of my friends, who had to face a far harder lot than mine. I felt dully that I had myself got quite as much as I could bear. In that grey hollow into which the universe had shrunk there were some—usually young men—who enjoyed it all, and breathed continually the air of adventure. The ordinary man went through it with fortitude and good humour as if it had been a kind of school, finding comfort in a new fellowship. To a few with exposed nerves and inward-turning eyes it was all an agony. To those who had had some taste of the rich variousness of the old life it meant bitter disappointment and a deadly *ennui*. But those who suffered most were, I think, the men who had already found their niche, who were approaching middle age, and whose bodies had not the resilience of youth. They felt acutely the physical strain; their minds were full of private anxieties; above all they saw the shattering of the house of life they had made for themselves, and despaired of building another.

From the start of the War I was clear that an old regime was passing away. That I did not regret, for the radicalism which is part of the Tory creed was coming uppermost, and I looked forward to a clearing out of much rubbish. But I realised that we were at the point of contact of a world vanishing and a world arriving, and that such a situation was apt to crush those who had to meet it. A new world would have to be made, and who would be left to make it? No man can have more than perhaps a score of intimate friends, and most of mine had gone, or were going. My youngest brother and my partner in business fell at Arras. Hugh Dawnay, whom I put first among the younger soldiers, died at First Ypres; Cecil Rawling, with whom, before the War, I had made plans for an attempt on Everest, fell as a brigadier at Passchendaele; my wife's cousin, Jack Stuart-Wortley, disappeared in the German advance of March 1918; Oxford contemporaries like Raymond Asquith and Bron Lucas, and younger friends like Charles Lister and the Grenfell twins, all were dead. Losses, which a few years before would have seemed cataclysmal, became a matter of course. One acquiesced in tragedy, but it was an acquiescence without hope or philosophy. There was no uplift of the spirit, such as is traditionally associated with battle.

I acquired a bitter detestation of war, less for its horrors than for its boredom and futility, and a contempt for its *panache*. To speak of glory seemed a horrid impiety. That was perhaps why I could not open Homer. I found that I could read very little, and that many things which used to charm me seemed meaningless, since they belonged to a dead world. My reading was chiefly in the Latin and Greek classics, which were beyond the caprice of time. I read and re-read Thucydides, for he also had lived among crumbling institutions; Virgil, for he had known both the cruelty and the mercy of life; Plato, above all, for he was seraphically free from the pettinesses which were at the root of our sorrows.

When I returned to England I gradually won a happier outlook. While in bed during the autumn months of 1914 I had begun a popular history of the War in monthly volumes, designed to keep my workpeople in employment, and its wide circulation induced the authorities to advise its continuance. This was a hard job in France, but it was easier in London—indeed, my difficulty was that I now knew too much and was often perplexed as to what I could print. Slowly I began to see the War as a gigantic cosmic drama, embracing every quarter of the globe and the whole orbit of man's life. Though it lacked the epic fervour and simplicity it had an apocalyptic splendour of design. This prospect, and my work, which lay largely in the study of the mind of other nations, gave me a new intellectual interest. Also I was acquiring a boundless admiration for human nature. It was a war, as I have written elsewhere, won he paid a visit to G.H.Q. and for a week, on Haig's instructions, I took him for an elaborate tour of the British Front. He talked much during those long cold journeys, brilliantly, persuasively, sometimes almost with inspiration. Had he had a more normal education and discipline he might have been a great man, for when unswayed by vanity he had sound judgment and a penetrating insight. . . . I saw at close quarters the intricate mechanism which directed the War at home, one of the strangest mixtures of amateur and professional, talent and charlatanry, the patriot and the *arriviste* which history has known, with behind it the dynamic figure of the Prime Minister, generating heat and somehow turning it into power. Of Mr. Lloyd George I have written elsewhere [1]; *proximus ardebat Ucalegon*; he was the flame at which all warmed, and many scorched, their hands.

I would pay tribute to one of the most brilliant, misunderstood, and tragically fated men of our time. Charles Masterman began by being overestimated, or rather estimated on the wrong lines, and he ended by being most unjustly decried. He came into Parliament at the election of 1906 in the van of the triumphant Liberals, a young Moses who was to lead the people to a new way of life. He had the idealist's ardour and a remarkable oratorical gift, and his sensitiveness to suffering was not mere rhetoric but a profound emotion. Then came his apprenticeship to the ordinary tasks of administration, and wholly different talents were revealed. Older members of his party spoke of him as having a heart of gold and a head full of feathers. It was a complete misunderstanding; much, but not all, of his idealism disappeared in the rut of office and was replaced by a mild cynicism, but he developed

[1] In *The King's Grace,* 1935.

notable administrative gifts, and did invaluable work for the Government in piloting some of their most controversial measures through the House. When we worked together during the War I found his judgment shrewd and bold and his mastery of detail impeccable. But I would stress above all things his loyalty. In his parliamentary career he was more faithful to his colleagues than they were to him. In his fidelity to principles and persons he put to shame the brittle loyalties of party.

I have some queer *macabre* recollections of those years —of meetings with odd people in odd places, of fantastic duties which a romancer would have rejected as beyond probability. I remember a dinner at my house in the spring of 1916, when I happened to be on leave, and a delegation from the Russian Duma was visiting England. I have forgotten some of the guests, but Arthur Balfour was present, and Maurice Baring, and Milyukov, the leader of the Cadets, and Protopopov. The last was a sick man and slept so badly in his hotel that I invited him to stay with me. He had great personal charm, but I think that even then he was a little mad. He professed to have learned some English poetry from his nurse, and as examples he repeated with tremendous gusto various nursery rhymes like "A Frog he would a-wooing go." A few months later he became the henchman of the Empress and Rasputin, and the proximate cause of the Russian Revolution, and in a year the Bolsheviks had him shot in prison.[1]

---

[1] I have other fantastic experiences in my recollection, and two of the most unpredictable belong to recent years and the American continent. In April 1937 I addressed crowded sessions of the Senate and the House of Representatives in Washington without having had the opportunity to prepare speeches. In September 1939 at Ottawa I was got out of bed in the small hours of a Sunday morning to declare war on Germany on Canada's behalf, and had staying in the house at the time a son of the late Emperor of Austria!

man lacked discipline, both intellectual and moral. Sometimes he was dangerous, for he was very vain; he had a gift, too, of making a situation more clear than God intended it to be, and therefore he had an undue influence upon civilian minds at home. More often he was simply futile, a brilliant child bombinating in the void. But if his defects were obvious so were his qualities, his courage, his humour, his unflagging gusto. He used to tell how he once overheard some Frenchmen discussing his appearance and trying to find the *mot juste*. "*Ce monsieur*," said one at last, "*a une physionomie à part*." The whole man was *à part*. I never met anyone in the least like him, and that long, lean, whimsical face, like a good-natured pike, will not soon be forgotten by his friends.

The soldiers whom I have known best in my life were Julian Byng and Douglas Haig. One evening in the year 1902 I found myself sitting on my haversack at a derelict station in the South African veld wondering where I should find a meal and a bed. A cloud of dust appeared on the horizon, and presently a mounted column arrived with Byng in command. He gave me supper, and from that hour dated a close friendship. His nature was compounded of a child-like delight in simple things, a resolute and clear-sighted sagacity, infinite kindliness and a profound religion. He had that best sort of humour which sees and rejoices in the homely whimsicalities of life. In the War he was a centre of legend, and most of the stories about him have the merit of being true. The most familiar tells how during the German advance in March 1918, when he was in command of the Third Army, he was sitting in his headquarters at Albert and was visited by a staff officer from G.H.Q. Every five minutes a telephone message was handed to him, with news of the retreat of one of his divisions. Julian studied the messages, and then, laying his hand on the pile, turned to the staff officer. "Did you ever hear," he asked, "of an admiral of my name?" Another belongs to the early days of the campaign when he commanded a cavalry division in the neighbourhood of Ypres. One evening, accompanied by a young A.D.C., he went for a walk in an unsalubrious bit of ground somewhere near Klein Zillebeke. Apparently in deep thought, he strolled unconcernedly among the craters, while shells fell unpleasantly close, and the A.D.C. became nervous for the safety of his charge and himself. "But I must not say a word," he thought. "He is working out some tremendous scheme." At last they reached a sunken road, and Julian beckoned the A.D.C. to him. "What do you think?" he asked. "Wouldn't the partridges come over here nicely?"

There can have been few commanders who were more rapturously adored by their men, and it was because of his rich, understanding humanity, what in Scotland is called "innerliness," and not because of any genial slackness, for he kept a tight rein on discipline. To whatever he commanded he gave his own "tone," whether a cavalry division, or the Canadian Corps, or the Third Army, or the Metropolitan Police. Like Sir Walter Scott, he talked to every man as if he were a blood relation. As Governor-General of Canada he met again the men who had served under him, and there is a Byng legend in the Dominion to-day which will always be part of its tradition. The tall figure in very old clothes, with a short pipe in his mouth, sitting on a gate talking to a prairie farmer, is a picture which Canada will long cherish. He had the key which instantaneously unlocks men's hearts.

Haig was a different and a far more complex being.

He was a member of my own Oxford college, and he was descended from one of the most famous of Border families; so he and I had a ready-made basis for friendship. Once in South Africa I carried despatches to him, and, oversleeping myself, was decanted at Colesberg platform on a bitter winter morning indecently clad in pyjamas and a British-warm. He received my apologies with the remark that Brasenose had never been a dressy college! I was for a time attached to G.H.Q. and saw a good deal of him there, and after the War, when he was settled at Bemersyde, I had ample opportunity for the study of a mind and character which no neat formula could assess. He became so much the subject of controversy that those who loved him, as I did, were inclined to a mere defiant eulogy. But eulogy was the last thing that so rare a personality sought or desired.

He was first and foremost a highly competent professional soldier. Now a soldier's professionalism differs from that of other crafts. He acquires a body of knowledge which may be varied and enlarged by new conditions, such as new weapons and new modes of transport, but which in essence is a closed technique. The reason is that, unlike art, law and medicine, there has in the past been little in the way of a philosophy of first principles behind it to stimulate evolution; a powerful mind might work brilliantly inside its limits with little impulse to alter the fundamentals. Change and expansion were consequently in the nature of a revolution, and were brought about either by a great genius, or—slowly and grudgingly—by some cataclysmic pressure of facts. Hence the more competent and better trained a soldier was, the more averse he would be to alter his traditional creed till its failure had been proven with utter finality.

This was the attitude of all the principal com-

manders, British, French and German, at the beginning
of the War. The campaign produced in the high
command no military genius of the first order, no
Napoleon, Marlborough or Lee, scarcely even a
Wellington, a Stonewall Jackson or a Sherman. Its
type was Grant. Hence changes of method had to
come by the sheer pressure of events after much tragic
trial and error. Haig was as slow to learn as any of his
colleagues, and he made grave mistakes. But he did learn.
Take one point, the use of cavalry ; having once opened
his mind, he showed himself notably receptive and
prescient. Most of the tactics of the final advance to
victory were his, and in the last great movement he
leaned upon Foch no more than Foch leaned upon him.
It is fair to say, I think, that his mind developed fast as
soon as circumstances permitted it to develop at all.

But in a soldier character is at least as vital as intellect,
and there can be no question about the quality of his
character. He had none of the lesser graces which make
a general popular with troops, and it took four years
for his armies to feel his personality.[1] To his friends
that personality in war was a revelation. They had
known him as an able, ambitious and industrious soldier,
handsome and fashionable, a good sportsman, the type
certain to succeed under normal conditions—in a word,
a conventional type. But in supreme command a new
man appeared. For one thing he spoke with a broader
accent—of the Borders, oddly enough, instead of his
native Fife. The religion of his childhood was recaptured, and a spirit naturally kindly and genial was
braced by a kind of Covenanting fervour to an austere

[1] He had not Sir John French's gift of speaking to the chance-met
soldier. Once, I remember, he tried it. There was a solitary private by
the roadside, whom he forced himself to address. *Haig:* "Well, my
man, where did you start the war?" *Private* (pale to the teeth): "I
swear to God, sir, I never started no war." It was his last attempt.

M

discipline and a constant sense of the divine fore-ordering of life. He had found deep wells from which to draw comfort. The self was obliterated, for I do not think that he ever thought of his own reputation. Unrhetorically, almost unconsciously, his country and what he held to be God's purpose became for him the transcendent realities.

This character, thus toughened and elevated, was highly tried. He had to feel his way in his task and was often conscious of blunders, more acutely conscious, I think, than most of his critics. He had difficulties with his allies, with his colleagues, with the home Government, though, let it be said, he had far less to complain of on the latter score than most soldiers of a democracy —Wellington in the Peninsula, for example, or Lee. He had repeated bitter disappointments. He had the wolf by the ears, and at first he clung to traditional methods, when a smaller man might have tried fantastic experiments which would have assuredly spelt disaster. He did not revise his plans until the old ones had been fully tested, and a new one had emerged of which his reason could approve. Under him we incurred heavy losses, but I believe that these losses would have been greater had he been the brilliant empiric like Nivelle or Henry Wilson. When the last great enemy attack came he took the main shock with a quiet resolution; when the moment arrived for the advance he never fumbled. He broke through the Hindenburg line in spite of the doubts of the British Cabinet, because he believed that only thus could the War be ended in time to save civilisation. He made the decision alone—one of the finest proofs of moral courage in the history of war. Haig cannot enter the small circle of the greater captains, but it may be argued that in the special circumstances of the campaign his special qualities were the ones most needed—patience, sobriety, balance of temper, unshakable fortitude. His best epitaph is the sentence which Pope wrote of Harley: "He was a steady man and a great firmness of soul."

There were no strong colours in his nature, but he diffused a gentle compelling radiance. As I have said, he was incapable of rhetoric, and his addresses to his troops, as in April 1918, were of a hodden-grey simplicity. His interests were limited. When eminent and cultivated guests came on a visit to G.H.Q., to prevent the Commander-in-Chief sitting tongue-tied, a kind of conversational *menu* had to be arranged. For example, Walter Pater, who had been his tutor, had once said something to him about style which he remembered, and it was desirable to lead the talk up to that. After the War he led the pleasant life of a Border country gentleman in the home of his ancestors, and a stranger, meeting him in the hunting-field or at a covert side, could never have guessed the storms he had ridden. His end came too soon—but happily, for there was no decline in his mental powers. On the very morning when I read of his death I received from him a copy of his "appreciation" of the War, now in the British Museum, to which he had added new and illuminating passages. In peace his main interest was in the future of the men who had fought under him, and he refused all rewards until he had convinced himself that they were not forgotten. "He will go to Heaven for that, said Corporal Trim."

III

The Armistice found me at the end of my tether and I straightway collapsed into bed. I was not fit to stand for Parliament at the ensuing election, nor did I want to, for the pre-War party labels seemed to me meaningless, so I withdrew from my candidature and induced my supporters to vote for my former opponent. It was not until the early spring of 1919 that I could crawl out of cover and survey the post-War scene.

To my surprise I found that I had recovered something of the exhilaration of youth. I was forty-three, but I seemed to have "found again my twentieth year." My reason indeed warned me that there was little cause for optimism. The War, the vastest disordering since the breakdown of the Pax Romana, must be followed by decades of suffering and penury. Many familiar things had gone, and many more would go. Britain had lost for good her old security in the world, and, like other peoples, she would have to struggle to preserve stability at home. I hoped for something from the League of Nations, but with diffidence, for the mechanism seemed to me futile without the appropriate spirit, and I did not find that spirit in the world. But I had a new confidence in human nature, in the plain man who for four years had carried the globe on his shoulders, with no gift of expression, unperplexed by philosophies, but infinitely loyal, enduring and unconquerable. I believed that, though it would be a slow business, he might be trusted somehow to remake the world, for he was eternally, in Shelley's words, "at enmity with nothingness and dissolution."

As the weeks passed I realised that that was happening which Canning noted after the Napoleonic wars; "the spires and turrets of ancient establishments began to reappear above the subsiding wave." There were times when one had the impression, soon alas! dispelled by reflection, that nothing had been lost except one's friends. The world had not become the drab wilderness that I had feared, and I felt again Bruno's *visibilium aeternus, immensus et innumerabilis affectus.*

I shall never forget my first visit to the country, to Warwickshire and Oxfordshire, in April 1919. In the early years of the War natural beauty had been to me a forbidden fruit. I was in the Salient during the second battle of Ypres, and the scent of hawthorn and lilac battling with the stink of poison-gas, and bird-song in the coverts heard in the pauses of the great guns, seemed to underline grimly the indifference of nature to human ills. I remember a June morning, too, in the Chilterns, the beauty of which seemed to me only a savage irony. Experiences in France, which at another time would have entranced me—flaming Picardy sunsets, fresh windy dawns, little towns dumb with snow under the winter moon—were things to which I had no title. I acquired a saner temper when my duties brought me back to England, but I still felt a brittleness in life and a profound insecurity, a sense that the treasures of the past and the joys of the natural world had become "too dear for my possessing." I walked warily, as if the ground under me were mined. I used to admire the detachment of Edward Grey, who would have observed the ways of wild duck though the skies were falling; indeed we sometimes did it together in St. James's Park when the outlook was black as Erebus. But on that April journey I recovered the past, and with it hope for the future. The War after all was only what Henry James called it, a "great interruption." I was almost back in Keats's Chamber of Maiden Thought. I felt like a man recovering from a fever, or like the mediaeval poet who, going into the fields after his frozen winter's vigil, abased himself before the miracle of spring.

> "Tears
> Are in his eyes, and in his ears
> The murmur of a thousand years."

CHAPTER VIII

AN IVORY TOWER AND ITS PROSPECT

I

THE War left me with an intense craving for a country life. It was partly that I wanted quiet after turmoil, the instinct that in the Middle Ages took men into monasteries. But it was also a new-found delight in the rhythm of nature, and in small homely things after so many alien immensities. In all times of public strife there has been this longing for rural peace; Chaucer had it, and Dunbar, and Izaak Walton:

> "Far from acquaintance kest thee
> Where country may digest thee . . .
> Thank God that so hath blest thee,
> And sit down, Robin, and rest thee."

So I sold my house in London and purchased the little manor house of Elsfield, four miles from the city of Oxford.

The house and the countryside were rich in history, and I had become most historically minded. My old interest in philosophy was ebbing. I had had enough for the moment of theories and speculations, and I had certainly had enough of changes. When the future is uncertain the mind turns naturally to the certainties of the past, and finds comfort in what is beyond the peril of change. History might be only what Napoleon called it, "agreed fiction," but at any rate it was agreed, and had the dignity of repose. I wanted the sense of continuity, the assurance that our contemporary blunders were endemic in human nature, that our new fads were very ancient heresies, that beloved things which were threatened had rocked not less heavily in the past.

In common with most of my countrymen I felt that for the time I had done with civic duty, and might reasonably return to my own affairs. That feeling, I think, explains the lack of public servants to-day, even more than the "lost generation." No doubt a great number of able young men died, but of those who survived only a small proportion took to public life; the majority turned resolutely to private business and stayed there. They refused to bury themselves in what T. E. Lawrence used to describe as the "shallow grave of public duty."

The intellectual atmosphere of the immediate post-War period was enough to drive the ordinary man into privacy. While plain folk everywhere set themselves sturdily to rebuild their world, the interpreting class, which Coleridge called the "clerisy," the people who should have influenced opinion, ran round their cages in vigorous pursuit of their tails. If they were futile they were also arrogant, and it was an odd kind of arrogance, for they had no creed to preach. The same type before the War had prostrated themselves in gaping admiration of the advance of physical science and the improvements in the material apparatus of life. There was little of that left. The War had shown that our mastery over physical forces might end in a nightmare, that mankind was becoming like an overgrown child armed with deadly weapons, a child with immense limbs and a tiny head. But this belated enlightenment seemed to drain their vitality. Just as many of the boys then leaving school, who had escaped war service, suffered from a kind of *accidie* and were inclined to look for "soft options" in life, so the interpreting class plumed themselves wearily on being hollow men living in a waste land. "A man may dwell so long upon a thought," Halifax wrote, "that it may take him prisoner"; and they had made a picture of the world and themselves from which they could not escape. They had no philosophy, if Plato's definition in the *Theaetetus* be right—"the mood of the philosopher is wonder; there is no other source of philosophy than this"—for wonder involves some vigour of spirit. They would admit no absolute values, being by profession atomisers, engaged in reducing the laborious structure of civilised life to a whirling nebula.

It was a difficult time for those who called themselves intellectuals. They found themselves living among the fears and uncertainties of the Middle Ages, without the support of the mediaeval faith. The belief in the perfectibility of man, the omnipotence of reason, and the certainty of progress, which began with the French Encyclopaedists and flourished among the brisk dogmatists of the nineteenth century, had more or less ended with the War. It was very clear that reason could be enchained, that human nature was showing no desire to be perfected, and that the pillars of civilisation were cracking and tilting. The inerrancy of science, too, which had sustained the Victorians, was proving a broken reed, for science was going back upon itself, cultivating doubts and substituting probabilities for certainties. The world of sense and time had become distressingly insecure, and they had no other world.

One section of this class, very vocal in speech and writing, cherished modernity as its peculiar grace, regarding the word as descriptive of quality, and not merely as denoting a stage in time. These people, who

ELSFIELD MANOR

HATFIELD MANOR

were usually young, had few of the genial characteristics of youth, and their extravagances were not
Plato's agreeable impertinences of juniors to seniors.[1]
They were a haunted race, who seemed to labour under
perpetual fear. Like a tenth-century monk who expected the world soon to end, they had ruled out of
their lives many normal human interests on the ground
that the times were too precarious for trifling. They
seemed to be eager to get rid of personal responsibility,
and therefore in politics—and in religion if they had
any—were inclined to extremes, and readily surrendered
their souls to an ancient church or a new prophet, an
International or a dictator. They were owlishly in
earnest and wholly humourless ; and, lacking moral and
intellectual balance, they were prone to violent changes.
It was the old story of the debauchee turned flagellant,
and a man who had made a name by raking in the
garbage heaps would suddenly become a precisian in
manners and morals. They had a limitless contempt for
whatever did not conform to their creed of the moment
and expressed it loudly, but their voices would suddenly
crack, and what began as a sneer would end as a sob.

Another section gave their minds to historical
portraiture—which might be more accurately described
as historical fiction, for they were without the scholar's
discipline and conscience. Lytton Strachey, their
fugleman, was an accomplished man of letters, but in
his followers his faults became monstrous and his
virtues disappeared. With slender talents, callow and
arrogant, their "facetious and rejoicing ignorance"
made a strange spectacle of the past. They were much
concerned with sex, and found sexual interest in
unusual places, dwelling upon it with a sly titter. They
were sansculottes who sought to deflate majestic reputa-

---

[1] νεανιεύματα ἰδιωτῶν εἰς ἄρχοντας. *Republic*, iii. 390.

tions, and reduce the great to a drab level of mediocrity, like the Jacobins who would have destroyed Chartres Cathedral because it dominated offensively their foolish little city.

There was also a curious deterioration in literary manners—it had nothing to do with morals. Frankness in literature is an admirable thing if, as at various times in our history, it keeps step with social habit; but when it strives to advance beyond it, it becomes a disagreeable pose. Among civilised people after the War the ordinary conventions held, but in literature, especially in fiction, a dull farmyard candour became fashionable, an insistence upon the functions of the body which had rarely artistic value.

> "No crab more active in the dirty dance,
> Downward to climb, and backward to advance."

These dull salacities had their comic as well as their offensive side, for novelists, who had been noted for their virginal decorum, would now interpolate little bits of irrelevant coarseness to show that Master Slender was also a man of mettle.

It all spelled a revolt against humanism, a return to the sourness of puritanism without its discipline and majesty. The old humanism was a revulsion from mediaeval doctrine of original sin and salvation by divine grace. It placed the centre of gravity in man and believed in progress and the perfectibility of the world. Against such a view, which was essentially un-Christian, there were bound to be many rebels, and its opponents, the great Puritans like Cromwell, found refuge in abasement before God. The new rebels did not greatly admire humanity, seeing chiefly its animal grossness, they did not believe in progress, and they had no high-pitched dreams of a coming golden age. Therefore they were rootless and unhappy, for they had not Cromwell's refuge. But gradually one seemed to discern the beginnings of a return to religion. There was not that spiritual awakening after the War which some had foreseen, but as the years passed there was a steady drift towards some form of faith. A proof was the number of distinguished converts to the Catholic Church; at the other end of the scale the Calvinism of Karl Barth; the revival of Thomism; the embittered puritanism of certain men of letters; and a variety of new evangels, some of them foolish enough, but all involving a stumbling quest for God. The glib agnostic had gone out of fashion.

In the prevalent intellectual anarchy there was also a craving for order and law. It was inevitable that this purpose would in certain circles be crudely interpreted, and order identified with uniformity on the communist pattern. The dream of a classless society was never very potent in Britain, for our people had Shakespeare's belief in the virtue of a rich heterogeneity.

> "Take but degree away, untune that string,
> And hark what discord follows."

But the craving in its least admirable form was to grow elsewhere in the world to an extent and at a pace which no one then foresaw. Men for the sake of security and order were to barter their souls. Ironic atonement was made for feudalism and the centuries of privilege when proud nations fell into abject bondage to inflamed and loquacious peasants.

II

Elsfield was like the dwelling of Axylos, the son of Teuthras, in the *Iliad*, a house by the roadside. It opened on the village street, but, being built on the slope of a hill, its back view was superb, covering the Cherwell valley and all the western Cotswold. The oldest part was alleged to have twelfth-century walls, contemporary with the little church; but its form was Jacobean and the rest was Oxford gothic of the 'seventies. The manor had had few owners since the days of the Saxon Aella: the Norman grantee, the Pudseys from Yorkshire, the Hores from East Anglia, and then until nearly the end of last century it was a kind of dower-house for the North family at Wroxton, further up the Cherwell.[1] It was a clearing in the forest long before the Conquest, and a clearing it remained, so that at the siege of Oxford the Parliament army used it as a gun-park.

England is full of patches which the tides of modernity have somehow missed, and Elsfield was such an one. Though only fifty-five miles by road from London, and an hour's walk from Oxford, it was as set in its ancient ways as an isle of the Hebrides. When I first went there my gamekeeper had never been in a railway train. At that time it was the only side of Oxford where there were no suburbs, for the college towers could be seen from our hill rising sheer from meadows, and there was the same moat of deep country between its mind and the outer world. Startling experiences passed from its people like water from a duck's back. My gardener had fought through the East African campaign and nearly died of fever, and another of my men had had four years in France, but for all the effect those adventures had on them they might never have left the parish. It was the same with the neighbouring hamlets, like Noke and Wood Eaton and Beckley.

Elsfield stood on the edge of the long ridge which

[1] The history of the parish has been written by Professor G. N. Clark of Oxford.

intervenes between the Chilterns and Cotswold, a ridge muffled in great woods, and dropping in the north to the fen of Otmoor; so our people were half-uplanders and half-woodlanders, and therefore dissociated both from the shepherd-folk of the high Cotswold and the valley-folk along Thames and Cherwell. They had their own ways, their own speech, their own pride of descent, for you will find the same names to-day in the villages as in mediaeval abbey-rolls, and they gripped like a vice on the past. From my lawn I looked over some thirty miles of woods and meadows to the dim ridges about Stow-on-the-Wold, and, except in the bareness of winter, there was not a house to be seen. That view was a symbol of our detachment.

It was a good countryside for the field naturalist. My garden soil was the coarse limestone called cornbrash, which gave place to Oxford clay in the meadows below. The flat top of the hill was sand. There was an abundance of water everywhere on the hillside. As a consequence of this geological variety the flora was notably rich; three hundred years ago Mr. Gerard of the *Herball* botanised in Stowood. To the bird-lover the place was a paradise. In my first summer a pair of peregrines— from Wales or the spire of Salisbury Cathedral—came every morning to hunt our fields. I have seen on the lawn at the same time pied, grey and yellow wagtails. A hobby nested in one of our spinneys. On my morning rides, when my horse's hooves were muffled in the grass, I twice saw a golden oriole. Otmoor, a couple of miles off, was a wonderful haunt of rare birds, and anything might appear by its reedy watercourses—bitterns, cranes, one winter a pair of storks. Dr. Plot at the end of the seventeenth century recorded a hoopoe's nest on Otmoor. I have never found the nest, but I have seen the bird there.

With one species of fowl my household became well acquainted. My eldest son from his early days was a passionate falconer. He kept hawks at Eton, for there is much latitude in that great republic, and at Oxford he was rarely without a bird on his wrist. I liked best the little kestrels who each summer sat and scolded on their perches on the lawn. He ended by becoming a real authority on the subject, and corresponded with fellow-falconers all over the world. It was the training of the birds that interested him, and he flew them only at vermin. Falcons are terribly fragile things, and we lived under the shadow of death, for the birds were always hanging themselves, or developing strange diseases. This was particularly true of his peregrines, but his goshawk, Jezebel, survived until he went to Uganda, when she was handed over to Lord Howard de Walden.

In my leisure at Elsfield I came under the spell which makes men local antiquaries. A predecessor had set the example, for Francis Wise, Radcliffe librarian and Dr. Johnson's friend, had once lived in the house. He had filled the garden with dubious antiques, including a Roman altar, which was examined by no less a person than Mommsen, and had designed a gardener's cottage in the style of a mediaeval chantry. Everything in that countryside is long-descended. Follow the ridge northward and you pass at Beckley the ruins of a hunting-lodge of the kings of England, and presently tread the floor of a Roman villa. Cross Otmoor by what at most seasons is the only practicable way, and you are traversing a Roman road, while in the hollow of one of our meadows are the remains of a fibula factory. Every one of our quaintly named little fields has appeared in deeds and chartularies for nine hundred years. The past came so close to the present that it was inevitable that I should delve happily and unskilfully in its corners. I was especially fascinated by the Civil War, in which Oxfordshire had been a famous terrain—with the actions at Islip bridge, Bletchingdon, Cropredy and Edgehill, and Charles's wild ride on that June evening when he slipped out from the city between Waller and Essex.

I resumed my walking habits, and of a Saturday would disappear on a lengthy tramp. My favourite course was the circuit of Otmoor, taking in its Seven Towns. That was the low-level route; the high-level route was longer—about thirty miles—and covered the circumjacent hills, Brill, Arncote, Gravelhill, and the rise of Wood Eaton. There was also an infinite variety of shorter courses up and down the Cherwell valley, and east and north into Bucks. In time I became more ambitious and used the motor-car to get me far afield, so that a day's walk might take me into distant shires and over the water-shed of Severn.

Our ridge was old forest land and it provided one of the two types of landscape which have always had a special charm for me. These types are the mountain-meadow and the woodland clearing. By the first I do not mean the Swiss alp or the Norwegian sacter pasture, for these are on too large a scale. I mean rather the little meadows which one stumbles across in certain up-land places—the "mountain lawns" of the poets—which have the charm of a garden in the wilderness. I can think of a hundred such—in Wales especially, and throughout the whole hill chain which runs from Vermont to the Carolinas. The other is the island of pasture, made by man's hands, in a sea of forest, and of such I have memories in south Germany, in New England, and above all in eastern Canada—places where the turf is greener by contrast with the inky pines, and which make a sanctuary for birds and flowers. Elsfield

was rich in those secret glades, sometimes only an acre
wide, but all ancient clearings whose turf had been
cropped for centuries. Summer never dulled their ver-
dure, for there was water in most of them, and in autumn
their fringes were a riot of berries.. One could find
primroses there every month of the year.

Now I "took sasine" of English soil, and learned to
know intimately what I had hitherto only admired.
Especially I came to respect the English countryman
who had been the backbone of our army in the War,
and has always been the backbone of the nation. I
delighted in his slow idiomatic speech, his firm hold on
the past, his fortitude and kindliness. Indeed, I think
those early years at Elsfield were the happiest in my
life, for I acquired a new loyalty and a new heritage,
having added the southern Midlands to the Scottish
Borders. I loved

> "with equal mind
> The southern sun, the northern wind,
> The lilied lowland watermead,
> And the grey hills that cradle Tweed ";

and felt amazingly rich in consequence. The procession
of the seasons was now part of my life, as it could not
be for a town-dweller, and to watch it gave me a keener
sense of the rhythm of things. I enjoyed every type of
scene and weather—autumn gales which blew down
Thames from the Bristol Channel, the first snow clouds
from the Chilterns, the long-lighted midsummer days
when sunrise trod on the heels of sunset, the woods
bathed in the clear radiance of April and alive with
bird-song. Riding on winter mornings I would see
the lights go out one by one in the villages of the plain,
or, returning in the twilight, watch them kindle, and
reflect that I lived apart from, and yet within hail of,
the sounding, glittering world.

J.N.S.B. AND HIS GOSHAWK JEZEBEL

On most days I went to my office in London, a longish daily journey, but it was worth while getting back late, even in winter, to the smell of wood smoke and the hooting of owls. Later, when I had given up business and entered Parliament, I arranged my life differently. From Monday afternoon until Friday I was in town and concerned exclusively with business and politics. From Friday evening until Monday at noon I was in sanctuary at Elsfield, a minor country gentleman with a taste for letters.

III

I was beginning to deserve the name of man of letters. As an author I was a link with the past, for in my extreme youth in the 'nineties I had contributed to the old *Yellow Book*. As an impecunious undergraduate I read manuscripts for John Lane, who was a good friend to me, and had the privilege of accepting Arnold Bennett's first book, *A Man from the North*. Then for a little my literary activities flagged, but in the post-War years I was responsible for a good deal of military history—the story of my family regiment, the Royal Scots Fusiliers; a record of the doings of the South African Infantry Brigade in France; and a memoir of my friends, the Grenfell twins, Francis and Riversdale, who fell in the first year of war. Meantime I had become a copious romancer. I suppose I was a natural story-teller, the kind of man who for the sake of his yarns would in prehistoric days have been given a seat by the fire and a special chunk of mammoth. I was always telling myself stories when I had nothing else to do—or rather, being told stories, for they seemed to work themselves out independently. I generally thought of a character or two, and then of a set of incidents, and the question was how my people would behave.

N

They had the knack of just squeezing out of unpleasant places and of bringing their doings to a rousing climax.

I was especially fascinated by the notion of hurried journeys. In the great romances of literature they provide some of the chief dramatic moments, and since the theme is common to Homer and the penny reciter it must appeal to a very ancient instinct in human nature. We live our lives under the twin categories of time and space, and when the two come into conflict we get the great moment. Whether failure or success is the result, life is sharpened, intensified, idealised. A long journey, even with the most lofty purpose, may be a dull thing to read of if it is made at leisure; but a hundred yards may be a breathless business if only a few seconds are granted to complete it. For then it becomes a sporting event, a race; and the interest which makes millions read of the Derby is the same, in a grosser form, as when we follow an expedition straining to relieve a beleaguered fort, or a man fleeing to a sanctuary with the avenger behind him.

In my undergraduate days I had tried my hand at historical novels, and had then some ambition to write fiction in the grand manner, by interpreting and clarifying a large piece of life. This ambition waned and, apart from a few short stories, I let fiction alone until 1910, when, being appalled as a publisher by the dullness of most boys' books, I thought I would attempt one of my own, based on my African experience. The result was *Prester John*, which has since become a school-reader in many languages. Early in 1914 I wrote *Salute to Adventurers*, the fruit of my enthusiasm for American history. In that book I described places in Virginia which I had never seen, and I was amazed, when I visited them later, to find how accurate had been my guesses.

Then, while pinned to my bed during the first months of war and compelled to keep my mind off too tragic realities, I gave myself to stories of adventure. I invented a young South African called Richard Hannay, who had traits copied from my friends, and I amused myself with considering what he would do in various emergencies. In *The Thirty-Nine Steps* he was spy-hunting in Britain; in *Greenmantle* he was on a mission to the East; and in *Mr. Standfast*, published in 1919, he was busy in Scotland and France. The first had an immediate success, and, since that kind of thing seemed to amuse my friends in the trenches, I was encouraged to continue. I gave Hannay certain companions—Peter Pienaar, a Dutch hunter; Sandy Arbuthnot, who was reminiscent of Aubrey Herbert; and an American gentleman, Mr. John S. Blenkiron. Soon these people became so real to me that I had to keep a constant eye on their doings. They slowly aged in my hands, and the tale of their more recent deeds will be found in *The Three Hostages*, *The Courts of the Morning* and *The Island of Sheep*.

I added others to my group of musketeers. There was Dickson McCunn, the retired grocer, and his ragamuffin boys from the Gorbals, whose saga is written in *Huntingtower*, *Castle Gay* and *The House of the Four Winds*. There was Sir Edward Leithen, an eminent lawyer, who is protagonist or narrator in *The Power House*, *John Macnab*, *The Dancing Floor* and *The Gap in the Curtain*; and in his particular group were the politician, Lord Lamancha, and Sir Archibald Roylance, airman, ornithologist and Scots laird. It was huge fun playing with my puppets, and to me they soon became very real flesh and blood. I never consciously invented with a pen in my hand; I waited until the story had told itself and then wrote it down, and, since it was already a finished thing, I wrote it fast. The books had a wide sale, both in English and in translations, and I always felt a little ashamed that profit should accrue from what had given me so much amusement. I had no purpose in such writing except to please myself, and even if my books had not found a single reader I would have felt amply repaid.

Besides these forthright tales of adventure I was busy with a very different kind of romance. The desire to recover the sense of continuity, which had brought me to Elsfield, prompted my first serious piece of fiction. It was called *The Path of the King*, and was based on the notion that no man knows his ancestry, and that kingly blood may lie dormant for centuries until the appointed time. The chapters began with a Viking's son lost in a raid, and ended audaciously with Abraham Lincoln.

After that I varied my tales of adventure with this kind of romance, over which I took a great deal of pains, and which seems to me the most successful of my attempts at imaginative creation. Being equally sensitive to the spells of time and of space, to a tract of years and a tract of landscape, I tried to discover the historical moment which best interpreted the *ethos* of a particular countryside, and to devise the appropriate legend. Just as certain old houses, like the inns at Burford and Queensferry, cried out to Robert Louis Stevenson to tell their tales, so I felt the clamour of certain scenes for an interpreter.

The best, I think, is *Witch Wood*, in which I wrote of the Tweedside parish of my youth at the time when the old Wood of Caledon had not wholly disappeared, and when the rigours of the new Calvinism were contending with the ancient secret rites of Diana. I believe that my picture is historically true, and I could have documented almost every sentence from my researches on

Montrose. In *The Free Fishers* I tried to catch the flavour of the windy shores of Fife at a time when smuggling and vagabondage were still rife. I had always felt keenly the romance of the Jacobite venture, but less in its familiar Scottish episodes than in the dreary ebb of the march to Derby, so I took that period for my attempt in *Midwinter* to catch the spell of the great midland forests and the Old England which lay everywhere just beyond the highroads and the plough-lands. Finally, in *The Blanket of the Dark* I chose the time when the monasteries fell and the enclosures began, and I brought all the valleys of Cotswold into the picture.

These were serious books and they must have puzzled many of the readers who were eager to follow the doings of Richard Hannay or Dickson McCunn. That is the trouble with an author who only writes to please himself; his product is not standardised, and the purchaser is often disappointed. I once had a letter from an Eton boy who, having a taste for a bustling yarn, was indignant at anything of mine which did not conform to that pattern. He earnestly begged me to "pull myself together."

Though my hand is vile and scribing has always bored me, I found the writing of my romances almost a relaxation. Less so my excursions in biography. The subject of my first was Montrose. From my Oxford days I had been fascinated by his military genius and the sorrows of his life, and I gradually began to read myself into his period. I found that the Whig historians had dismissed him as at the best a bandit of genius, and had beatified the theocrats who opposed him. To this view I could not assent, and as my studies progressed I came to the conclusion that he was the most balanced and prescient mind in Scotland at the time, as well as the greatest of Scottish soldiers. Materials for his life had been collected by Mark Napier with an enthusiasm which was not always critical, and I decided to go over them again, and try to present an authentic picture of a very great man. In 1913 I published a short sketch, which presently went out of print, and after the War, when my military histories had been completed, I set myself to elaborate the portrait. The book was issued in 1928 and I am happy to think that my view of Montrose, foreshadowed by Carlyle and presented briefly in their histories by S. R. Gardiner and Andrew Lang, is now generally accepted. I could ask for no greater honour than to help to restore to his country's pantheon the hero of my youth.

Cromwell was bound to follow. I had long shared Lord Rosebery's view of him as the greatest of Englishmen, and, when I began to study his campaigns, I felt that as a soldier he was very near the first rank. I had the supreme advantage of having been brought up in a Calvinistic atmosphere, so I was able to write of his religious life with some understanding. For several years I lived chiefly in the seventeenth century, reading acres of its divinity and many hundreds of its pamphlets. Cromwell with all his imperfections seemed to me not only admirable but lovable, and I tried in my book to present the warm human side of him. I cannot claim that there was anything in my work which could not be found in Gardiner and Firth, but I think I elaborated certain neglected aspects and I took special pains with the background.

When *Cromwell* was published in 1934 the subject had become acutely topical, for dictators were arising in Europe who claimed, without warrant, to follow in his steps. This made me return to what had been an undergraduate ambition, a portrait of Augustus. I had already done a good deal of work on the subject, and my first two winters in Canada gave me leisure to re-read the Latin and Greek texts. I have rarely found more enjoyment in a task, for I was going over again carefully the ground which I had scampered across in my youth. Augustus seemed to me to embody all the virtues of a dictator, when a dictator was needed, and to have tried valiantly to provide against the perils. The book was kindly received by scholars in Britain, America and on the Continent, though my Italian friends jibbed at some of my political deductions.

In my book on Sir Walter Scott, published in the centenary year of his death, I tried not only to pay tribute to the best-loved of Borderers, but to repeat my literary *credo*. All these four books were, indeed, in a sense a confession of faith, for they enabled me to define my own creed on many matters of doctrine and practice, and thereby cleared my mind. They were a kind of diary, too, a chronicle of my successive interests and occupations. They were laborious affairs compared to my facile novels, but they were also a relaxation, for they gave me a background into which I could escape from contemporary futilities, a watch-tower from which I had a long prospect, and could see modern problems in juster proportions. That is the supreme value of history. The study of it is the best guarantee against repeating it.

IV

Reading has always filled so large a part of my life that for a page or two I may be allowed to set down my literary vicissitudes. It is a sad tale, for it records a steady narrowing of interests. In the 'nineties, when I first discovered the world of books, I had a most

catholic taste in them. I was attracted by every new
venture, I had few dislikes, my purpose was exploration
rather than judgment, orthodoxy had no claims on me,
and I identified appreciation with enjoyment. I was
Montaigne's *ondoyant et divers* reader, undulating and
diverse.

Then—some time in my early twenties—the arteries
of my taste seemed to narrow and harden. I became
more fastidious, but with an eye less on eternal canons
of excellence than on my own pleasure. I was now a
critic, but on a purely subjective basis. Certain things
satisfied me and certain things did not, and I was
inclined to limit myself to the former. Since I knew
what these were in the older literature and had no
certainty of finding them in the new, I became conservative in my reading. As a publisher I had to keep
a watchful eye on contemporary letters, but there my
motive was commercial; for my pleasure I went to
old fields. I speak, of course, of imaginative work. I
was an assiduous student of the moderns in philosophy
and history.

Not being a critic I was not called upon to formulate
the reasons for my preferences, but I was conscious that
I had standards of a sort. One was a belief in what
the French call *ordonnance*, the supreme importance of
an ordered discipline both in matter and style. Another
was a certain austerity—I disliked writing which was
luscious and overripe. A third was a distrust of extreme
facility; a work of art, I thought, should be carved in
marble, not in soapstone. There were other half-
conscious principles, and the whole batch constituted
a strict, dry and rather priggish canon, which kept me
from taking any real interest in the literature of my own
day. One or two Romans (Virgil especially), Shakespeare and Wordsworth pretty well contented me

among the poets, and in prose, apart from history and philosophy, I had recourse chiefly to the seventeenth-century writers. I had become what Dr. Johnson called Gray, a "barren rascal."

During the War my general reading was confined to a few classics, but after 1918, feeling rejuvenated and enterprising, I did my best to get on terms with my contemporaries. Alas! I had put it off too long. My ear simply could not attune itself to their rhythms, or lack of rhythms. Much of the verse seemed to me unmelodious journalism. Often it was a pastiche of Donne, but it seemed to reproduce only his tortured conceits, and not his sudden flute notes and moments of shattering profundity. I have always been a poor reader of fiction—perhaps because I could tell myself my own stories—and I was baffled by the immense, shambling novels that poured steadily from the press in Britain and America.

The trouble was that my intelligence admitted the merit of much that filled the rest of me with *ennui*. Proust, for example. I disliked his hothouse world, but it was idle to deny his supreme skill in disentangling subtle threads of thought and emotion. It was what Henry James had striven to do, and partially succeeded in, before he fell into the tortuous arabesques of his later manner. There may be limits to the value of hitting a nail on the head, but it is better than fumbling with an evasive tin-tack. Again, I had read as a duty the principal works of the Russian novelists, and—with the exception of *War and Peace* and one or two of Tourgeniev's—was resolved never to attempt them again. I suffered from a radical defeat of sympathy. Their merits were beyond doubt, but their method and the whole world which they represented seemed to me ineffably dismal.

Not that I did not admire much contemporary work. I thought Virginia Woolf, as a critic, the best since Matthew Arnold—wiser and juster, indeed, than Arnold. I esteemed certain writers (principally American, like Sinclair Lewis and Booth Tarkington) who seemed to have the visualising power and the gift of absorbing, torrential narrative which mark the good novelist. To go a little further back, Mr. H. G. Wells' studies of certain phases of English life, in books like *Kipps*, *The Wheels of Chance* and *Mr. Polly*, were destined, I thought, to live as long as the English tradition endured. But the rebels and experimentalists for the most part left me cold. "The life of reason," Santayana has written, "is our heritage and exists only through tradition. Now the misfortune of revolutionists is that they are disinherited, and their folly is that they wish to be disinherited even more than they are."

My serious preferences I was always ready to defend. But I could also take pleasure in the second-, third- and even the fourth-rate on purely sentimental grounds. I believe that the taste in literature of most people sets fairly early in life, and in essentials does not alter, except in the case of a few superior minds which remain always receptive and yet anchored to eternal values. What delights in an impressionable youth gives inevitably a lasting bias to the judgment. A music lover who can appreciate the austerest merits may have also an irrational liking for ditties which have no artistic credentials. So, in literature, oddments are carried over from youth and continue to please, not because of their intrinsic quality but because they were first read or heard on happy occasions, and the memory of them recalls those blessed moments. It is pure sentimentality, but how many of us are free from it?

My memory is full of such light baggage. Stanzas of Swinburne, whom I do not greatly admire, remind me of summer mornings when I shouted them on a hill-top, and still please because of the hill-top, not the poetry. In the 'nineties Austin Dobson and others had made popular various exercises in old French metrical forms like the ballade, the rondeau and the villanelle; even Robert Bridges succumbed to the fashion. There was no great value in such confections, but I have a lingering taste for them, since they are entwined with memories of golden afternoons in cool, green Oxfordshire backwaters. Some of W. E. Henley's lyrics are often in my mind because they were the viaticum of an unforgettable spring walking tour. I have the same feeling about certain songs of R. L. Stevenson and Rudyard Kipling's early work. So I am in this position :—I believe I can judge fairly the greater books which all my life have been my companions; I am attached to certain things produced in my youth which, but for their sentimental associations, would probably not appeal to me; the modern work most loudly acclaimed my traditionalist mind is simply not competent to judge at all.

Apart from what our fathers called *belles-lettres* I have continued to be a voracious reader. In my day there have been no books, no *Das Kapital* or *Origin of Species*, which have opened up new avenues of thought. There has been no Hegel to attempt a new system of world-philosophy. Except for F. H. Bradley's *Appearance and Reality* I do not think any book has been published which our descendants will regard as a philosophical classic. But there have been seminal works in various related branches of thought, such as Freud's in psychology, and those of Einstein and his colleagues in a type of physics which almost fulfils Pope's prophecy and "of metaphysics begs defence." This latter subject I regard with a fascinated awe, but from afar off, for I have not the key with which to enter the city. My knowledge of mathematics stops with a desperate finality just when the difficulties begin. The new physicist has a grammar of his own, for his substantives are equations with which the reader must be familiar before he can follow the argument.

For some years I have found my chief interest in history, since in the fog in which we live I get comfort from tracing the puzzled lives of those who traversed the same road. As in philosophy, so in history; we have had no venture on the grand scale; Mr. G. M. Trevelyan's *England under Queen Anne* is the nearest approach to it. Perhaps such work is now less easy, because of a more scientific view of evidence and an austerer conscience in the historian. The work of the quarriers and masons has become so intricate that the architects have been compelled to limit the scale of their buildings. But I have seen one heresy relinquished. Few historians would now assent without qualification to J. B. Bury's famous dogma, "History is a science— no less and no more." It is a science, but it is a great deal more. It is an art, a synthesis rather than a compilation, an interpretation as well as a chronicle. The historian, if he is to do justice to the past, must have a constructive imagination and a reasonable mastery of words. The scientist must be joined to the man-of-letters.

One heartening movement I can detect—a greater consideration for the average man. There have been brilliant specimens of synoptic history, which summarises a long tract of time, such as Mr. Herbert Fisher's *Europe*, Mr. George Trevelyan's *England*, and Mr. S. E. Morison's *United States*. The philosophies have made an honest attempt to descend from the schools to the market-place. All the principal thinkers of the last thirty years have a more or less popular appeal : Bergson in France, Croce in Italy, William James and Santayana in America ; sometimes indeed the literary graces are so luxuriant as to obscure the thought. Valiant attempts have even been made to expound the cloudy trophies of the new physics. It has been pre-eminently the age of the *vulgarisateur* in the best sense of that word. I think the tendency wholly admirable. Lord Rutherford used to say that no conclusion which he ever reached was of any use to him until he could put it into plain English, into language understood by the ordinary man. Attempts to present the history of the world as an inter-related intelligible process, or to give a bird's-eye view of the long march of the sciences, may be faulty in detail, with many arbitrary judgments, but they do furnish principles of interpretation which enable the reader to find at any rate *one* way in the world of thought—perhaps a little later to make his *own* way.[1] In this task the *vulgarisateur* may be preparing the soil for a rich future harvest, just as the work of the Sophists cleared the ground for Plato.

V

Living in the country I escaped the close social intercourse of London. Apart from Oxford and country neighbours, I was dependent for society on friends whom I visited and who visited me. Of these, fortu-

---

[1] I would instance not only Mr. H. G. Wells' celebrated compilation, but also Mr. S. E. M. Joad's various guides to philosophy. They seem to me remarkable achievements, for not only are the different creeds outlined with a notable fairness, but the emphasis is put on the questions asked rather than the solutions, and that is the right kind of introduction.

nately, many are still alive, but I would pay my tribute to four who have gone.

"How shall I name you, immortal, mild, proud shadows?"

After his short ambassadorial term in Washington, Edward Grey came little to London. His health had become a serious business, since to his failing eyesight other bodily ailments were added. When I first knew him in my undergraduate days I thought him the most fortunate of mortals, for he had everything—health, beauty, easy means, a great reputation, innumerable friends, the gift of succeeding in whatever he tried, whether in sport or public affairs. Before he died I was often reminded of those eerie words which Herodotus puts into the mouth of Amasis: "I know that the gods are jealous, for I cannot remember that I ever heard of any man who, having been constantly successful, did not at last utterly perish." One by one his sources of happiness vanished. He lost a beloved wife; he saw his work as peacemaker close in the bloodiest of wars; his eyesight and his general health failed; his country home was burnt down; his intimate friends died before their time; a second marriage gave him only short-lived comfort, for it soon ended with his wife's death.

Yet he did not cease to be happy, for he built a new life out of the wreckage of the old. He could no longer browse among books, but he took to writing them, and learned the satisfaction of being explicit in print as well as in speech. Trout fishing was no more for him, but for a time he could still fish for salmon with his friend, Frank Pember, the Warden of All Souls, in certain convenient Highland rivers. He could not watch birds at a distance, but he had his colony of ducks at Fallodon, and he became a wizard in detecting birds' song. In what seemed to me to be a single note he could discern a blend of several birds.

Under the buffetings of life he never winced or complained, and the spectacle of his gentle fortitude was both a heartbreak and an inspiration. More than any man I know he possessed his soul. Most of us have some friend whom above all others we would wish our sons to resemble. I have no doubt as to my choice, and I am glad to think that I was able to associate him with a memorable occasion in the life of my eldest boy. When John, who was an ardent bird-lover and fisherman, came of age, I gave a small dinner for him at the House of Commons, and Edward Grey came down from Northumberland to take the chair and propose his health. It was a happy chance that a boy should be speeded on his journey in life by the man whom in all the world he most revered.

Henry Newbolt died when he was well on in the seventies, but he never became middle-aged. Everything about him remained boyish—his slim figure, his lean alert face, his endearing, almost ingenuous, ardour, everything except his grey hair. I had known him a little before 1914, and in the last year of the War I found in him a most able colleague. But though he did well by his generation he never quite belonged to it. Providence had cast him for a bard, a companion of men-at-arms and the chronicler of their deeds. He found his niche in letters in a kind of half-lyric, half-ballad, the best of which must live since they are enshrined in the popular memory. But for him that was only half a life. He would have liked, himself, to move in the thick of great deeds. It seems ungenerous to say of one who had so much happiness in the world that he was not quite at home in it, but I think it is true that, apart from his poetry, he never found work which wholly satisfied him. I can picture him more easily as a minstrel singing of Border raids in which he had shared, or a *jongleur* in the trail of a crusade, or like Volcker of Alsace in the *Niebelungenlied*, with his sword-fiddle-bow whose every stroke was a note of music.

In conversation he had few superiors. He was not a great architect of talk like Arthur Balfour, but a contributor, always in perfect tune with the occasion. In this also he was a little outside his age, belonging rather to the era of breakfasts, when busy men began their day with scholarly talk. I do not mean the solemn meals of that deposit of the glacial age, the Philosophic Radicals, or the scarcely less solemn feasts at which Macaulay pontificated—a character in *Sybil* complains bitterly that only Liberals ever breakfasted out !—but the later and gentler affairs which did not wholly go out of fashion until the close of last century. Their place has been taken by dining-clubs, like Grillion's, the Literary Society, and The Club, and there Henry was at his best. He was happiest on literary topics, and of the three men of letters I have known who could talk well I should put him first. Edmund Gosse had moments of petulance and uncertain temper; St. Loe Strachey was too copious, apt to drown a topic with a spate of words; but Henry Newbolt had always a nice sense of the relevant and unfailing intellectual courtesy. I liked to hear him quote poetry in his low crooning recitative; it was like overhearing a delightful child repeating to himself his favourite pieces.

I first came to know Frederick Scott Oliver just after the publication of his book on Alexander Hamilton. He was engaged, like myself, in trying to work out a reasonable philosophy of empire, and I was attracted to him by his freedom from party bias and his acute historical sense. Also he was a fellow Borderer. His health was poor, but his ruddy complexion and clear eyes gave him the look of a Border shepherd. His strong, finely modelled face was not unlike Alexander Hamilton's. In a peruke he would have been the model of some eighteenth-century gentleman from a canvas of Sir Joshua.

For a decade he was the ablest pamphleteer in Britain. His *Alexander Hamilton* was in a sense a pamphlet, for it had a direct topical moral. His writings on the Ulster question and his *Ordeal by Battle* were real pamphlets, in which political views were set out with an eloquence and a precision long absent from the literature of politics. After the Armistice his health worsened, and he gradually withdrew from business, in which he had been very successful, and gave up his remaining years to the study of British policy in the first half of the eighteenth century—a task which combined political philosophy and history proper. He had bought the estate of Edgerston, which lies at the top of the Jed valley and runs up to the watershed of Cheviot. In that beautiful place he united the life of the scholar and of the country gentleman, and it is in that environment that I shall always think of him, striding about in his rough clothes to examine his young trees, or sitting in the circular library upstairs, which was scented with tobacco and old calf, and looked out over gardens to the bent of the hills.

Oliver's mind had two sides—one strictly logical, delighting in close and compact argument, and the other imaginative and intuitive. He was not one who overvalued ratiocination, for he held that in the greater matters of life the mind must fling itself forward beyond its data, and that the possession of this instinct was what

o

constituted the difference between the great and the less great among mankind. Such a power he believed to be found chiefly in simple souls, and this explained his admiration for soldiers. He was contemptuous of the hyper-subtle and the intellectually arrogant; the clever fool seemed to him the worst of all fools. He believed that the ordinary man was the best judge of most things, and might, if lawyers and pedants could be kept out of the way, be trusted to govern the country. The worst vice was seeing the trees and missing the wood, but it was a vice of clever, not of plain, people.

He used to attribute this conviction to his business experience, but it came from something deeper, something far back in his Border ancestry. There was a good deal in him of the mystic and the poet. He transfigured every political subject he wrote on— tariff reform, Ireland, military training—by opening up imaginative vistas. He might start with the pose of a commonplace man wearily repeating truisms, but he ended startlingly as a seer. History became his favourite study because it gave his imagination room for the reconstruction of men's souls, and because it showed truth in action. Principles he valued high, but he saw them not as dogmas but as pictures and deeds.

This conjoint power of visualising and divining made him a brilliant writer, and at moments almost a great one. He was an admirable painter of historical portraits, and he was skilled in tracking the progress of a doctrine. His style was eminently simple and clear, but capable also of a strong eloquence; his general urbanity had its moments of tenderness, but it could harden, too, into deadly satire.

His published writings, owing partly to his ill-health and partly to a fastidiousness which made him produce

slowly, give no real impression of the fertility and
originality of his mind and the delightfulness of his
society. He had the Border quality, of which Sir
Walter Scott is the great example, of intellectual
generosity and geniality. His conversation was a joy
to his friends. He had all the Baconian requirements;
he was a full man from wide reading and much thought;
an exact man from his scrupulous logic; and a ready
man from his native wit. And behind the colour and
light there was a friendly warmth which made it good
to be with him. He never dogmatised; his sharp
dialectic made him a noted pricker of bubbles; he had
the gift of impromptu perfection of phrase, so that his
talk was as finished as his prose. His humour, though
irony and satire were among his weapons, was for the
most part tolerant and debonair, and he had an acute
sense of farce and fun.

Oliver did not write because he liked writing, but
because he had causes to plead. A preacher at heart,
he testified at all times to the truth that was in him. He
loved his country deeply, and strove to serve her by
lifting contemporary disputes into a larger air, and to
seek guidance for the future by a patient diagnosis of
the present and a wise reading of the past. He never
wrote merely for artistic effect, but always to convince
—to break down some lie or to establish some verity.
That is why he wrote so well. That is why he has had,
I think, a real and enduring influence on political
thought. He made out of politics a philosophy—
though he disliked the word—and his wisdom will not
die, though the causes which he served may change.

I do not profess to have understood T. E. Lawrence
fully, still less to be able to portray him; there is no
brush fine enough to catch the subtleties of his mind,

no aerial viewpoint high enough to bring into one picture the manifold of his character.

Before the War I had heard of him from D. G. Hogarth, and so many of my friends, like Alan Dawnay, George Lloyd and Aubrey Herbert, served with him in the East that he became a familiar name to me; but I do not think that I met him before the summer of 1920. Then we found that we had much in common besides Hogarth's friendship—an admiration for the work of C. E. Doughty, including his epics; similar tastes in literature; the same philosophy of empire.[1]

Until his death I saw him perhaps half a dozen times a year while he was in England. He had gathered round him a pleasant coterie, most of whom I knew. But we never worked together, though we once projected a joint-editing of the Gadarene poets—there were others from Gadara besides Meleager. He would turn up without warning at Elsfield at any time of the day or night on his motor-cycle Boanerges, and depart as swiftly and mysteriously as he came.

Yet in a sense I knew him better than many people whom I met daily. If you were once admitted to his intimacy you became one of his family, and he of yours; he used you and expected to be used by you; he gave of himself with the liberality of a good child. There was always much of the child in him. He spoke and wrote to children as a coeval. He had a delightful impishness. Even when he was miserable and suffering he could rejoice in a comic situation, and he found many in the ranks of the R.A.F. and the Tank Corps. What better comedy than for a fine scholar to be

---

[1] "I think there's a great future for the British Empire as a voluntary association, and I'd like to have Treaty States on a big scale attached to it. . . . We are so big a firm that we can offer unique conditions to small businesses to associate with us." *Letters*, p. 578.

examined as to his literacy by the ordinary education officer? And the game of hide-and-seek which he played with the newspapers amused him as much as it annoyed him.

When I first knew him he was in the trough of depression owing to what he thought to be the failure of his work for the Arabs, which involved for him a breach of honour. Mr. Churchill's policy eventually comforted him, but it could not heal the wound. Physically he looked slight, but, as boxers say, he stripped well, and he was as strong as many people twice his size, while he had a bodily toughness and endurance far beyond anything I have ever met. In 1920 his whole being was in grave disequilibrium. You cannot in any case be nine times wounded, four times in an air crash, have many bouts of fever and dysentery, and finally at the age of twenty-nine take Damascus at the head of an Arab army, without living pretty near the edge of your strength. But he had been endowed also with a highly keyed nervous system which gave him an infinite capacity for both pleasure and pain, but never gave him ease. There was a fissure in his nature—eternal war between what might be called the Desert and the Sown—on the one side art and books and friends and leisure and a modest cosiness; on the other action, leadership, the austerity of space.

His character has been a quarry for the analysts and I would not add to their number. It is simplest to say that he was a mixture of contradictories which never were—perhaps could never have been—harmonised. His qualities lacked integration. He had moods of vanity and moods of abasement; immense self-confidence and immense diffidence. He had a fastidious taste which was often faulty. The gentlest and most lovable of beings with his chivalry and considerateness, he could also be ruthless. I can imagine him, though the possessor of an austere conscience, crashing through all the minor moralities to win his end. That is to say, he was a great man of action with some "sedition in his powers."

For the better part of three years he was a leader of men and a maker of nations. Military students have done ample justice to his gifts as a soldier. Perhaps his contribution to the art of war has been a little over-stated, but beyond question he foreshadowed a new strategy and tactics—audacity in surprise, the destruction of material rather than of men, blows at the enemy's nerve centre and therefore at his will to resist. And he could put his doctrine into effect with speed and precision. If he had come out of the War with a sound nervous system and his vitality unimpaired, he might have led the nation to a new way of life. For he had a magnetic power which made people follow him blindly, and I have seen that in his eye which could have made, or quelled, a revolution. He had also an astonishing gift for detail. He knew more about the history and the technique of war than any general I have ever met. He understood down to the last decimal every weapon he employed and every tool he used. He was a master both of the vision and of the fact.

What deflected him from his natural career of action? For deflected he was; he made deliberately *lo gran rifiuto*; he cut himself off from the sphere in which he was born to excel. It is idle to speculate on what would have happened if he had ended the War with perfect balance and undamaged nerves; if he had he would not have been Lawrence. There was a fissure in him from the start; the dream and the business did not march together; his will was not always the servant of his intelligence; he was an agonist, a self-tormentor,

who ran to meet suffering halfway. This was due,
I think, partly to a twist of puritanism, partly to the
fact that, as he often confessed, pain stimulated his
mind; but it was abnormal and unwholesome. He
was a great analyst of himself, but he never probed the
secret of this crack in the firing. Sometimes he put it
down to his war experiences, sometimes to his post-
War disillusionment, when he was inclined to talk the
familiar nonsense about youth having been betrayed
by age. But I think it was always there, and it tended
to gape under stress. When there was no call to action
he was torn by his divided thoughts. "The War was
good," he once wrote, "by drawing over our depths
that hot surface wish to do or win something."

He was disillusioned, too, about mundane glory,
disillusioned too early. "I wasn't a King or Prime
Minister, but I made 'em and played with 'em, and
after that there was not much more in that direction for
me to do." The man of action in him gave him an
appetite for fame, even for publicity, and the other side
of him made him despise himself for the craving. His
conscience forbade him to take any reward for his
War services, but there were times when he thought it
a morbid conscience. So, pulled hither and thither by
noble and contradictory impulses, he had moods when
he hated life. "Oh, Lord, I am so tired! I want so
much to lie down, to sleep and die. Die is best because
there is no réveillé. I want to forget my sins and the
world's weariness."

He craved, like a mediaeval monk, for discipline and
seclusion. To use a phrase of his own, he was done
with trying to blow up trains and bridges, and was
thinking of the Well at the World's End. He wanted
padlocks, as Hogarth said, and that was why he enlisted
in the R.A.F. as a mechanic. It was a true instinct, for,

unless after 1922 he had found mechanical work under discipline, the fissure might have become a gulf. I remember that at that time I came across some words written by the Sir Walter Raleigh of our day about the Elizabethan Raleigh, who was a collateral kinsman of Lawrence. "The irony of human affairs possesses his contemplation. . . . The business of man on this earth seems trivial and insignificant against the vast desert of eternity."

He had found refuge from the life of action in another kind of activity, for he had always an itch to write. He was contemplating the *Seven Pillars* as early as September 1917, and he had no sooner entered the Air Force than he planned a book on his experiences. "Writing has been my inmost self all my life," he wrote in his last years, "and I can never put my full strength into anything else." This interest brought him after the War into literary and artistic circles. In one way this was very good for him, since it gave him a host of new interests and much welcome companionship, but I fear that it also increased his tendency to introspection. What was an intellectual pastime to those cultivated ingenious friends of his might to him be deadly serious. But one thing it did—it made him write.

To me he seems to be a great writer who never quite wrote a great book. All his writing was a sort of purgation, a clearing from his mind of perilous stuff, and consequently the artistic purpose was often diverted by personal needs. The *Seven Pillars* is ostensibly the story of a campaign and it contains brilliant pieces of story-telling ; but, as he said of it himself, it is "intensely sophisticated." It is a shapeless book and it lacks the compulsion of the best narrative, for he is always wandering off down the corridors of his own mind. The style has its great moments, but it has also its lapses into adjectival rhetoric. The *Mint* is a *tour de force*, an astonishing achievement in exact photography; no rhetoric here, but everything hard, cold, metallic and cruel. His power of depicting squalor is uncanny, though there is nothing in the *Mint*, I think, which equals a later passage describing a troop-ship on its way to India[1]; that fairly takes the breath away by its sheer brutality. In the *Mint* he weaves words and phrases from the gutter—*les gros mots*—into a most artful pattern. But I cannot think the book a success. It lacks relief and half-tones; also shape. In his own phrase it is a "case-book; not a work of art but a document."

I never cared for his version of the *Odyssey*, for I did not share his view that that poem was Wardour Street. Lawrence had had the ideal experience for an Homeric scholar. "For years we were digging up a city of roughly the Odysseus period. I have handled the weapons, armour, utensils of those times, explored their houses, planned their cities. I have hunted wild boars and watched wild lions, sailed the Aegean (and sailed ships), bent bows, lived with pastoral peoples, woven textiles, built boats and killed many men." But he was not simple-souled enough to translate Homer, so he invented a pre-Raphaelite Homer whom he could translate. I believe that the *Letters* will rank as high as any of his books, because they show nearly all the facets of his character; and he never wrote better prose than his description of the bleak sea coast of Buchan.[2]

His fame will endure, and as time goes on the world may understand him better; as he wrote of Thomas Hardy, "a generation will pass before the sky will be perfectly clear of clouds for his shining." I last saw him at the end of March 1935, when on a push-bike he turned up at Elsfield one Sunday morning and spent a

[1] *Letters*, p. 502. [2] *Ibid.*, p. 699.

long day with me. He was on his way from Bridlington
to his Dorsetshire cottage. He looked brilliantly well,
with a weather-beaten skin, a clear eye, and a forearm
like a blacksmith's. His nerves, too, seemed to be completely at ease. He had no plans and described himself
as like a leaf fallen from a tree in autumn, but he was
looking forward avidly to leisure. He spoke of public
affairs and his friends with perfect wisdom and charity.
When he left I told my wife that at last I was happy
about him and believed that he might become again
the great man of action—might organise, perhaps, our
imperfect national defences. She shook her head. "He
is looking at the world as God must look at it," she
said, "and a man cannot do that and live." . . . A few
weeks later he was dead.

I am not a very tractable person or much of a hero-
worshipper, but I could have followed Lawrence over
the edge of the world. I loved him for himself, and
also because there seemed to be reborn in him all the
lost friends of my youth. If genius be, in Emerson's
phrase, a "stellar and undiminishable something," whose
origin is a mystery and whose essence cannot be defined,
then he was the only man of genius I have ever known.

CHAPTER IX

PARLIAMENT

AFTER some six years of my ivory tower I grew restless. I rejoiced as much as ever in the prospect from it, but I came to feel that it should be a sanctuary to return to and not a heritage for continuous habitation. In addition to the work of my firm I held several directorships, but I did not find that business absorbed all my energies; while my writing, which gave me enormous pleasure, would have lost its charm for me unless kept as a relaxation. The fatigue of the War, moral and mental, was passing, and my bodily ailments could be kept within bounds. The truth is that in my late forties I experienced a ridiculous resurgence of youth. In Scotland I was as active as ever on the hill, and in my early morning rides in Oxfordshire I seemed to recapture the precise emotions of twenty-one. The very tunes I had hummed then were back on my lips. Reason told me that it was folly, that I was only Donne's "aged childe and grey-headed Infant"; but I had not a single grey hair, and I was unfeignedly grateful for this return, even if illusory, of what had been a most happy youth.

That horrid possession, a social conscience, also began to prick me. My forecast of the grim consequences of the War had not been quite realised, but I believed that they were only retarded. I clung to a hope in the League of Nations and expounded it to many audiences, but my confidence was declining; I did not believe that such an institution could be effective straight from its birth, and I did not find the spirit abroad in the world which would encourage an organic growth. I had an ugly fear that its foundations were on sand, and that the first storm would overthrow it.

When I examined my political faith I found that my strongest belief was in democracy according to my own definition. Democracy—the essential thing as distinguished from this or that democratic government —was primarily an attitude of mind, a spiritual testament, and not an economic structure or a political machine. The testament involved certain basic beliefs— that the personality was sacrosanct, which was the meaning of liberty; that policy should be settled by free discussion; that normally a minority should be ready to yield to a majority, which in turn should respect a minority's sacred things. It seemed to me that democracy had been in the past too narrowly defined and had been identified illogically with some particular economic or political system such as *laissez-faire* or British parliamentaryism. I could imagine a democracy which economically was largely socialist and which had not our constitutional pattern.

Believing this, I had come to feel that the faith, if it were to continue, must set its house in order. Its essential value was not questioned, but its efficiency had declined, since it had been clogged by irrelevancies. There was a great deal of false democracy about, the kind of thing dreaded by the great American federalists like Alexander Hamilton and John Adams. Also I feared another war, for force is democracy's eternal foe. Señor de Madariaga seemed to me to have written wise words: "a democracy that goes to war, if beaten, loses its liberty at the hands of its adversary; if victorious it loses its liberty at its own hands." But most of all I was alarmed lest the creed should lose its glamour. It was too much taken for granted; and I thought that it might perish from the sheer *ennui* of its votaries. I could not guess that in a year or two it would become once again the oriflamme of a crusade, a cause to be fought for against odds.

For the democracies, which then included Germany, it was a dull world. The grandiose experiment in Russia had taken away all interest from the socialism which was merely academic. Except in America, which seemed to be in a fair way to rake in the wealth of the globe, the ordinary man was struggling with private problems so difficult that he had no time for public affairs. The high post-War visions had gone, and the prevalent mood was, at the best, a stoical resolution.

> "Life still
> Leaves human efforts scope.
> But, since life teems with ill,
> Nurse no extravagant hope ;
> Because thou must not dream, thou need'st not then despair."

I

In those six years I did not quite rid myself of political interests. I had some office or other in many of the Oxford undergraduate clubs, and on Sunday afternoons a multitude of young men used to come to tea. There was a legend in the family that wherever one went on the globe one would meet somebody who had been to Elsfield. These guests were of every type—Blues, hunting men, scholars, Union orators, economists, poets—and of every creed from Jacobitism to communism. We discussed politics, and I was often asked to advise about careers, so perforce I had to keep in touch with the political world. More than once I was offered a constituency, and when it was proposed that I should follow Mr. Bonar Law in Central Glasgow

I had to give the matter serious thought. Early in 1927
Sir Henry Craik, the senior Member for the Scottish
Universities, died, and I was invited to succeed him.
It was the kind of constituency which suited me, for
I was warned that my health would not stand the
ordinary business of electioneering. In the election
which ensued I was opposed by a socialist who forfeited
his deposit. In the eight years of my membership I had
only to face one other contested election, when I was
returned by a very large majority.

It would be hard to imagine a more perfect seat.
The electors were the graduates of the four Universities,
St. Andrews, Glasgow, Aberdeen and Edinburgh.
The method was proportional representation, the
voting was by post, and the constituents were scattered
all over the world. I was never asked for a favour—
rarely even to procure a seat in the Members' Gallery.
Except on the Prayer Book question no constituent
ever cavilled at my doings. They gave me perfect
confidence and the amplest freedom. I was elected
as a Conservative, for, believing in party government,
I disliked the name of Independent. But I held that a
university member should sit a little loose to parties,
and I was independent in fact if not in name.

I had often listened to parliamentary debates, but it is
one thing to be in the gallery and quite another to be on
the floor of the House. My historical reading had
given me a reverence for parliamentary tradition, and
I was not disillusioned. On paper the whole lay-out
is absurd. There are seats for only about three-fourths
of the members, and these seats are uncomfortable;
the ventilation leaves the head hot and the feet cold;
half the time is spent in dragging wearily into and out
of lobbies, voting on matters about which few members
know anything; advertising mountebanks can waste a

deal of time ; debates can be as dull as a social science congress in the provinces, which, according to Matthew Arnold, filled the soul with "an unutterable sense of lamentation and mourning and woe." But speeches are shorter and of a far higher quality than in any other legislative assembly with which I am acquainted, and, while many members recite pieces for the benefit of their local papers, there are hours of close debating, and now and then a high emotional scene.

But I was puzzled at first to account for its repute. The practical business of law-making and administration would have been better and more speedily done by a committee of civil servants or industrialists, or, for that matter, by the notable experts to be found in the House of Lords. On the side of general policy and principles a group of professors would have provided more illuminating discussions. There are few real experts, and these few were not regarded too respectfully, except now and then on service questions. The debates were confessedly and intentionally the work of amateurs. What made it all so impressive and, in its way, so effective ? Partly the long tradition behind it. As one looked round the members one reflected that men just like them, no better informed or abler, had preserved our liberties and helped to build our Empire. The House wrought under the august canopy of its past. Partly the tremendous practical importance of those often limp debates. A decision set a huge machine in motion and influenced the lives of millions. But chiefly, I think, the fact that the House was truly representative. It was the people of Britain who were governing, not a batch of supermen. Those halting dogmas, those shy heroics, those sudden outbursts of hard sense were precisely the thoughts and emotions of the ordinary man, whom Burke believed to be in the long run wiser than his leaders. Beyond doubt the House was a microcosm of the people.

Nevertheless I have seldom disliked anything so much as speaking in it. It was like addressing a gathering of shades, who might at any moment disappear into limbo unless they were clutched by the hair. I felt that nobody wanted to listen to me, that I was only tolerated out of courtesy, and that each of my hearers was longing for me to sit down that he might himself be called. Only on rare occasions did I have an audience with which I felt at ease. On public platforms I was fairly happy, but not often in Parliament.

Yet I was fortunate, and was always well treated. My maiden speech, delivered two months after my election, was something of an occasion. The Lord Chancellor had introduced in the Lords a bill to amend the Parliament Act, which proposed a reformed Second Chamber and the restoration of certain powers lost in 1911. To me and to many of the younger Conservatives this seemed to be a policy which would rouse endless controversy in the country. The Parliament Act was working well enough, and we did not believe in the cry about the need for barriers against revolution; if the people really wanted revolution no paper safeguards could stop them. I arranged to make my *début* in the Commons on Lord Cave's proposal, and to my consternation my purpose was advertised beforehand in the Press, so that I had a double reason for nervousness. I lunched that day, I remember, with Mr. Neville Chamberlain, who said that he thanked heaven that no such fate had befallen him.

When the moment came it was worse even than I had feared. I spoke fourth, in the tea hour, and rose in an almost empty House. I had prepared a careful speech, but my first sentences sounded duller than human nature could bear, and my voice a hideous croak. Then my nervousness departed and boredom succeeded. I feared that I might have to stop and yawn. But suddenly I realised, from the surprised look of the only occupant of the Treasury bench, that I was speaking against the Government and my own party, and that gave me a slight fillip. Then I perceived that the House was filling up, and presently that it was packed, with a crowd below the Bar. After that I began to enjoy myself and, greatly daring, I ventured to conclude with a solemn rhetorical appeal to respect the spirit of the constitution. Mr. Lloyd George, who followed, did me the honour to repeat my arguments in his own words. No more was heard of the Lord Chancellor's scheme, for the Whips knew that if it had been pressed several hundred Conservatives would have joined me in the Opposition lobby.

That was an occasion to me of great personal interest, but a far more dramatic one was the first Prayer Book debate in December 1927. The revised book had been accepted by the House of Lords, where it was believed to be most in danger, and it was generally assumed that it would have an easy passage in the Commons. On the contrary it was rejected by a large majority, after a debate which showed the House at its best; it was defeated by Irish and Scottish votes, just as the proposal whose failure caused the Disruption of 1843 in the Scottish Church was defeated by English votes. The chief Government spokesman made the mistake of treating the subject in a jocose man-of-the-world style, and he was met by earnest evangelical appeals which stirred up the latent protestantism of the most careless members. I knew a good deal about the subject and I laboured to expound what seemed to me the true Reformation spirit of freedom. My effort was futile,

P

for argument had no chance against the emotional power of a very old tradition. But I enjoyed speaking in the tense atmosphere, with many friends regarding me with white faces and angry eyes.

When I entered the House I decided that I had no desire for the ordinary *cursus honorum*. A minor post would only have complicated my life, and I was too senior to begin to try for Cabinet office. So I had no reason to put myself forward, and I spoke only on subjects where I had special knowledge or a special interest. These were most Scottish questions; anything to do with education; certain problems of Empire; and the Zionist experiment, for which Arthur Balfour had aroused my enthusiasm. I attempted two private bills, one to regulate greyhound racing, which failed, and another to prevent the sale of British song-birds, which succeeded. I rarely spoke more than half a dozen times in a session, for I had no wish to make set speeches, while to intervene effectively in a debate meant a long wait for an opportunity for which I had simply not the time. Outside the House my most successful effort was the movement to raise the limit of the school age.

Though I was an undistinguished Member of Parliament, I was a contented one, and I enjoyed every moment of my eight years there. The customary platitudes about the House of Commons happen to be true. Individual members may be ill-bred; the House itself has a fine taste and breeding, and a sure instinct in matters of conduct. It will always include people who are foolish, hasty, humourless; but collectively it is rarely other than patient, urbane and wise. It is nicely discriminating, for while it will tolerate an agreeable buffoon and an honest donkey, it will not give its confidence except to sterling character and talent. *Securus judicat.* The flashy platform demagogue has to change his methods if he is to win its favour. It demands specific qualities—a certain decency in debate and a certain respect for itself and its ancient ritual. The sansculotte who refuses its demands is speedily silenced, for the House has immense powers of neglect and disapproval. The man who has won fame in some other walk of life, like the public service, business, science or literature, is given a respectful hearing, but he has to show the specific House of Commons gifts before he is accepted. It is a friendly body, but as a judge of what it likes it is unbending ; it will never forsake him whom it once accepts, or accept one who has been weighed and found wanting.

In my time, as I have said, there were no great political storms blowing. We had the eternal problems of unemployment and poverty, the business of adjusting the relations of master and man, polishing up the educational apparatus, and giving sops to distressed agriculture. Some reforms were effected, occasional squalls ruffled the political calm, stolid aspirants climbed the ladder of office, and the world jogged along not very comfortably but without any great to-do. In 1931 came the depression which jostled Britain off the gold standard and brought a National Government into being. After that politics were duller than ever. The ordinary citizen was behaving heroically, but the drama was outside the Palace of Westminster. I remember being puzzled by the flatness of everything and wondering uneasily if it were not the calm before the storm. Something monstrous seemed about to emerge from the economic pit into which the world was slipping. I longed for someone of prophetic strain, someone like Mr. Gladstone, to trouble the waters even at the expense of our peace of mind. I would have been happier if I could have found a leader, whose creed I fully shared and whom I could devoutly follow.

But if political life was stagnant, I found a perpetual interest in the House itself, and I acquired that respect for it as a body which Oliver Cromwell learned during the Short Parliament. My own party was full of young or youngish men who might have led a life of amusement, but who, instead, sat till all hours through dull debates and gave laborious days to their constituencies. Such members were for the most part liberal, often radical, in their political views, and they seemed to me to be the most valuable element in public life—holding to what was worth holding to in the legacy of the past, but always prepared to jettison lumber. There were a few genuine reactionaries, not country gentlemen but business magnates, who were not much liked, and who woke to life only in the Budget season. The most futile type were the Labour intellectuals, a batch of whom came in at the election of 1929. They were not quite able enough to be impressive, they were drearily dogmatic, and they were regarded with suspicion by the ordinary Labour member, with whom they had simply no points of contact. That seemed to me a pity, for they had something to give the trade unionists, and much to get from them. As for the latter, I found them the most interesting section of the House. They might be clumsy in handling dogmas, but all their lives they had been in contact with realities, and each of them was a master of a special knowledge. They were the most genuinely English thing in public life, with all the English foibles and virtues. Also they spoke racily and idiomatically. It was a delight to me, after the ordinary clipped talk of the public schools and universities, to hear speech which had a relish of country nooks and long-descended provincial ways.

Their Scottish colleagues were different—more speculative and impulsive, better educated and better read.
All of them were my friends, but especially the Glasgow
contingent, who, deeply suspect at first, soon won a
distinguished place in the House's esteem, and greatly
enlivened its debates. No members more fully represented their constituencies, for they knew every man,
woman and child in them, and gave up laborious week-
ends to the study on the spot of the problems of poverty.
Woe to him who spoke loosely on the subject and was
pounced upon by those experts ! James Maxton, too,
with his beautiful husky voice, seemed more able than
any other member to capture at will the attention and
the affection of the House. When I resigned my seat
in April 1935 I had many regrets, but the chief, I think,
was that, while I was likely to meet most of my
colleagues elsewhere, I would find it less easy to see
my Glasgow friends.

My years in Parliament left me a more convinced
believer than ever in democracy, but convinced, too,
that the democratic technique wanted overhauling. I
remembered Burke's words: "There ever is within
Parliament itself a power of renovating its principles
and effecting a self-reformation which no other place
of government has ever contained. . . . Public troubles
have often called upon this country to look into its
constitution. It has ever been bettered by such a
revision." I was not an advocate of stronger checks
on hasty legislation ; these seemed to me strong enough
already, for we had not one Second Chamber, but many
—the House of Lords, the Civil Service, the City, the
great local Government machine. I accepted adult
suffrage, but I felt that votes should be weighted—that
of the married man as against the bachelor, of the man
with a family as against the childless ; I thought that

the voting power of inexperienced youth if left un-
balanced might compel undue oscillations in the body-
politic.   Again, I thought that the rigid territorial
basis for elections was out of date.   It might continue
in part as a framework, but the Universities' precedent
should be followed, and there should be additional
representation for great economic, cultural and professional interests; as it was, a trade unionist had virtually
a double vote.   But my strongest conviction was that
the area of public service should be extended, and
that the ordinary citizen should be given the chance
of an active share in the work of administration.   I
believed that the policy represented by organisations like
the B.B.C., the Port of London Authority, and the
Central Electricity Board, was our natural line of development—public utilities privately administered but
authorised and ultimately controlled by Government.

Happily we do not idolise our public men.   They are
St. Sebastians stuck up aloft for critical arrows; even
when we admire them we treat them irreverently; we
show our gratitude by a friendly ribaldry, and in
moments of annoyance they are our first cock-shies.
Owen Seaman once told me that he had to come back
to London early on a Monday morning, and was compelled to take a workman's train.   It was the year when
Crippen, the murderer, had been arrested in Canada,
and that and the Ulster troubles filled the columns of
the Press.   He found himself in a compartment full of
honest men smoking their pipes and reading their
halfpenny papers.   At last one of them flung down his
journal in disgust.   "Wot I says," he exclaimed, "is to
'ell with the lot of 'em—Asquith and Lloyd George and
Carson and Crippen—the 'ole bleedin' lot!"   Upon
which there was a general protest.   "'Ere, wot 'arm's
old Crippen done?"   You will find in France, in the

United States, and even in parts of the Dominions, a real cynicism about the value of their type of government, a distrust of all engaged in it, and a general boredom with the whole business. It is different in Britain. Here our surface ribaldry covers a sincere respect, and in recent years, when parliamentary government has been overthrown elsewhere, I think we have come to cherish ours more than ever. Public life is regarded as the crown of a career, and to young men it is the worthiest ambition. Politics is still the greatest and the most honourable adventure.

II

During my years in Parliament I had one curious interlude. In 1933 and 1934 I was Lord High Commissioner to the General Assembly of the Church of Scotland in succession to Sir Iain Colquhoun. The King's Commissioner opens and closes the Assembly, appears daily at its meetings, and fulfils a multitude of other engagements; for a fortnight he lives in the Palace of Holyroodhouse, where he entertains the Church and the World according to his means and his inclination.

I gladly accepted the office, for the Scottish Church had always been a principal part of my background. I was born and brought up in a manse. I was an elder of the Kirk, my historical studies had lain to some extent in Scottish church history, and I had had a small part in bringing about the union of the United Free Church (of which my father had been a minister) with the Church of Scotland. It was an office thickly encrusted with history. In the seventeenth century the Lord High Commissioner presided over the Scottish Parliament as well as the General Assembly, and a stormy time he had of it. (I remembered Hamilton at the epoch-making Glasgow Assembly of 1639.) Since the Union of 1707 he presides at the Assembly alone. But memories of early sturt and strife still cling to him. On the night of his arrival, when the Scots nobility are invited to a state dinner, he receives from the Lord Provost the keys of the city of Edinburgh; he himself chooses the password for the Palace guards; the Lord Provost and the Sheriff of the Lothians are given the highest precedence;—all relics of the past when the King's Commissioner took his life in his hands and had at any cost to mollify the local dignitaries. The same atmosphere hangs over the Assembly itself. The proceedings are opened with an historic ritual, and the close has in it the whole history of the Scottish Kirk, which has always claimed, and is now admitted by statute, to be completely self-governing. The High Commissioner formally declares the sederunt closed and promises to report to the King that everything has been done decently and in order. The Moderator then rises and has the last word, appointing the date of the next Assembly, "in the name of Our Lord Jesus Christ, *the only Head of this Church.*"

The Lord High Commissioner is the sole subject in Great Britain who on occasion represents His Majesty, and he must therefore conduct himself high and disposedly. Holyroodhouse used to be the last word in shabby discomfort; the High Commissioner had to bring his own plate, linen and other accessories, and bivouac in windy chambers where the rats scampered. Now it is like a well-appointed country house, and I think the west drawing-room, which looks out on Arthur's Seat, one of the pleasantest rooms I have ever entered. The High Commissioner and his wife are for a fortnight Their Graces, and, besides the Purse Bearer, are attended

by a lady-in-waiting, by several maids-of-honour, and
by four A.D.C.'s. During my two years of office I
had as my A.D.C.'s representatives of ancient Scottish
houses—Lord Clydesdale and his brother, Lord Nigel
Douglas-Hamilton ; Captain Duncan Macrae of Eilean
Donan ; and my future son-in-law Captain Brian
Fairfax-Lucy (a Cameron of Mamore). They all wore
kilts of the old pattern, and made a most impressive
bodyguard. I shall not soon forget those dinners in the
great gallery of the Palace, where sometimes a hundred
sat at table—the lingering spring sunshine competing
with the candles, the dark walls covered with the
portraits of the Kings of Scotland (daubs two hundred
years old, but impressive in the twilight), the toast of
the King, followed by the National Anthem, and that
of the Church of Scotland, followed by Old Hundred,
the four pipers of the Argylls, who strutted round the
table and then played a pibroch for my special delecta-
tion. On those nights old ghosts came out of secret
places.

III

Between 1927 and 1935 the stage was emptied of
most of the figures who had been prominent when I
first became interested in politics. Milner and Curzon
died before I entered the House ; Asquith and Arthur
Balfour, Finlay and Sumner and Buckmaster while I
was a member. All of them were in the Lords ; only
Austen Chamberlain and Mr. Lloyd George, of the
pre-War statesmen, still sat in the Commons, and the
latter spent much of his time at his Sutton farm in his
new role of Cincinnatus.

One friend of my youth was in the Cabinet when I
came to St. Stephen's, and three years later all parties
mourned his untimely death. When I went up to

Oxford F. E. Smith was a law don at Merton, imping his wings for the most brilliant legal flight of our day. When he spoke in the Union he swept away opposition like a river in spate. I met him in the political clubs, and I had the benefit of his advocacy when, with other unfortunates, I had some trouble with the police during the visit of King Edward VII (then Prince of Wales) to Blenheim. When I returned from South Africa I found that he had settled as a "local" at Liverpool and had already built up a large practice. On the northern circuit I used to stay with him at his house in the Wirral, and spend a cheerful week-end among dogs and horses. I remember how deeply I was impressed by his appearances in court. Disregarding the folly of solicitors, he refused to argue each and every point, but concentrated on the vital ones; wherefore he was beloved by judges, whose time he never wasted.

He entered Parliament in the 1906 election, migrated to London, and presently was a resplendent figure both in the Law Courts and the House of Commons. Everything he undertook he did easily, as if with his left hand, and with a superb gesture of unconcern. He was Aristotle's Magnificent Man, the last exponent of the eighteenth-century Grand Manner. He was consciously shaping his career according to a long-settled plan, and he took a boyish pleasure in the masterful way in which he made stage follow stage. Wholly incapable of pretence and humbug and time-serving, he had strong views on public questions which he candidly avowed and faithfully acted upon. He liked the good things of life and made no bones about it; ginger remained for him hot in the mouth, and he refused to relinquish cakes and ale because of the frowns of the anaemic. He had his own strict code of honour, hard as stone and plain as a pikestaff, and he never departed from it. One of its articles was loyalty to friendship. At the start he imperilled his chances at the Bar because he stood by an unpopular acquaintance. He would go out of his way at his busiest to help a friend. He used to speak for me in my Border constituency before the War, and arrive at the last possible moment, when I had given up hope. I had a house far up in the moors, from whose door one could see four miles of road, and I ought to have contracted heart disease from my Sister-Anne watches on that doorstep!

He was in every sense an extraordinary man according to Sydney Smith's definition: "The meaning of an extraordinary man is that he is eight men in one man; that he has as much wit as if he had no sense, and as much sense as if he had no wit; that his conduct is as judicious as if he were the dullest of human beings, and his imagination as brilliant as if he were irretrievably ruined." F. E. had plenty of foibles and plenty of critics, but, as has been well said, it is only at the tree loaded with fruit that people throw stones. He had talents of the first order, and in a dazzling variety. First and foremost he was a great lawyer—a great advocate and a great judge. He had an intellect of remarkable range and power, capable of the nicest subtleties and the broadest and most luminous common sense. He could embody his conclusions, too, in clear, nervous prose. I do not think that he was a very good writer in the general way, he had too few notes in his scale; but he was a master of judicial statement. Then he was a great orator. Not in the highest rank, perhaps, for here, too, he had a limited range, and I was never much moved by his solemnities; but in supple argument and devastating controversial skill he had no equal in our time. He had a beautiful voice and his sentences seemed to flow with a contemptuous ease. The fluency of the ordinary man suggests the shallow and the ineffective, but his proclaimed an insolent mastery. I have more than once been with him on election platforms, and his handling of interrupters and hecklers was a cruel piece of artistry ; it must have taken them weeks to recover.

The Magnificent Man is apt to lack the small prudential virtues. F. E. took no thought for the morrow ; he was resolved to get what he sought by the sheer weight of brains and will, and not by any tactical adroitness. I question whether, if he had lived, he would have gone much further ; certainly he would never have been Prime Minister, for he was too much the brilliant individualist for our queer synthetic polity. There has been no one quite like him in our history, for audacious figures like Thurlow had usually something rotten and cankered about them, whereas F. E. had most of the wholesome virtues. Sometimes he seemed to cultivate a kind of Regency grossness, but the coarseness of grain was superficial ; he was capable of the most delicate consideration and chivalry. Above all he had magnanimity ; next to a stout ally he loved a stout opponent. No architect of a career was ever less jealous of other builders. An ambition very near his heart was to be Chancellor of Oxford University, but when Lord Cave died it seemed to the committee of Conservatives who were concerned with the nomination that F. E. was not a possible candidate. I was given the unpleasant task of breaking the news to him. "My dear John," he said, "I wholly agree. What Oxford needs in the present crisis of her fortunes is a decorous façade, and that unhappily I cannot provide." To some he seemed to play the game of life for common and earthy stakes, but who among us can on this account cast a stone ?—and in any case the triviality of the stakes was redeemed by the brilliance and the humanity of the player.

I knew Ramsay Macdonald long before I entered Parliament. Indeed, before I took that step I had some talk with him as to what room there was for anybody like myself in public life. I was in the House when he led the Opposition; during the Labour Government of 1929-1931; and from the day when he became Prime Minister of a National Government to the day he retired. In the last two years of his premiership I saw much of him, for during the session we walked together round St. James's Park on several mornings in the week, and I frequently breakfasted with him and did my best to help a very tired man to arrange his difficult days.

He will be a hard personality for historians to judge, since the evidence, to a writer a hundred years hence, will seem a mass of contradictions. He was the chief maker of the Labour party, and according to his critics he did his best to destroy it—*suarum legum auctor ac subversor*. Before he took office he preached an emotional socialism, but in his later years he tended towards a creed scarcely distinguishable from left-centre conservatism. In 1914, at the outbreak of War, he was in opposition to the bulk of his party and to the vast majority of the British people, but no man was less of a pacifist. There were moments when he was Jacobin and sansculotte, and moments when his affections were with an *ancien régime*. Most of his life was spent with very plain folk, but his taste was fastidious, his courtesy of an old-fashioned elaboration, and—to quote from some novel whose title I have forgotten—he "had the so-called aristocratic appearance which is common in England among the middle classes, but unknown among the old nobility."

I think that some of these contradictions can be explained. He had the starkest kind of courage, and if he were challenged or coerced he was apt to be forced into an opposition which did not represent his real views. That is certainly true of his behaviour in the War. Again, his critics said that, though his business was to succour the under-dog, he disliked the breed. That is not true. His sympathies were always with the under-dog, and he disliked it only when it became smug and patronising and talked bad economics. Yet I think that here lay his great limitation. In one of his letters Rupert Brooke wrote that he could "watch a dirty, middle-aged tradesman in a railway carriage for hours, and love every dirty, greasy, sulky wrinkle in his weak chin, and every button on his spotted, unclean waistcoat." Ramsay Macdonald lacked this catholic, enjoying zest for human nature, this kindly affection for the commonplace, which may be called benevolence, or, better still, loving-kindness, the quality of Shakespeare and Walter Scott. It may have been due to some harsh experience in his youth, but he had developed what seemed to me to be an undue fastidiousness. He was too ready to despise. He loved plain folk, but they must be his own kind of plain folk with his own background. Of the ordinary stupid stuff of democracy he could be as intolerant as Coriolanus.

He had all the qualities of a leader, fearlessness, decision, a temperamental mastery; but it was the irony of fate which made him leader of the Labour party. There he had to deal with honest men most of whom had drab backgrounds and narrow outlooks, people with whom he could share nothing. Worse, he had to deal with the half-baked, the minor intellectuals, and he knew too well the dismal shallows of their minds. With the really able men of the Left he made no contact. He used to profess an admiration for science and scientists, but his own mind had nothing of the scientific bent. He simply did not understand the language of modern economics.

I can only speak of him as I knew him, and that was in his decline. I never heard him in his great days when he was a famous platform orator and a formidable debater. He had still the oratorical habit, and would drift into rhetorical cadences, but he had lost his old copiousness and had to drag his thoughts and words from a deep well, so that the result was often a sad anti-climax. His alleged vanity seemed to me to be largely sensitiveness. The struggle of his early years had made him suspicious and too quick to imagine affronts. Also he had a queer romantic kink which made him see melodrama in perfectly humdrum affairs. He could not help picturing himself in dramatic parts. To the end there was an endearing innocence about him.

Indeed if I had to choose one epithet for him it would be "endearing." There was a sombre gentleness which fascinated me. In his last years when mind and body were almost worn out, two things never failed him—courage and courtesy. The whole man was a romance, almost an anachronism. To understand him one had to understand the Scottish Celt, with his ferocious pride, his love of pageantry and poetry, his sentiment about the past, his odd contradictory loyalties. He would have made an excellent Highland chief three hundred years ago, and a heroic Jacobite refugee. That is why he was a successful Foreign Secretary, for his imagination enabled him to understand large grandiose things, the conflict of nations, the strife of continents. Now and then the curtain would be drawn back and something would be revealed of a lonely inward-looking soul. I remember that when the National

Government was formed in 1931, the Scots in London gave him a dinner, and in his speech he let his recollection wander back to his boyhood and told of his happiness when a harvest-worker had been kind to him long ago. I shall not soon forget the wistfulness with which he revived that old, dim memory.

The man was principally a poet—a poet who, like Cecil Rhodes, had not the gift of song. When his days of struggle were over and he found himself in a high place, he did not quite know what to do with his power, for his was a kingdom of dreams, not of things and men. The silliest charge levelled against him was snobbishness. He liked cultivated, long-descended people and beautiful things, and had the honesty to admit it. But the true definition of a snob is one who craves for what separates men rather than for what unites them, and of that type Ramsay Macdonald was the extreme opposite. He had no real wish to be any kind of grandee. The things which were dearest to him were the things which are happily found in the widest commonalty—old friends, the folk of his native parish, the songs and tales of his youth, the seasonal beauties of nature. He had tramped over all my Border hills and knew every shepherd by name, and once, when he was the most talked of man in Europe, he suggested that he and I should go off for a week's walking there. "I want some pleasure," he said, "before the lean years begin.'

It is fitting to pass from Ramsay Macdonald to King George V, for between the two there was a sincere friendship. I was first brought into association with the King in the latter part of the War when, as part of my official duties, I was occasionally summoned to discuss with him public opinion in foreign nations. What struck me was his eager interest, his quick apprehension and his capacious memory. As with many royal personages, what to the ordinary man was abstract history was to him a personal affair, like a family chronicle, and he was extraordinarily quick in detecting historical parallels. I was not less impressed by his courage. He never lost heart, and his fortitude was not a dead, stolid thing, for there was always something about it of the buoyant and the debonair.

He had a ready sense of humour, of the kind often found among good sportsmen. Verbal wit did not interest him, but he had a robust appreciation of the comedies of life. He was a great reader, reading rather for substance than for style. He did me the honour to be amused by my romances, and used to make acute criticisms on questions of fact. Of one, a poaching story of the Highlands, he gave me a penetrating analysis, but he approved of it sufficiently to present many copies of it to his friends.

The sportsman was always strong in him, for he loved not only the practice of an art in which he excelled, but the whole out-of-doors world and the pageant of nature. Akin to this taste was his liking for those who lived close to nature. Like Walter Scott, he rejoiced that "nothing worth having or caring about in this world is uncommon." He understood plain people and was in turn understood by them, and that was the secret of his strength. Few things pleased or moved him more than to be told of the pithy sayings of simple folk, and of episodes which revealed the divine spark in them. In 1923 when he visited the Borders and passed through Peebles, an old shepherd's wife tramped ten miles from a hill glen to greet him. When I asked her why she had undertaken such a journey her reply was "We maun boo to the buss that bields us." [1]

[1] "We must bow to the bush that shields us."

Q

I told this to the King, and it stuck in his memory, for he often quoted it.

He had one key of access to all hearts, his sincere love of his fellows. He could be explosive and denunciatory, but always with a twinkle in his eye. He had in a full degree what Clarendon attributed to England, "its old good manners, its old good humour, and its old good nature." Soberly and unrhetorically it can be written of him that he loved humanity. Therefore he was a shrewd judge of character, which no cynic can ever be. He never rode rough-shod over anyone's feelings, and he was tender even to prejudices. He was immensely considerate of all those who served him. When he summoned a Minister to his presence, he endeavoured not to overburden the days of a busy man. In his long illness of 1928-1929 he was constantly thinking of the comfort of his doctors and nurses.

After that illness his health was a guarded flame, and sometimes the need for restrictions irked him. But to the world he always presented a smiling front. If anything, he became more gentle, and there was perhaps a greater benignity in his kind, worn face and frosty blue eyes. He was, if possible, more charitable in his judgments, more thoughtful for others. When I received at his hands an appointment to a great imperial post, he gave me wise advice. One thing he impressed upon me was to be sympathetic to the French people in Canada, and jealously to respect their traditions and their language. On the very day of his death I received a message from him bidding me remember that ski-ing was not a safe pursuit for a middle-aged man!

It will be for the historian of the future to expound the work he did in the world. In this brief note I am concerned only with the personality of the man, a personality greater perhaps than any of his achievements, a personality which was in itself an achievement. His simplicity, honesty, and warm human sympathy made themselves felt not only in the Empire, but throughout the globe, so that millions who owed him no allegiance seemed to know and love him. For he was a pillar of all that was stable and honourable and of good report in a distracted world. In the United States he was never, in conversation or in the Press, called the "king of England," but the "king"; for them there was only one King; the Throne of Britain long ago lost their allegiance, but not their hearts. The same was true of almost every nation. It is to the credit of mankind that it responds to what is best in itself, when that best—which rarely happens—is so pinnacled that none can miss it. He feared God and loved and served his people, and, through them, all peoples. In Carlyle's phrase about Scott, no sounder piece of manhood was fashioned in our generation, for he had in him both warmth and light.

"Blest are those
Whose blood and judgment are so well commingled."

CHAPTER X

FIRST AND LAST THINGS

I

TO anyone whose imagination has been caught by ancient Rome one picture must keep recurring. It is the living-room of a country house—farm or villa— in which, among objects of domestic use, a space was reserved for the images of the dead. I do not mean the grandiose *lararium* of the rich, but the modest household where there was no room to segregate the family busts. I picture those wax memorials, often rude and discoloured, lit by the glow of the hearth-fire when the storm howled without, catching the sun on a bright morning, and drawing the wondering eyes of the children when an elder spoke of the past and jerked a thumb upwards towards some ancestor. In such a life the dead remained in a real sense within the family circle. Piety was nourished not by the memory only but by the eye.

So among these chapters it may be permitted to allot one to the pictures which, as we grow older, acquire a sharper outline than the contemporary scene—those family recollections which are the first, and also, I think, the last, things in a man's memory. As one ages, the memory seems to be inverted and recent events to grow dim in the same proportion as ancient happenings become clear. To-day, for instance, I am a little hazy about the Great War but very clear about the South African campaign. And I seem to live more intimately with those who died long ago than with men and women whom I see every day. Lockhart's lines are less a precept for conduct than the recognition of a fact in human psychology:

> "Be constant to the dead,
> The dead cannot deceive."

My father died in his early sixties when I was in my thirty-seventh year. His strong physique was worn out by unceasing toil in a slum parish, an endless round of sermons and addresses, and visits at all hours to the sick and sorrowful. He had retired to his native Tweeddale, where he had a brief leisure among the scenes of his youth before he died peacefully in his sleep. For the last dozen years of his life I saw less of him, for my own life was spent in London or abroad. The picture in my memory belongs to my childhood, amplified a little by the reflections of adolescence.

As a young man he had bushy whiskers and must have looked very much like Matthew Arnold, but as time passed these grew smaller until they vanished altogether. He had the ruddy complexion of a countryman, and that air of gentle, wondering cheerfulness which God sometimes gives to His servants:

> "The good are always the merry,
> Save by an evil chance."

When I first met Charles Gore I observed in him the same benign, surprised enjoyment of the mere fact of living.

My father had been a good classical scholar, and he remained a voracious reader. He had a notable memory for poetry and could repeat every Border ballad that was ever printed and many still unpublished. He had a profound knowledge of Scottish songs, both words and tunes, and I could wish that I had taken down from

him some of the traditional fragments. He was also
an excellent field botanist. He had read much history
and was an unashamed partisan. The past to him was
a design in snow and ink, one long contest between
villains of admitted villainy and honest men. His
dividing line was oddly drawn. In the eighteenth
century the Jacobites were for him the children of
light; in the seventeenth the Covenanters. For the
latter indeed he cherished a fervent private cult,
admitting no flaw in their perfection. But his children
observed that his special admiration was reserved for
those among the Covenanters who had something of
the Cavalier romance—Hackstoun of Rathillet, the
Black MacMichael, Paton of Meadowhead—and he
would permit no criticism of Montrose.

It was odd that he should have been by profession a
theologian, for he was wholly lacking in philosophical
interest or aptitude. But a stalwart theologian of the
old school he was, rejoicing in the clamped and riveted
Calvinistic logic and eager to defend it against all
comers. In church politics he belonged to the extreme
Conservative wing, and it was his delight, when a
member of the Annual Assembly, to stir up all the strife
he could by indicting for heresy some popular preacher
or professor. There was no ill-feeling in the matter,
and he might profoundly respect the heretic, but he
conceived it his duty to defend the faith of his fathers
against every innovator. Partly the interest was
intellectual. He liked a clear pattern and a clean logic,
however austere. He greatly admired the Puritan
divine and he had a special liking for the later Jonathan
Edwards. Partly it was sentimental—a love of old
ways and a fast-vanishing world. Partly it was the
reaction against two things which he whole-heartedly
disliked—a glib modernism and the worship of fashion.

He had no belief in compromises and a facile liberalism ;
he never cherished the illusion that the Christian life
was an easy thing, and on this score he had to testify
against many false prophets. He had a complete distrust of current fashions and of the worship of the
"voice of the people" and the "spirit of the age" and
such fetishes. He believed that a majority was usually
wrong, and he would have been terrified to find himself
on a side which was superior in numbers. He had the
same taste as his children for things old and unpopular
and shabby.

But, except as regards dogma, he had little of the
conventional Calvinistic temper. He had no sympathy
with the legalism of that creed, the notion of a contract
between God and man drawn up by some celestial con-
veyancer. I could wish that he had lived to read Karl
Barth, for their views had much in common. In the
beleaguered city of the Faith he thought it his duty now
and then to man a gun on the dogmatic ramparts, but
more of his time was devoted to easing the life of the
civilians and strengthening their hope. What he
preached for forty years was a very simple and comforting gospel. His evangel had neither the hysteria nor
the smugness of ordinary revivalism. He believed
profoundly in the fact of "conversion," the turning
of the face to a new course. But, the first step having
been taken, he would insist upon the arduousness of
the pilgrimage as well as upon its moments of high
vision and its ultimate reward. His religion was
tender and humane, but it was also well-girded. He
had no love for those who took their ease in Zion.

To his children he was a companion rather than a
mentor ; or, to put it otherwise, his life was the example,
not his precepts, for he rarely preached to us. He could
judge sternly but never harshly. He hated lying and

cowardice, and he was distrustful of large professions. He was nervous about the value of youthful piety and used to rejoice that his family, bad as they were, were not prigs. For cant, and indeed for all rhetoric, he had a strong distaste. Beginning life as a Liberal he lost his confidence in Mr. Gladstone after Gordon's death in Khartoum, and the Home Rule question drove him to the Unionist side. He detected in Ulster some kinship with his beloved Covenanters.

My father was an instance of what I think was commoner among the Puritans than is generally supposed—a stiff dogmatic theology which in practice was mellowed by common sense and kindliness and was conjoined with a perpetual delight in the innocent pleasures of life. He was like that seventeenth-century Scots minister who besought his flock to thank God, if for nothing else, for a good day for the lambs. He could preach a tough doctrinal sermon with anybody; but his discourses which remain in my memory were those spoken at the close of the half-yearly Communions, when he invited his hearers, very simply and solemnly, to share his own happiness.

For he was above all things a happy man. Straitened means and a laborious life did not weaken his relish for common joys. He found acute delight in the simplest things, for he savoured them with a clean palate. Like the old preacher he could exclaim, "All this—and Heaven too." He had always the background of an assured faith to correct man's sense of the fragility of his hopes. Also he had none of the little fears and frustrations which are apt to cloud enjoyment. I do not think that he was afraid of anything—except of finding himself in a majority. He was wholly without ambition. He did not know the meaning of class-consciousness; he would have stood confidently before

kings, and was quite incapable of deferring to anybody
except the very old and the very poor. He was not, I
suppose, the conventional saint, for he was not over-
much interested in his own soul. But he was something
of the apostle, and, if it be virtue to diffuse a healing
grace and to lighten the load of all who cross your
path, then he was the best man I have ever known.

II

My father was a true son of Mary; my mother own
daughter to Martha. Had she had his character the
household must have crashed, and if he had been like
her, childhood would have been a less wonderful thing
for all of us.

Not many sons and mothers can have understood
each other better than she and I; indeed, in my adolescence we sometimes arrived at that point of complete
comprehension known as a misunderstanding. We
had no quarrels, for to each of us that would have been
like quarrelling with oneself, but we had many arguments. Instinctively we seemed to grasp the undis-
closed and hardly realised things which were at the back
of the other's mind. As I grew older what had been
a little frightening became an immense comfort, for
we were aware that in seeking sympathy there was no
need for elaborate explanations. We knew each other
too well.

My mother was married at seventeen, and had at once
to take charge of a kirk and a manse, to which was soon
added a family. A Scots minister must be something
of a diplomat if he is to keep his congregation in good
temper; my father had about as much diplomacy as
a rhinoceros, for he was utterly regardless of popular
opinion, so my mother had to be ceaselessly observant,

and an habitual smoother of ruffled feathers. The
family income was small, and my father had no sense
of homely realities. We children used to say that he
might have been a great general, for it would have been
impossible for an opponent to guess what he was going
to do next. So the management of the household fell
wholly on my mother. Both tasks she willingly undertook and — against great odds — succeeded in. She
brought up her family in comfort, and saw to it that they
lacked no reasonable opportunities. Successive congre-
gations were handled so adroitly that my father's
defects in tact were covered and the charm of his
personality given full play.

Having found her task in life my mother became a
rigid specialist. Her world was the Church, or rather
a little section of the Church. Her ambitions were
narrowly ecclesiastical. A popular preacher, a famous
theologian seemed to her the height of human greatness
—a view which was not shared by her family. My
father's lack of such ambitions was to her, I think, a
sorrow. Yet in theology she had no real interest, and
her religion depended little upon dogma and much on
her generous human instincts. The Church to her was
like a secular profession, a field for administrative talent,
not a mystic brotherhood. She had a passion for church
services, which were to her a form of ritual; so many
in the week were a proper recognition of the claims of
religion. So was the reading of the requisite number of
chapters from the Bible and other devotional literature.
My father rarely spoke of religious matters outside the
pulpit; from my mother's conversation they were
never absent; such references were in her eyes a
testimony, a proper acknowledgment of man's frailty
and dependence. She would have been very happy in
the Church of Rome, with its clear schedule of duties,

or in any faith where merit could be acquired by an
infinity of small devotional acts. Her clear practical
intelligence was at ease only among things concrete and
defined. She was as little of a mystic as a Scotswoman
can be.

She was a possessive mother and fiercely maternal.
The bodily and spiritual well-being of her flock was
never out of her mind. She nursed its members
devotedly through their illnesses, and my carriage
accident, which involved nearly a year in bed, must
have taken severe toll of her strength. She lived in a
perpetual expectation of disaster, not to herself but to
her children, and wore out her strength with needless
anxieties; but when disaster did come she faced it with
coolness and courage. She must have had a remarkable
talent for administration to make a tiny income go so
far, and to steer my father among the pitfalls of his
profession. Her success was largely due, as I have said,
to a rigid specialisation on two things, family and
Church. In a bookish household she alone was totally
uninterested in literature. Public affairs only affected
her if they affected her kirk.

But her passionate possessiveness was never allowed
to become a vice. She had no desire to mollycoddle us.
As children we were given much liberty of action,
though it cost her anxious hours, and as we grew older
and had to shape our careers she never tried to interfere
with our decisions. She longed to keep us near her,
but she did not complain when we scattered like wood-
cock over the globe. Her view seems to have been
that, while humanity was a frail thing, at the mercy
of the Devil and wholly dependent upon God, the
particular specimens that belonged to her were as much
to be trusted as any other, and a lack of trust would
have meant a lack of faith in the Almighty.

About the middle of her life she fell into bad health, and pernicious anaemia brought her to death's door. For four years she was a very sick woman until she was cured by the genius of Sir Almroth Wright. This time of ill-health was also a time of sorrow. In 1911 my father died, my brother William in 1912, and five years later her youngest son, Alastair, fell in the Great War. For a little it looked as if she would sink under the double burden of bereavement and sickness.

But a miracle happened. She rose above her sorrows and her frailty, and the last twenty years of her life were not only, I think, the happiest, but the most active. She died in her eighty-first year, having been about her usual avocations almost up to the last day. She had become very small and slight, but her bodily energy put youth to shame, and it was matched by a like activity of mind. While church affairs were still her chief preoccupation, she developed a new interest in secular politics. Her preferences in human nature had once been circumscribed, except where there was a call for charity, but now they covered all sorts and conditions. She made intimate friends of devout Catholics, and of people with no religion at all. The old house at Peebles, above the bridge of Tweed, where she lived with my sister and brother, became a port of call for the whole shire, indeed for the whole Lowlands. Young people came to her for counsel and their elders for sympathy, and none went empty away.

Only then I began to realise how remarkable were my mother's powers of mind as well as of heart. She had a really penetrating intelligence. In the ordinary business of life she was apt to deal in moral and religious platitudes and in the prudential maxims, which the Scots call "owercomes" and which flourished especially in her family. But when things became serious all this went by the board, and she judged a situation with a mathematical clarity. She had a wild subtlety of her own which gave her a wide prospect over human nature, and she could assess character with an acumen none the less infallible because charity was never absent. My one complaint was that in practice she was too charitable. No tramp was ever turned away from her door, and her tenderness towards bores was the despair of her family.

In these last years, as I have said, her interests broadened. Literature was no longer despised, nor politics, and she condescended to read some of my own speeches and romances. She longed to travel, and when well over seventy she was always imploring me to take her by air to Palestine. In her eightieth year she visited me in Canada and covered a large part of the Canadian East. The truth is that the world, which had once been a bugbear, was now regarded more kindly. She discovered a surprising number of unexpected "temples of the Holy Ghost." Her great moments, I think, were my tenures of the office of Lord High Commissioner in Edinburgh, where she found the Church and the World in the friendliest accord.

To the end she remained a countrywoman—a Border countrywoman. She had the country dislike of over-statement and the country love of pricking bubbles. She feared praise as the Greeks feared Nemesis. Lord Baldwin once said kind things to her about a speech of mine, to which she replied that at any rate it was short! She had the robust humour of the Border glens, robust and yet subtle. Like most country folk she scarcely knew the name of a bird or a plant, but she was entirely at home with nature and talked to dogs, cattle and horses as if they were blood relations. She had the

lovable country habit of going nowhere without carrying gifts, generally some simple kind of country
produce. If her beloved little ghost should ever visit its
familiar places I think that it will have a basket on its
arm—fresh eggs, perhaps, or new churned butter, or a
picking of gooseberries.

III

Two of my brothers died in their early youth.

Alastair, the youngest, fell at the head of his company
of Royal Scots Fusiliers on the first morning of the
battle of Arras. He was one of those people who seemed
to have been born especially for the Great War. Cheerful, dreamy, absent-minded, he went creditably through
the stages of school and college, and decided on
chartered accountancy as his profession. But he
never seemed to take any of these things quite
seriously, as if he were waiting for another kind of
summons.

Coming at the end of the family, he had a different
upbringing from the rest of us. Even in his teens he was
far-travelled, having been to South Africa, to the
Continent, and many times to London. He had therefore a width of interests denied to us. He steadfastly
refused to be much concerned about his future, as if he
had a premonition that that future would be short.
Half the time he moved in a world of his own. On a
moorland ramble, as a child, he would walk by himself, telling himself stories, and excitedly repeating
poetry with which his memory was stored. Sir
Walter Scott's confession might have been his: "Since
I was five years old I cannot remember the time when I
had not some ideal part to play for my own solitary
amusement." When he grew up he was extra-

ordinarily happy with children and was an adored uncle to my own brood.

He was twenty when the War broke out, and at once joined a battalion of Cameron Highlanders, where for some months, in the Hampshire mud, he cut a strange figure in all the uniform that could be provided—shocking old blue trousers, and a red tunic made in 1880 and apparently designed for a giant! Then he obtained a commission in the Royal Scots Fusiliers, and went to France with them at the close of 1915. He was wounded in the spring of 1916 and did not return to duty until the autumn of that year. On Easter Monday, 1917, he was killed at Arras.

I have said that he was born for the Great War. In August 1914 he found himself, and entered upon the task to which he was dedicated. He had a remarkable gift for managing men, especially bad characters, and he endeared himself to all who served with him. He was never out of temper or depressed, and wherever he was he diffused an air of confidence and hope. I remember that when I occasionally ran across him during the last stages of the battle of the Somme I thought him the only cheerful thing in a grey world. He managed to get the best out of everybody, and won a general affection because he himself gave out so much of it. I wonder if the future historian will realise how much of the strength of the British army was due to the boys of twenty who brought the kindly ardour of youth into the business of war and died before they could lose their freshness.

When he was a child he was a devotee of *Cyrano de Bergerac*, and his favourite scene was that "under the walls of Arras." I remember how he would declaim, "Who are these men that rush on death?" and thunder forth the answer, "Cadets of Gascony are we." He did not dream that it would be his fate to fall on an April morning under the walls of Arras.

My brother William was also "to find perfection in short space." Had he lived until the War he would probably have died in it, for he would assuredly have found some way of serving, and in that holocaust of youth his loss would not have seemed so grievous a thing as it did in the soft years of peace. Destiny struck too soon.

He was five years my junior, so it was not until we were grown up that we became in the full sense companions. As a boy he was gravely and consistently pugnacious. Without haste and without rest he fought his way through the youth of the place to an unchallenged pre-eminence. One of his fingers was permanently crooked in consequence. Yet he was the gentlest of mortals, and would take endless pains to succour a starving cat or a homeless dog.

About the age of sixteen he suddenly woke up and decided upon his profession. It must be the Indian Civil Service, about which he cherished a romance. He planned out his course—first Glasgow University with a scholarship, then Oxford with a scholarship—and, never having done a stroke of work at school, he became forthwith a most assiduous student. He won his scholarships; at Oxford got good seconds in both classics and history, and passed high into the Indian service. He also played association football with success, and made his mark in the political clubs. He was vice-secretary of the Canning, and at the annual dinner in 1903 he had the difficult task of proposing Sir Edward Carson's health in the midst of the controversy between that statesman and Mr. George Wyndham over the Irish Land Purchase Act. In 1902,

LIEUTENANT ALASTAIR BUCHAN, ROYAL SCOTS FUSILIERS

a year before Mr. Chamberlain made his famous pronouncement, he acquired great prestige by propounding similar proposals—an episode to which a good deal of space is devoted in the published history of the club.

His three years at Oxford were a happy time. He spent them in rooms in college, first in a top storey in the New Quad, and then in the rooms which I had before him (and my eldest son after me) on the first floor in the north-eastern corner of the Old Quad, the rooms where Bishop Heber entertained Sir Walter Scott, and where on a summer's day the sunlight filters softly through the chequered greenery of the great chestnut in Exeter gardens. For all his passion for wet moorlands and windswept hills he fell deeply in love with the beauty of an Oxford summer, when, in long days among the lilied reaches of the Cherwell, a boy may dream of the untravelled road which lies before him. Oxford, for those with no clear outlook on the future, is apt to be a lotus-eating land from which there comes a rude awakening. But to one whose path in life is determined it is a place of pure delight, the consummation of a happy youth. Such an one leaves it with regret, but it is a regret untinged with melancholy. He carries with him into the arid places of the East the memory of a cool and fragrant world, the shrine of his boyish memories, the epitome of that homeland in whose cause he spends his strength.

In India he certainly spent his strength. After holding various administrative posts in Bengal, he became the registrar of agricultural banks and a pioneer of rural co-operation. There was a chivalrous strain in him which arrayed him on the side of anything which was distressed. At Glasgow he had been a conspicuous partisan of a professor who became unpopular during

R

the South African War, and in India his sympathies went out to the peasant who seemed to have a hard deal in life. He made it his mission to save him from the moneylender, and in the few years of work permitted to him he laid lasting foundations.

In the early summer of 1912 he came home on his first long leave. The autumn before he had gone on a lengthy trek in the Sikkim Himalayas—he wrote an admirable account of it in *Blackwood's Magazine*—and there he may have picked up some infection which slowly poisoned his blood. At any rate he seemed a changed man, easily tired and complaining of odd pains. The doctors could make nothing of him, but daily he lost strength until in October he was in a nursing home. There his life slowly ebbed :

> "through long days of labouring breath
> He watched the world grow small and far
> And met the constant eyes of death,
> And haply knew how kind they are."

It is a bitter thing, when mind and spirit are strong and ambition high, to surrender youth and the hope of achievement. My brother faced the sacrifice with a splendid fortitude.

I have known many brave men, but I have never known a braver. I have seen many devout servants of their country, but none more single-hearted. I have known many gentle hearts, but none more filled with the supreme Christian virtue of courtesy. There is a tablet to his memory in the ante-chapel of Brasenose on which is inscribed a sentence adapted from Landor :

> "Patriae quaesivit gloriam, videt Dei."

CHAPTER XI

MY AMERICA

I

THE title of this chapter exactly defines its contents. It presents the American scene as it appears to one observer—a point of view which does not claim to be that mysterious thing, objective truth. There will be no attempt to portray the "typical" American, for I have never known one. I have met a multitude of individuals, but I should not dare to take any one of them as representing his country—of being that other mysterious thing, the average man. You can point to certain qualities which are more widely distributed in America than elsewhere, but you will scarcely find human beings who possess all these qualities. One good American will have most of them; another, equally good and not less representative, may have few or none. So I shall eschew generalities. If you cannot indict a nation, no more can you label it like a museum piece.

Half the misunderstandings between Britain and America are due to the fact that neither will regard the other as what it is—in an important sense of the word— a foreign country. Each thinks of the other as a part of itself which has somehow gone off the lines. An Englishman is always inclined to resent the unfamiliar when it is found under conditions for which he thinks he has some responsibility. He can appreciate complete and utter strangeness, and indeed show himself highly sympathetic towards it; but for variations upon his own ways—divergencies in speech, food, clothes, social habits—he has little tolerance. He is not very happy even in his own colonies and dominions, and in America he can be uncommonly ill at ease.

On a higher level, when it comes to assessing spiritual values, he often shows the same mixture of surprise and disappointment. America has lapsed from the family tradition; what would have been pardonable and even commendable in a foreigner is blameworthy in a cousin. Matthew Arnold, for example, was critical of certain American traits, not on their merits but because they were out of tune with that essential European tradition of which he considered himself the guardian. The American critic can be not less intolerant, and for much the same reason. His expositions of England are often like sermons preached in a Home for Fallen Women, the point being that she has fallen, that her defects are a discredit to her relations, that she has let down her kin, and suffered the old home to fall into disrepute. This fretfulness can only be cured, I think, by a frank recognition of the real foreignness of the two peoples. No doubt they had a common ancestor, but he is of little avail against the passage of time and the estranging seas.

II

I first discovered America through books. Not the tales of Indians and the Wild West which entranced my boyhood; those seemed to belong to no particular quarter of the globe, but to an indefinable land of romance, and I was not cognisant of any nation behind them. But when I became interested in literature I came strongly under the spell of New England. Its culture seemed to me to include what was best in Europe's, winnowed and clarified. Perhaps it was especially fitted to attract youth, for it was not too difficult or too recondite, but followed the "main march of the human affections," and it had the morning freshness of a young people. Its cheerfulness atoned for its occasional bleakness and anaemia. Lowell was the kind of critic I wanted, learned, rational, never freakish, always intelligible. Emerson's gnomic wisdom was a sound manual for adolescence, and of Thoreau I became—and for long remained—an ardent disciple. To a Scot of my upbringing there was something congenial in the simplicity, the mild austerity and the girded discipline of the New England tradition. I felt that it had been derived from the same sources as our own.

Then, while I was at Oxford, I read Colonel Henderson's *Stonewall Jackson* and became a student of the American Civil War. I cannot say what especially attracted me to that campaign : partly, no doubt, the romance of it, the chivalry and the supreme heroism ; partly its extraordinary technical interest, both military and political; but chiefly, I think, because I fell in love with the protagonists. I had found the kind of man that I could whole-heartedly admire. Since those days my study of the Civil War has continued, I have visited most of its battlefields, I have followed the trail of its great marches, I have read widely in its literature ; indeed, my memory has become so stored with its details that I have often found myself able to tell the descendants of its leaders facts about their forebears of which they had never heard.

My interest soon extended from the soldiers to the civilians, and I acquired a new admiration for Abraham Lincoln. Then it was enlarged to include the rest of America's history—the first settlements, the crossing of the Appalachians, the Revolution, the building of the West. Soon America, instead of being the unstoried land which it appears to most English travellers, became for me the home of a long tradition and studded with sacred places. I dare to say that no American was ever more thrilled by the prospect of seeing Westminster Abbey and the Tower, Winchester and Oxford, than I was by the thought of Valley Forge and the Shenandoah and the Wilderness.

I came first into the United States by way of Canada, a good way to enter, for English eyes are already habituated to the shagginess of the landscape and can begin to realise its beauties. My first reflection was that no one had told me how lovely the country was. I mean *lovely*, not vast and magnificent. I am not thinking of the Grand Canyon and the Yosemite and the Pacific coast, but of the ordinary rural landscape. There is much of the land which I have not seen, but in the east and the south and the north-west I have collected a gallery of delectable pictures. I think of the farms which are clearings in the Vermont and New Hampshire hills, the flowery summer meadows, the lush cow-pastures with an occasional stump to remind one that it is old forest land, the quiet lakes and the singing streams, the friendly accessible mountains; the little country towns of Massachusetts and Connecticut with their village greens and elms and two-century-old churches and court-houses; the secret glens of the Adirondacks and the mountain-meadows of the Blue Ridge; the long-settled champaign of Maryland and Pennsylvania; Virginian manors more old-England perhaps than anything we have at home; the exquisite links with the past like much of Boston and Charleston and all of Annapolis; the sun-burnt aromatic ranges of Montana and Wyoming; the Pacific shores where from snow mountains fishable streams descend through some of the noblest timber on earth to an enchanted sea.

It is a country most of which I feel to be in a special

sense "habitable," designed for homes, adapted to human uses, a friendly land. I like, too, the way in which the nomenclature reflects its history, its racial varieties, its odd cultural mixtures, the grandiose and the homespun rubbing shoulders. That is how places should be named. I have no objection to Mechanics- ville and Higginsville and Utica and Syracuse. They are a legitimate part of the record. And behind are the hoar-ancient memorials of the first dwellers, names like symphonies—Susquehanna, Ticonderoga, Shenandoah, Wyoming.

III

"Ah, my cabbages !" Henry Adams wrote, "when will you ever fathom the American? Never in your sweet lives." He proceeds in his genial way to make epigrams about his own New Englanders: "Impro- vised Europeans we were and—Lord God!—how thin !"—"Thank God I never was cheerful. I come from the happy stock of the Mathers, who, as you remember, passed sweet mornings reflecting on the goodness of God and the damnation of infants." Where an Adams scrupled to tread it is not for a stranger to rush in. But I would humbly suggest a correction to one reading which, I think, has the authority of Robert Louis Stevenson. America is, no doubt, a vast country, though it can be comfortably put inside Canada. But it is not in every part a country of wide horizons. Dwellers on the Blue Ridge, on the prairies, and on the Western ranges may indeed live habitually with huge spaces of land and sky, but most of America, and some of its most famous parts, is pockety, snug and cosy, a sanctuary rather than a watch- tower. To people so domiciled its vastness must be like the mathematicians' space-time, a concept apprehended by the mind and not a percept of the eye. "The largeness of Nature and of this nation were monstrous without a corresponding largeness and generosity of the spirit of the citizen." That is one of Walt Whitman's best-known sayings, but let us remember that the bigness of their country is for most Americans something to be learned and imaginatively understood, and not a natural deduction from cohabiting with physical immensities.

Racially they are the most variegated people on earth. The preponderance of the Anglo-Saxon stock disappeared in the Civil War. Look to-day at any list of names in a society or a profession and you will find that, except in the navy, the bulk are from the continent of Europe. In his day Matthew Arnold thought that the chief source of the strength of the American people lay in their homogeneity and the absence of sharply defined classes, which made revolution unthinkable. Other observers, like Henry James, have deplored the lack of such homogeneity and wished for their country the "close and complete consciousness of the Scots." (I pause to note that I cannot imagine a more nightmare conception. What would happen to the world if 130,000,000 Scotsmen, with their tight, compact nationalism, were living in the same country?) I am inclined to query the alleged absence of classes, for I have never been in any part of the United States where class distinctions did not hold. There is an easy friendliness of manner which conceals a strong class pride, and the basis of that pride is not always, or oftenest, plutocratic. Apart from the social snobbery of the big cities there seems to be everywhere an innocent love of grades and distinctions which is enough to make a communist weep. I have known places in the South where there was a magnificent aristocratic egalitarianism. Inside a charmed circle all were equal.

The village postmistress, having had the right kind of great-great-grandmother, was an honoured member of society, while the immigrant millionaire, who had built himself a palace, might as well have been dead. And this is true not only of the New England F.F.M.'s and the Virginian F.F.V.'s, the districts with long traditions, but of the raw little townships in the Middle West. They, too, have their "best" people who had ancestors, though the family tree may only have sprouted for two generations.

No country can show such a wide range of type and character, and I am so constituted that in nearly all I find something to interest and attract me. This is more than a temperamental bias, for I am very ready to give reasons for my liking. I am as much alive as anyone to the weak and ugly things in American life : areas, both urban and rural, where the human economy has gone rotten ; the melting-pot which does not always melt ; the eternal coloured problem ; a constitutional machine which I cannot think adequately represents the efficient good sense of the American people ; a brand of journalism which fatigues with its ruthless snappiness and uses a speech so disintegrated that it is incapable of expressing any serious thought or emotion ; the imbecile patter of high-pressure salesmanship ; an academic jargon, used chiefly by psychologists and sociologists, which is hideous and almost meaningless. Honest Americans do not deny these blemishes ; indeed they are apt to exaggerate them, for they are by far the sternest critics of their own country. For myself, I would make a double plea in extenuation. These are defects from which to-day no nation is exempt, for they are the fruits of a mechanical civilisation, which perhaps are more patent in America, since everything there is on a large scale. Again, you can set an achievement very much the same in kind against nearly every failure. If her historic apparatus of government is cranky she is capable of meeting the "instant need of things" with brilliant improvisations. Against economic plague-spots she can set great experiments in charity; against journalistic baby-talk a standard of popular writing in her best papers which is a model of idiom and perspicuity; against catch-penny trade methods many solidly founded, perfectly organised commercial enterprises; against the jargon of the half-educated professor much noble English prose in the great tradition. That is why it is so foolish to generalise about America. You no sooner construct a rule than it is shattered by the exceptions.

As I have said, I have a liking for almost every kind of American (except the kind who decry their country). I have even a sneaking fondness for Georgie Babbitt, which I fancy is shared by his creator. But there are two types which I value especially, and which I have never met elsewhere in quite the same form. One is the pioneer. No doubt the physical frontier of the United States is now closed, but the pioneer still lives, though the day of the covered wagon is over. I have met him in the New England hills, where he is grave, sardonic, deliberate in speech; in the South, where he has a ready smile and a soft caressing way of talking; in the ranges of the West, the cow-puncher with his gentle voice and his clear, friendly eyes which have not been dulled by reading print—the real thing, far removed from the vulgarities of film and fiction. At his best, I think, I have found him as a newcomer in Canada, where he is pushing north into districts like the Peace River, pioneering in the old sense. By what signs is he to be known? Principally by the fact that he is wholly secure, that he possesses his soul, that he is the true philosopher. He is one of the few aristocrats left in the world. He has a right sense of the values of life, because his cosmos embraces both nature and man. I think he is the most steadfast human being now alive.

The other type is at the opposite end of the social scale, the creature of a complex society who at the same time is not dominated by it, but, while reaping its benefits, stands a little aloof. In the older countries culture, as a rule, leaves some irregularity like an excrescence in a shapely tree-trunk, some irrational bias, some petulance or prejudice. You have to go to America, I think, for the wholly civilised man who has not lost his natural vigour or agreeable idiosyncrasies, but who sees life in its true proportions and he has a fine balance of mind and spirit. It is a character hard to define, but anyone with a wide American acquaintance will know what I mean. They are people in whom education has not stunted any natural growth or fostered any abnormality. They are Greek in their justness of outlook, but Northern in their gusto. Their eyes are shrewd and candid, but always friendly. As examples I would cite, among friends who are dead, the names of Robert Bacon, Walter Page, Newton Baker and Dwight Morrow.

But I am less concerned with special types than with the American people as a whole. Let me try to set down certain qualities, which seem to me to flourish more lustily in the United States than elsewhere. Again, let me repeat, I speak of America only as I know it ; an observer with a different experience might not agree with my conclusions.

First I would select what, for want of a better word, I should call homeliness. It is significant that the ordinary dwelling, though it be only a shack in the woods, is called not a house, but a home. This means that the family, the ultimate social unit, is given its proper status as the foundation of society. Even among the richer classes I seem to find a certain pleasing domesticity. English people of the same rank are separated by layers of servants from the basic work of the household, and know very little about it. In America the kitchen is not too far away from the drawing-room, and it is recognised, as Heraclitus said, that the gods may dwell there. But I am thinking chiefly of the ordinary folk, especially those of narrow means. It is often said that Americans are a nomad race, and it is true that they are very ready to shift their camp; but the camp, however bare, is always a home.[1] The cohesion of the family is close, even when its members are scattered. This is due partly to the tradition of the first settlers, a handful in an unknown land; partly to the history of the frontier, where the hearth-fire burnt brighter when all around was cold and darkness. The later immigrants from Europe, feeling at last secure, were able for the first time to establish a family base, and they cherished it zealously. This ardent domesticity has had its bad effects on American literature, inducing a sentimentality which makes a too crude frontal attack on the emotions, and which has produced as a reaction a not less sentimental "toughness." But as a social cement it is beyond price. There have been many to laugh at the dullness and pettiness of the "small town." From what I know of small-town life elsewhere, I suspect obtuseness in the satirists.

Second, I would choose the sincere and widespread

---

[1] In the Civil War homesickness was so serious a malady that the "printed forms for medical reports contained an entry for nostalgia precisely as for pneumonia." Douglas Freeman, *The South to Posterity*, 4.

J.B., 1937, EAGLE FACE, AS A CHIEF OF THE BLOOD INDIANS

friendliness of the people. Americans are interested in
the human race, and in each other. Deriving doubtless
from the old frontier days, there is a general helpfulness,
which I have not found in the same degree elsewhere.
A homesteader in Dakota will accompany a traveller
for miles to set him on the right road. The neighbours
will rally round one of their number in distress with
the loyalty of a Highland clan. This friendliness is not
a self-conscious duty so much as an instinct. A squatter
in a cabin will share his scanty provender and never
dream that he is doing anything unusual.

American hospitality, long as I have enjoyed it, still
leaves me breathless. The lavishness with which a busy
man will give up precious time to entertain a stranger
to whom he is in no way bound, remains for me one
of the wonders of the world. No doubt this friendliness,
since it is an established custom, has its fake side. The
endless brotherhoods and sodalities into which people
brigade themselves encourage a geniality which is more
a mannerism than an index of character, a tiresome,
noisy, back-slapping heartiness. But that is the exception, not the rule. Americans like company, but
though they are gregarious they do not lose themselves
in the crowd. Waves of mass-emotion may sweep
the country, but they are transient things and do
not submerge for long the stubborn rock of indi-
vidualism. That is to say, people can be led but they
will not be driven. Their love of human companionship is based not on self-distrust, but on a genuine liking
for their kind. With them the sense of a common
humanity is a warm and constant instinct, and not a
doctrine of the schools or a slogan of the hustings.

Lastly—and this may seem a paradox—I maintain
that they are fundamentally modest. Their interest
in others is a proof of it; the Aristotelian Magnificent

Man was interested in nobody but himself. As a nation they are said to be sensitive to criticism; that surely is modesty, for the truly arrogant care nothing for the opinion of other people. Above all they can laugh at themselves, which is not possible for the immodest. They are their own shrewdest and most ribald critics. It is charged against them that they are inclined to boast unduly about those achievements and about the greatness of their country, but a smug glorying in them is found only in the American of the caricaturist. They rejoice in showing their marvels to a visitor with the gusto of children exhibiting their toys to a stranger, an innocent desire, without any unfriendly gloating, to make others partakers in their satisfaction. If now and then they are guilty of bombast it is surely a venial fault. The excited American talks of his land very much, I suspect, as the Elizabethans in their cups talked of England. The foreigner who strayed into the Mermaid tavern must often have listened to heroics which upset his temper.

The native genius, in humour, and in many of the public and private relations of life, is for overstatement, a high-coloured, imaginative, paradoxical extravagance. The British gift is for understatement. Both are legitimate figures of speech. They serve the same purpose, for they call attention to a fact by startling the hearer, since manifestly they are not the plain truth. Personally I delight in both mannerisms and would not for the world have their possessors reject them. They serve the same purpose in another and a subtler sense, for they can be used to bring novel and terrible things within the pale of homely experience. I remember on the Western Front in 1918 that two divisions, British and American, aligned side by side, suffered a heavy shelling. An American sergeant described it in racy and imaginative speech which would have been appropriate to the Day of Judgment. A British sergeant merely observed that "Kaiser 'ad been a bit 'asty." Each had a twinkle in his eye; each in his national idiom was making frightfulness endurable by domesticating it.

IV

The United States is the richest, and, both actually and potentially, the most powerful State on the globe. She has much, I believe, to give to the world; indeed, to her hands is chiefly entrusted the shaping of the future. If democracy in the broadest and truest sense is to survive, it will be mainly because of her guardianship. For, with all her imperfections, she has a clearer view than any other people of the democratic fundamentals.

She starts from the right basis, for she combines a firm grip on the past with a quick sense of present needs and a bold outlook on the future. This she owes to her history; the combination of the British tradition with the necessities of a new land; the New England township and the Virginian manor *plus* the Frontier. Much of that tradition was relinquished as irrelevant to her needs, but much remains: a talent for law which is not incompatible with a lawless practice; respect for a certain type of excellence in character which has made her great men uncommonly like our own; a disposition to compromise, but only after a good deal of arguing; an intense dislike of dictation. To these instincts the long frontier struggles added courage in the face of novelties, adaptability, enterprise, a doggedness which was never lumpish, but alert and expectant.

That is the historic basis of America's democracy, and to-day she is the chief exponent of a creed which I believe on the whole to be the best in this imperfect world. She is the chief exponent for two reasons. The first is her size ; she exhibits its technique in large type, so that he who runs may read. More important, she exhibits it in its most intelligible form, so that its constituents are obvious. Democracy has become with many an unpleasing parrot-cry, and, as I have urged elsewhere in this book, it is well to be clear what it means. It is primarily a spiritual testament, from which certain political and economic orders naturally follow. But the essence is the testament ; the orders may change while the testament stands. This testament, this ideal of citizenship, she owes to no one teacher. There was a time when I fervently admired Alexander Hamilton and could not away with Jefferson ; the latter only began to interest me, I think, after I had seen the University of Virginia which he created. But I deprecate partisanship in those ultimate matters. The democratic testament derives from Hamilton as well as from Jefferson.

It has two main characteristics. The first is that the ordinary man believes in himself and in his ability, along with his fellows, to govern his country. It is when a people loses its self-confidence that it surrenders its soul to a dictator or an oligarchy. In Mr. Walter Lippmann's tremendous metaphor, it welcomes manacles to prevent its hands shaking. The second is the belief, which is fundamental also in Christianity, of the worth of every human soul—the worth, not the equality. This is partly an honest emotion, and partly a reasoned principle—that something may be made out of anybody, and that there is something likeable about everybody if you look for it—or, in canonical words, that ultimately there is nothing common or unclean.

The democratic testament is one lesson that America

THE PRESIDENT OF THE UNITED STATES AND THE
GOVERNOR-GENERAL OF CANADA—QUEBEC, 1936

has to teach the world. A second is a new reading of nationalism. Some day and somehow the people must discover a way to brigade themselves for peace. Now there are on the globe only two proven large-scale organisations of social units, the United States and the British Empire. The latter is not for export, and could not be duplicated; its strength depends upon a thousand-year-old monarchy and a store of unformulated traditions. But the United States was the conscious work of men's hands, and a task which has once been performed can be performed again. She is the supreme example of a federation in being, a federation which recognises the rights and individuality of the parts, but accepts the overriding interests of the whole. To achieve this compromise she fought a desperate war. If the world is ever to have prosperity and peace, there must be some kind of federation—I will not say of democracies, but of States which accept the reign of Law. In such a task she seems to me to be the pre-destined leader. Vigorous as her patriotism is, she has escaped the jealous, barricadoed nationalism of the Old World. Disraeli, so often a prophet in spite of himself, in 1863, at a critical moment of the Civil War, spoke memorable words:

"There is a grave misapprehension, both in the ranks of Her Majesty's Government and of Her Majesty's Opposition, as to what constitutes the true meaning of the American democracy. The American democracy is not made up of the scum of the great industrial cities of the United States, nor of an exhausted middle class that speculates in stocks and calls that progress. The American democracy is made up of something far more stable, that may ultimately decide the fate of the two Americas and of Europe."

S

For forty years I have regarded America not only with a student's interest in a fascinating problem, but with the affection of one to whom she has become almost a second motherland. Among her citizens I count many of my closest friends; I have known all her Presidents, save one, since Theodore Roosevelt, and all her ambassadors to the Court of St. James's since John Hay; for four and a half years I have been her neighbour in Canada. But I am not blind to the grave problems which confront her. Democracy, after all, is a negative thing. It provides a fair field for the Good Life, but it is not in itself the Good Life. In these days when lovers of freedom may have to fight for their cause, the hope is that the ideal of the Good Life, in which alone freedom has any meaning, will acquire a stronger potency. It is the task of civilisation to raise every citizen above want, but in so doing to permit a free development and avoid the slavery of the beehive and the ant-heap. A humane economic policy must not be allowed to diminish the stature of man's spirit. It is because I believe that in the American people the two impulses are of equal strength that I see her in the vanguard of that slow upward trend, undulant or spiral, which to-day is our modest definition of progress. Her major prophet is still Whitman. "Everything comes out of the dirt—everything; everything comes out of the people, everyday people, the people as you find them and leave them; people, people, just people!"

It is only out of the dirt that things grow.

CHAPTER XII

THE OTHER SIDE OF THE HILL

I

SIR WALTER SCOTT had a pleasant phrase for middle life; he called it reaching the other side of the hill. It is a stage which no doubt has its drawbacks. The wind is not so good, the limbs are not so tireless as in the ascent; the stride is shortened, and since we are descending we must be careful in placing the feet. But on the upward road the view was blocked by the slopes and there was no far prospect to be had except by looking backwards. Now the course is mercifully adapted to failing legs, we can rest and reflect since the summit has been passed, and there is a wide country before us, though the horizon is mist and shadow.

These chapters have been written several thousand miles from England, in a country of new problems and hopes, where the mind has, none the less, been clouded by the secular anxieties of Europe. Half-detached and half-embroiled, Canada's position seems to me much like my own. I have in my lifetime passed from an era of peace through various unsettled stages into a world which, in Sir Thomas More's phrase, is "ruffled and fallen into a wildness," but I retain enough of the disengagement of the earlier world to refuse to surrender my right to cheerfulness. I was brought up in times when one was not ashamed to be happy, and I have never learned the art of discontent. I preserve my devotion to things "afar from the sphere of our sorrow." It seems to me that those who loudly proclaim their disenchantment with life have never been really enchanted by it. Their complaints about the low levels they dwell in ring hollow, for they have not known the uplands.

The memories of a happy past are in themselves a solid possession :

> "Is it so small a thing
> To have enjoy'd the sun,
> To have lived light in the spring ?"

The possession is the more valuable if such memories are readily evoked, so that past and present dwell in friendly proximity. This gift has always been mine. I cannot recover the vigour of youth for my limbs, but through memory I can recapture something of its ardour for my mind. The smell of wood-smoke and heather, for instance, or a whiff of salt will recall shining morning-lands of the spirit.

But this world of recollection demands gentle handling. It is brittle, like all spiritual things. If too coarsely approached the bloom will be rubbed off it like the down on a butterfly's wing. It will endure only in clear and bracing weather. If used as an opiate for the mind it becomes a vulgar drug of commerce. Moreover, "we receive but what we give." It demands a certain tolerant, charitable, enjoying habit of thought, quick to observe and to distil the soul of goodness. The rhetor Dio of Prusa said of Homer that he "praised almost everything—animals and plants, water and earth, weapons and horses. He passed over nothing without somehow honouring and glorifying it. Even the one man whom he abused, Thersites, he called 'a clear-voiced speaker.'"

I have small patience with the antiquarian habit

which magnifies the past and belittles the present. It is a vicious business to look backward unless the feet are set steadfastly on a forward road. Change is inevitable, at once a penalty and a privilege. The greatest of the Ionian philosophers wrote: "It is necessary that things should pass away into that from which they are born. For things must pay one another the penalty of compensation for their injustice according to the ordinances of time." An open and flexible mind, which recognises the need of transformation and faithfully sets itself to apprehend new conditions, is a prerequisite of man's usefulness. But those who take my point of view will try to bring all change into harmony with the fundamentals drawn from the past. If the past to a man is nothing but a dead hand, then in common honesty he must be an advocate of revolution. But if it is regarded as the matrix of present and future, whose potency takes many forms but is not diminished, then he will cherish it scrupulously and labour to read its lessons, and shun the heady short-cuts which end only in blank walls. He will realise that in the cycle to which we belong we can see only a fraction of the curve, and that properly to appraise the curve and therefore to look ahead, we may have to look back a few centuries to its beginning.

Regard for the past has been therefore both an article of my creed and a principal source of my pleasure in life. But I realise that, while the philosophical doctrine is inexpugnable, connoisseurship in memories is a more debatable business. They are brittle, as I have said, and clumsy hands can destroy them. They may conduct to a maudlin sentimentality. They are also not without a disruptive power, for storms can be brewed by delicious things like salt air and sunshine. If I have escaped these perils (as I trust I have) it is because my life has been so much more one of action than of contemplation. If I philosophised it had to be done like the Athenians of Pericles ἄνευ μαλακίας. I am very conscious of the pathos of lost things. It is only human to regret the passing of even the shadow of what once was great; we shall always hear the voice along the Aegean capes announcing the death of Pan, and the one eye-ancient, who was Odin, telling King Olaf Tryggvason tales of a vanished world. But I suppose I have a prosaic fibre in me, and though I sigh I do not sigh too deeply or too long. Devotion to the past should be like a salad with vinegar; it should have just enough melancholy in it to keep it from cloying.

My lifetime has included more drastic changes in manners and customs and modes of thought than can be shown, I think, by any similar period in history. The mechanical apparatus of living has been transformed. At twenty I thought it an adventure to take a bicycle over certain Highland hill-roads; at sixty I was flying across the pack-ice in the Arctic! Creeds in politics, in economics, in many branches of science have gone into the melting-pot, and it is not yet clear what is to succeed them. The old classes have been levelled down, and new class distinctions have appeared in many lands based on something much crueller and coarser than the former inequalities.

It is an ugly and comfortless world, but it is a world not without hope—a better world in spite of its confusion than the one that in despondent moods I have foreseen. The things which we value may be overlaid and obscured, but I do not think they will be destroyed at the root. My worst nightmare has removed itself. Let me set down the points of that fearsome wildfowl.

II

All of us in the last War had moments when we felt the stable universe dissolving about us. We were like pilgrims who, journeying on a road to an assured and desirable goal, suddenly found themselves on the edge of a precipice with nothing beyond but a great void. The common way of describing such moods was to say that our civilisation had become insecure and was in danger of perishing.

What did we mean by civilisation? The little comforts which made life easy and pleasant and gave us leisure; an ordered ritual which enabled us to plan for the future? But our dread was based upon something deeper than the loss of such amenities. By civilisation we meant especially the rule of law which gave us freedom to possess our souls. What we feared was a welter of anarchy which would reduce life to its bare rudiments. We defined civilisation as something more than the cushioned life made possible by science. It was not a mechanical apparatus but a spirit. The Greeks of the fifth century before Christ had an existence so simple that to our modern appetites it seems almost brutish. They lived chiefly on fruits and vegetables, their clothes were plain, their amusements were few, their transport was rudimentary, but no one can deny their high civilisation. So most of us came to define civilisation as the free development of the personality. That involved physical conditions of life lifted above the primitive man's struggle for bread. It involved an ordered society and the rule of law. But, since these things are negative only, it involved also a soul to develop, a mind which could rejoice in the things of the mind, an impulse towards spiritual perfection.

Clearly such an inner life would not be possible if our whole complex material apparatus were wrecked and we returned to primitive conditions. It demanded an existence raised above the level of urgent bodily wants. What mind prehistoric man possessed must have been wholly engrossed in getting food for himself and his family, in sheltering from the weather, and in saving his skin from the clutches of a sabre-toothed tiger or the malevolence of a neighbour with a club. We can all remember expeditions in the wilds when we were reduced to the extremes of bodily fatigue and could think of nothing except food and rest. For most of us the urgency of physical needs puts an effective damper on any mental activity. Primeval man cannot have had much of an intellectual life. Beyond doubt a return to barbarism, to primitive physical conditions, would play havoc with civilisation.

I was never really afraid that this would happen. The modern appurtenances of life seemed to be too firmly established, and the face of the world had been too fully remodelled to meet human needs. I found it impossible to conceive that those inventions on which our community rests could suddenly vanish and reduce us to the days of flint and steel and wooden spades and mud cabins. But imaginative novelists bemused themselves with this conception, and pictured a war which laid the whole world waste and left the few survivors in the condition of the cave man. They called it a return to the Dark Ages, by which they meant that epoch in our history which lasted from the fifth century, when the Roman Empire was crumbling, to the eleventh, when the Middle Ages began to develop their own culture.

What were those Dark Ages, those six centuries during which a curtain seemed to descend upon

Europe? The invasion of the wild Germanic and Slavonic peoples destroyed the civic life of the western world, the writ of Rome ceased to run, and her central authority crumbled. She had devised a host of inventions which made life comfortable and intercourse between nations easy; clothes and fine furniture and pictures and books and statuary; a noble architecture, and a plumbing system unsurpassed until modern America; methods of transport unmatched until a century or so ago; a legal fabric which is still largely our code; a civil service which at its best was probably as efficient as anything the world has known. All this went, and in most parts of Europe the forests overpowered the vineyards and corn-lands, the famous cities lost half their people, and the public buildings fell into ruins. Instead of the imperial law and the imperial bureaucracy new governments were formed by shaggy warriors, who either held to their own customs or gave the Roman code a tribal twist. There was little security for life and property, since the Pax Romana was no more. A man's hand had once again to keep his head. The world shrank into little pockets of humanity which knew nothing about their neighbours. Food and drink and housing were reduced to their beggarly elements, and clothes to a barbaric bareness or a barbaric gaudiness. Civilisation, remember, is a complex thing, or rather a thing which attains simplicity through complexity. The life of the Dark Ages was rudimentary, and, being rudimentary, ended in being unbelievably complex.

A curtain of darkness seemed to have settled upon a world which had once been so shining and varied. But there were many points of light in that darkness. There was first of all the Christian Church which, behind all its political caprices and theological pedantries, did preserve a continuous tradition of civilisation and the spiritual life. Throughout those centuries it produced saints and missionaries whose names we still honour. It produced poets whose hymns we still sing, and in many a monastery tucked away in the forests there were scholars who studied more than the Church Fathers. Much of the literature of Greece and Rome survived in obscure places. Aristotle, or a part of him, was not forgotten, and men could get to Plato through St. Augustine. Moreover, some subtle impact of the old classical tradition was inciting the new masters of the world to a kind of intellectual activity. The invaders who had wrecked the Roman Empire were beginning to devise a law, a poetry, a political philosophy of their own.

Therefore I think that the right way to look at the Dark Ages is as a time of darkness indeed, but with lights cherished in many places which in the end were to combine into a new dawn. The great Mediterranean tradition was obscured but not destroyed; or, to change the metaphor, the world was a field lying fallow, the soil was rich, the seed had been preserved, and one day there was to be a wide sowing and a bountiful harvest.

So I did not dread a return of the Dark Ages. For one thing I did not believe that that particular kind of retrogression was possible; for another I did not think that it would be such a terrible thing after all. My nightmare, when I was afflicted by nightmares, was of something very different. My fear was not barbarism, which is civilisation submerged or not yet born, but de-civilisation, which is civilisation gone rotten.

A certain type of flimsy romantic has been too ready with abuse of a mechanical age, just as a certain type of imaginative writer with a smattering of science has been too gross in his adulation. The machine, when

mastered and directed by the human spirit, may lead
to a noble enlargement of life. Enterprises which make
roads across pathless mountains, collect the waters over
a hundred thousand miles to set the desert blossoming,
build harbours on harbourless coasts, tame the elements
to man's uses—these are the equivalent to-day of the
great explorations and adventures of the past. So, too,
the patient work of research laboratories, where to the
student a new and startling truth may leap at any
moment from the void. Those who achieve such
things are as much imaginative creators as any poet, as
much conquerors as any king. If a man so dominates
a machine that it becomes part of him he may thereby
pass out of a narrow world to an ampler ether. The
true airman is one of the freest of God's creatures, for he
has used a machine to carry him beyond the pale of the
Machine. He is a creator and not a mechanic, a master
and not a slave.

But suppose that science has gained all its major
victories, and that there remain only little polishings and
adjustments. It has wrested from nature a full provision
for human life, so that there is no longer need for long
spells of monotonous toil and a bitter struggle for bread.
Victory having been won, the impulse to construct has
gone. The world has become a huge, dapper, smooth-
running mechanism. Would that be the perfecting of
civilisation ? Would it not rather mean de-civilisation,
a loss of the supreme values of life ?

In my nightmare I could picture such a world. I
assumed—no doubt an impossible assumption—that
mankind was as amply provided for as the inmates of
a well-managed orphanage. New inventions and a
perfecting of transport had caused the whole earth to
huddle together. There was no corner of the globe
left unexplored and unexploited, no geographical

mysteries to fire the imagination. Broad highways crowded with automobiles threaded the remotest lands, and overhead great air-liners carried week-end tourists to the wilds of Africa and Asia. Everywhere there were guest-houses and luxury hotels and wayside camps and filling-stations. What once were the savage tribes of Equatoria and Polynesia were now in reserves as an attraction to trippers, who bought from them curios and holiday mementoes. The globe, too, was full of pleasure-cities where people could escape the rigour of their own climate and enjoy perpetual holiday.

In such a world everyone would have leisure. But everyone would be restless, for there would be no spiritual discipline in life. Some kind of mechanical philosophy of politics would have triumphed, and everybody would have his neat little part in the state machine. Everybody would be comfortable, but since there could be no great demand for intellectual exertion everybody would be also slightly idiotic. Their shallow minds would be easily bored, and therefore unstable. Their life would be largely a quest for amusement. The raffish existence led to-day by certain groups would have become the normal existence of large sections of society.

Some kind of intellectual life no doubt would remain, though the old political disputes would have cancelled each other out, and the world would not have the stimulus of a contest of political ideals, which is, after all, a spiritual thing. Scientists and philosophers would still spin theories about the universe. Art would be in the hands of coteries, and literature dominated by *petites chapelles*. There would be religion, too, of a kind, in glossy upholstered churches with elaborate music. It would be a feverish, bustling world, self-satisfied and yet malcontent, and under the mask of a riotous life there would be death at the heart. The soil of human nature, which in the Dark Ages lay fallow, would now be worked out. Men would go everywhere and live nowhere; know everything and understand nothing. In the perpetual hurry of life there would be no chance of quiet for the soul. In the tumult of a jazz existence what hope would there be for the still small voices of the prophets and philosophers and poets? A world which claimed to be a triumph of the human personality would in truth have killed that personality. In such a bagman's paradise, where life would be rationalised and aided with every material comfort, there would be little satisfaction for the immortal part of man. It would be a new Vanity Fair with Mr. Talkative as the chief figure on the town council. The essence of civilisation lies in man's defiance of an impersonal universe. It makes no difference that a mechanised universe may be his own creation if he allows his handiwork to enslave him. Not for the first time in history have the idols that humanity has shaped for its own ends become its master.

It is a nightmare which may well terrify us, and sometimes I have thought that it was not altogether a nightmare, for it was the logical culmination of certain tendencies which were strong amongst us. It was not the return of the Dark Ages that I feared, but the coming of a too garish age, when life would be lived in the glare of neon lamps and the spirit would have no solitude.

But something has happened. A civilisation bemused by an opulent materialism has been met by a rude challenge. The free peoples have been challenged by the serfs. The gutters have exuded a poison which bids fair to infect the world. The beggar-on-horseback rides more roughshod over the helpless than the cavalier. A combination of multitudes who have lost their nerve and a junta of arrogant demagogues has shattered the comity of nations. The European tradition has been confronted with an Asiatic revolt, with its historic accompaniment of janissaries and assassins. There is in it all, too, an ugly pathological savour, as if a mature society were being assailed by diseased and vicious children.

For centuries we have enjoyed certain blessings; a stable law, before which the poor man and the rich man were equal; freedom within that law to believe what we pleased, to write what we pleased, to say what we pleased; a system of government which gave the ultimate power to the ordinary man. We have lived by toleration, rational compromise and freely expressed opinion, and we have lived very well. But we had come to take these blessings for granted, like the air we breathed. They had lost all glamour for us since they had become too familiar. Indeed, it was a mark of the intellectual to be rather critical and contemptuous of them. Paradoxical young men acquired a cheap reputation by sneering at the liberal spirit in politics, and questioning the value of free discussion, toleration and compromise.

To-day we have seen those principles challenged in the fundamentals, not by a few arm-chair theorists, but by great Powers supported by great armies. We have suddenly discovered that what we took for the enduring presuppositions of our life are in danger of being destroyed. To-day we value freedom, I think, as we have not valued it before. Just as a man never appreciates his home so much as when he is compelled to leave it, so now we realise our inestimable blessings when they are threatened. We have been shaken out of our smugness and warned of a great peril, and in that warning lies our salvation. The dictators have done us a marvellous service in reminding us of the true values of life.

III

These chapters are meant as a record of how the surface of life has appeared to one pilgrim at different stages. They do not contain a confession of faith, in religion, philosophy, or the business of government. I admit an undercurrent of optimism, which, it has been said, is in good times a luxury but in bad times a necessity. With me such cheerfulness, as I prefer to call it, is not a creed to adopt or reject, but a habit of mind, a temperamental bias, a pre-condition of perception and thought. And it in turn derives from the kind of youth I had. For youth to continue, so that it illumines middle life and old age and pleasantly binds the years together, it must have been spacious, with wide horizons and a tonic air; happy, too, in spite of all the heart-breaks of adolescence. For what it can give to the later phases of life are zest and freedom, and such gifts are impossible if it was itself bound and frustrate.

In my lifetime I seem to note a change which is a graver thing than our other discontents, which, indeed, is in a large measure the cause of them. The outlook of youth has been narrowed, doors have been sealed, channels have silted up, there is less choice of routes at the cross-roads.

This affects principally the middle class. Let me define that odious word. At one end of the social scale is the plutocracy, whose sons will be sufficiently well dowered to indulge their fancy. If they enter a profession they have the security of means behind them. At the other end are the wage-earning classes, who in their health and wealth are largely the care of the State. Between come the "middling folk" in many gradations; their characteristics are that they have to earn their living, since they have no accumulated fortunes, that the State has little responsibility for them, that they have a reasonable average of culture and certain strong traditions in customs, manners and conduct. The class contains most of the knowledge and skill in the nation. Also, since our nominal aristocracy has been so copiously diluted, it contains most of the older stocks, the people with the longest proven descent.

For this great class the world has become more rigid than I remember it. A young man seems to me to have fewer avenues open to him, and fewer chances in these avenues. I leave out of account the pre-eminence of mind or character which we call genius, for that will always hew out a course. I am speaking of youth of reasonable capacity and moderate ambitions, which seeks a calling with hope and daylight in it, which is capable of a great effort of patience but must have a glimpse of some attainable goal.

Wherever I look I seem to detect a deepening and narrowing of ruts. Technological progress, to be sure, has increased their number, but too few emerge into open country. The older universities have now returned to the mediaeval practice, and by way of new scholarships are far more accessible to those of scanty means. But what lies at the end of a university course? A high standard of attainment will no doubt take one into the upper walks of the teaching profession, and a moderate standard perhaps into the civil service, but besides that—what? Too often the only choice is some minor scholastic or clerical job in which a man is apt to stick fast for the rest of his days. Business is now accepted as a calling for those who have received a liberal education. But does business to-day give an active man without capital the chances it offered a couple of generations ago? Has it not become so desperately specialised that an ambitious entrant may all his life be condemned to be a minor cog in a huge machine? At the bottom of the class the position is worse. The clerk who begins on a pittance may have nothing to look forward to except small yearly increases till he reaches in middle age an income which will just support a household. He has, too, a haunting sense of economic insecurity, for the State takes no interest in his troubles.

The difficulty is not that the path from the log cabin to the White House is not made easy; that will always need vigorous axework and a stout heart. It is that society has become so rigid that average youth is deprived of those modest hopes which are its peculiar grace and the source of its value. And this narrowing of opportunity has come about when its mental outlook has been infinitely broadened. A dozen new means of enlightenment have opened up the world to it and vastly stimulated its interests. The clerk of fifty years ago had no ambition beyond a little house in the suburbs, and was content if he saw himself on the way to its attainment; the same man to-day, educated, open-eyed, imaginative, chafes bitterly at his confinement in a groove which may be far narrower than that of his predecessors.

The result in the end must be revolution, the most dangerous kind, a revolution of the middle classes. It is on their discontent that the dictators to-day have based their power. The working classes do not come into the picture; partly because, being nearer the margin of subsistence, they are more likely to be content with

T

what meets their immediate needs and gives them present security; partly because, having less education, they do not suffer from the unsatisfied cravings of the educated. The dictators have won their power largely by an appeal, not to a suffering proletariat but to the forgotten "little man" of the middle classes whom reformers in the past have accountably neglected. They have given him a sense of dignity and importance, and ópened vistas for him. They have brought him into the inner fold of the State when hitherto he has been a disconsidered outsider. Black and execrable as is most of their work, they have this to their credit; they have restored pride and confidence to large sections of a class which had begun to despair. There lies their strength— and also their doom, when it is realised that the horizon they have revealed to youth is no more than a painted back-cloth.

I have had much to do with young men on several continents and in many countries, and I regard this shrinking of opportunity as one of the gravest facts of our age. It will remain an urgent matter long after the guns are silent. Somehow or other we must make our social and economic world more fluid. We must widen the approaches so that honest ambition and honourable discontent may have elbow-room. The world must remain an oyster for youth to open. If not, youth will cease to be young, and that will be the end of everything.

There is another side to the problem. With all our reservoir of skill and knowledge there is a lamentable dearth to-day of the higher talent. Or rather, while this talent must exist, it is uncommonly difficult to lay one's hand on it. Anyone who has had experience in such matters knows how hard it often is to find men for the higher posts in finance, industry, journalism and academic and political life. Admittedly the talent is somewhere, if we have any confidence in our fellow-men, but how to find it? The Miltons may remain for ever mute and inglorious, the Hampdens only village worthies. If our society were more open-meshed and elastic it should be possible for a shining gift to reveal itself before it is too late. Were I a multi-millionaire I would devote my fortune to making an inquisition for the discovery of genius, so that those fitted to be our leaders should get their feet out of the mire in time to help the world. For in the last resort it is not the machine that matters, but the man.

IV

The dominant thought of youth is the bigness of the world, of age its smallness. As we grow older we escape from the tyranny of matter and recognise that the true centre of gravity is in the mind. Also we lose that sense of relativity, which is so useful in normal life, provided it does not sour into cynicism, and come more and more to acclaim absolute things—goodness, truth, beauty. From a wise American scholar I take this sentence: "The tragedy of man is that he has de-veloped an intelligence eager to uncover mysteries, but not strong enough to penetrate them. With minds but slightly evolved beyond those of our animal relations, we are tortured with precocious desires, and pose questions which we are sometimes capable of asking but rarely are able to answer." With the recognition of our limitations comes a glimpse of the majesty of the "Power not ourselves." Religion is born when we accept the ultimate frustration of mere human effort, and at the same time realise the strength which comes from union with superhuman reality.

To-day the quality of our religion is being put to the test. The conflict is not only between the graces of civilisation and the rawness of barbarism. More is being challenged than the system of ethics which we believe to be the basis of our laws and liberties. I am of Blake's view: "Man must and will have some religion; if he has not the religion of Jesus he will have the religion of Satan, and will erect a synagogue of Satan." There have been high civilisations in the past which have not been Christian, but in the world as we know it I believe that civilisation must have a Christian basis, and must ultimately rest on the Christian Church. To-day the Faith is being attacked, and the attack is succeeding. Thirty years ago Europe was nominally a Christian continent. It is no longer so. In Europe, as in the era before Constantine, Christianity is in a minority. What Gladstone wrote seventy years ago, in a moment of depression, has become a shattering truth: "I am convinced that the welfare of mankind does not now depend on the State and the world of politics; the real battle is being fought in the world of thought, where a deadly attack is made with great tenacity of purpose and over a wide field upon the greatest treasure of mankind, the belief in God and the Gospel of Christ."

The Christian in name has in recent years been growing cold in his devotion. Our achievement in perfecting life's material apparatus has produced a mood of self-confidence and pride. Our peril has been indifference, and that is a grave peril, for rust will crumble a metal when hammer blows will only harden it. I believe— and this is my crowning optimism—that the challenge with which we are now faced may restore to us that manly humility which alone gives power. It may bring us back to God. In that case our victory is assured.   The Faith is an anvil which has worn out many hammers.

We are condemned to fumble in these times, for the mist is too thick to see far down the road.   But in all our uncertainty we can have Cromwell's hope.   "To be a Seeker is to be of the best sect next to a Finder, and such an one shall every faithful, humble Seeker be at the end."   So, as a tail-piece to this book, I would transcribe a sentence of Henry Adams: "After all, man knows mighty little, and may some day learn enough of his own ignorance to fall down and pray." Dogmatism gives place to questioning, and questioning in the end to prayer.

THE END

This valediction ends *Memory Hold-the-Door* as its author left it ready for publication.   The next work he planned was to be a book about fishing.   Only the two chapters that follow were completed and were found among his papers with the pencilled title:

Pilgrim's Rest

PILGRIM'S REST

VALLEYS OF SPRINGS OF RIVERS

"Praised art Thou, my Lord, of Sister Water,
for manifold is her use, and humble is she, and
precious and pure."

ST. FRANCIS.

CHAPTER I

THE SPRINGS

I

IF fishing, as I maintain, be not only a craft but a way of life, then a fisherman must begin young. A small boy desires some tangible reward for his adventures. He has the British soldier's innocent passion for loot. So in the spring he will collect eggs, and in the autumn bring back mushrooms, and nuts and berries, and if he live in a land of streams he will begin early to try and catch fish. When about the age of nine I first plied a rod I was confined by my lack of skill to a narrow arena. The sophisticated trout of Tweed and the lower reaches of the burns were beyond me, and my hope lay in the slender runlets far up in the heather.

Those runlets were a long way off, so I only reached them in the brisk spring weather, when even short legs could manage a half-score of miles. Now this is the way of the upper Tweedside hills. Their tops, which are commonly in the neighbourhood of 2500 feet, are not peaks but a tableland. The plateau may be pitted with peat haggs or be a field of coarse bent, but always in its hollows there are stretches of mountain gravel, the milk-white debris of quartz. In those hollows there is also stagnant water, sometimes a true bog hole, sometimes only a moisture in the shingle. This water, drawn from the rains and the snows, sinks into the soil and feeds the eternal springs, ice-cold and diamond bright, which a few hundred feet below the summit begin to well out of the hillsides.

The well-heads take different forms. Sometimes there is a little ravine where patches of old snowdrifts linger until early summer, and there the fountain is commonly a pool in the rocks. More often it is the centre of a patch of bright green moss on the open hill, a tiny cup of water haunted by water beetles, whence a trickle seeps downward through sphagnum and rush, sundew and butterwort and grass of Parnassus. Presently both types have found their destined channel and a miniature glen is the consequence, where at first the water spouts at a steep angle and the pools are precarious things on the lip of cascades. But soon the ground flattens and the runlet has become a burn, less dependent on the law of gravity, and picking its course among bent and blaeberries and heather, the habitation of small dark trout, a fishable water.

To reach this kind of stream as a child I had usually to cross a watershed, and therefore the bald summits appear in all my recollections. There grew cloud-berries, which are not found below the 2000-feet line, bright red at first, but ripening to amber, the material of the best jam in the world. There also one met the graceful little blue hawk, the merlin. I frequented the place chiefly in April, when the skies were often grey and the air sharp, but when a mild west wind blew and the world leaped suddenly into spring. Down in the little glens there was a turmoil of nesting birds—ring ouzels and water ouzels, an infinity of meadow pipits, grouse and black game, and above all the curlew. The spring cry of the last was the true voice of the wilderness—*pooeeli, pooeeli—kirlew—wha-up*. It was eerie, fantastic, untamable, but it had none of the savagery of the buzzard's mew or the raven's croak. It was the voice of a habitable wilderness not wholly inimical to man.

At the age of nine my only lure was the worm. I could not cast a fly properly, and on the lower waters I made myself too conspicuous. But in those little hill runlets rush and heather provided a natural cover, and the fish were innocent things. I would drop my worm in a pool and let it float down the hidden stream until there came a check and a small trout was swung high over my head. If it came off the hook it was as often as not lost in the thick herbage. Now and then it was too heavy for such treatment—half a pound in weight perhaps—in which case it was dragged clumsily ashore. This was the beggarly element of fishing, but both exciting and satisfying. I have had as many as four dozen in a day, to be fried for breakfast in oatmeal and eaten bones and all. To call such takings a "basket" would be a misnomer, for I did not possess a creel, but carried my catch in my pockets or threaded through the gills on rushes.

In April and May I never felt lonely, for the birds were cheerful companions. But when the summer quiet fell on them I used to have fits of panic in the silence and solitude. The worst places for this were the glens where there was no heather, but only moss and bent and turf, for heather, especially when charred in patches by moorburn, was to me a half-human thing. Greenness, utter, absolute greenness, has all my life seemed to me uncanny, and the places which in my memory are infested with a certain awe are the green places. Take the Devil's Beef Tub, the green pit in the hills on the road from Tweed to the head of Annan. Rudyard Kipling once told me that, far as he had wandered, and much as he had seen, this uncanny hollow seemed more than any other spot to be consecrated to the old gods. The haunted chasm in *Kubla Khan* was in a Green hill. There was a song popular on the Border called *The wild glen sae green.* It was in such green "hopes," as we called them, that sometimes I came to the edge of fear. If there were sheep in sight I was never afraid. But if there were no sheep about, and a shoulder of hill shut out the world, I became conscious that I was alone in an *enclosed* place without the company of bird or beast. Then the terror of solitude laid hold of me, and I fled incontinent until I reached a herd's cottage.

It was in one of those childish expeditions that I first realised the wonders of dawn. Someone had told me that the trout in summer took best in the dark before sunrise, and one day I crept out of bed, dressed in the mirk, and slipped from the house when everyone was asleep. Having no watch I had miscalculated the time, and had started far too soon, for I seemed to be walking for hours before, from the watershed ridge, I saw the first flush in the east. The journey was achieved with a quaking heart, for I had heard tales of midnight gatherings of weasels which to anyone who fell in with them meant death. However, there were no weasels, and when I sat on a rock and watched the east turn from grey to rose-pink and then to banded crimson, and the great golden orb spring from beyond the furthest hills, I felt like Cortez staring at the Pacific. Fishing was impossible for me that morning, for I had had all the adventure I wanted for the day. The glory of the spectacle and a gnawing hunger sent me home forthwith, a small being both entranced and awed.

Since then I have seen the sun rise in many places—West Highland dawns over the wintry Glasgow streets as I plodded to college; moorland dawns when I awoke chilled and famished beside some Galloway loch; the superb pageants which greet the mountaineer when he breakfasts on some high saddle of rock or snow; dawns in the African bush or on the high veld, when the dew lay heavy and the morning scents were like spices; eerie dawns in Flanders and Picardy when the sun sprang out of enemy country to the sound of enemy guns; dawns over ocean and prairie and desert. One of the misfortunes of advancing age is that you get out of touch with the sunrise. You take it for granted, and it is over and done with before you settle yourself for the daily routine. That is one reason, I think, why, as we grow older, the days seem shorter. We miss the high moments of their beginning.

II

Below the clefts of their source and the round cups of the "hopes" begin the glens which the burns have sculptured out of the *massif* of the hills. Now the streams become important, for they are the key of the landscape.

From my earliest youth I have been what the Greeks called a "nympholept," one who was under the spell of running waters. It was in terms of them that I read the countryside. My topography was a scheme of glens and valleys and watersheds. I would walk miles to see the debouchment of some burn with whose head-waters I was familiar, or track to its source some affluent whose lowland career I had followed. There was no tributary of the upper Tweed that I could not name, and, when I came to possess a bicycle, the same was true of the adjacent waters of Clyde and Annan, Ettrick and Yarrow. At any time in my childhood I could have drawn a map of my neighbourhood, which, so far as the streams went, would have been scrupulously exact.

Ever since then I have translated, like Michael Drayton in *Polyolbion*, every land with which I was connected into the speech of its rivers. A hill country was simple enough, but the flat English lowlands were at first a little puzzling, and I have never found it easy in places where the valleys were ill-defined. But even there I was true to my fad. South Africa to me was not the Cape peninsula and the Karroo and the high veld and the bushveld, but the valleys of the Orange, the Vaal, the Caledon, the Tugela, the Limpopo and the Zambesi, and I could never rest there till I knew what exiguous streams drained what arid places. Even Switzerland was not pictured as mountain ranges, but as river valleys shadowed by clusters of peaks. The eastern seaboard of America is for me not a group of states and cities, but the courses of the Kennebec, the Connecticut, the Hudson, the Delaware, the Susquehanna, the Potomac and the James. Canada I found most satisfying, with the superb trough of the St. Lawrence, the streams that radiate into Hudson's Bay from east, south and west, the gigantic Mackenzie seaming the North with its tributaries, and the fierce rivers that cut their way through the Rockies and the Coast range to the western sea.

The streams are now past their infancy and in their first youth. In my experience I have found them of two types, the "highland" and the "lowland." In the first the waters fall steeply in pools, which are often long dark slits in little rock canyons. Dwarf birch and alder and mountain ash stud the rock walls, and now and then draw together into copses. Such streams are a genus by themselves and not miniature rivers, as are the second type, the more languid "lowland" waters. In the latter the fall is slight, and many yards of almost motionless current may intervene between the pools. Such pools are commonly long and shallow, with a stream at the head and tail, and their shores are often shelves of gravel.

They imitate exactly, on a small scale, the habits of the larger rivers. The first kind is to be found in any mountain land, like the Highlands, or Galloway, or Wales, and now and then in the gentler Tweedside hills, wherever these are rough and heathery. The second is the more familiar, and I have fished many scores of the type from Galloway to Berwick, and from the Cheviots to Devon.

The worm was useful in exploring the deeper pools after rain, but it was now that I first took to the fly. I began in the "highland" type, the lovely Powsail which joins Tweed at Merlin's Grave below Drummelzier village. Its pools were deep and clear, and into each tumbled a small cataract, so I found it easier to fish up than down stream—a valuable lesson for the fly-fisher. It was an elementary business with little art in it, for the casts were perforce short, and the configuration of the land enabled the angler to keep well in cover. My flies never varied from a couple of plain black hackles (which we called "black spiders"), on coarsish gut. From April to August the pools were the best chance, in September the little runs and stickles. The fish averaged three or four to the pound, and I had never anything beyond a pound weight.

This was in the "highland" type. In the "lowland" the prospects of good fish were greater, but there was also an excellent chance of no fish at all. For such streams would sink in dry weather to the slenderest trickles. Then, I regret to say, I would altogether abandon the rod and take to my naked hands, having behind me the authority of John Bunyan :

> "Yet fish there be that neither Hook, nor Line,
> Nor Snare, nor Net, nor Engine can make thine;
> They must be grop't for, and be tickled too,
> Or they will not be catch't, whate'er you do."

I was an expert "guddler," scooping up trout from below stones in the channel and under the deep-cut banks. These "lowland" burns could become degraded indeed, choked with rubbish in passing a farmyard, or at the outlet of a village. But sometimes, when they looped through a broad pasture-land, they afforded pools and streams from which trout could only be taken by casting fine and far. They had occasional big fish, too, for, though it was never my luck, I have seen trout of two pounds and more taken from them. I was ill-equipped for fly-fishing, since my rod was the two upper joints of my grandfather's salmon rod, my reel and line were indifferent, and my gut was far too coarse for slender waters and bright weather. But it was there and then that the possibilities of the art began to dawn on me, and fly-fishing became for me a necessity of life.

I liked those hobbledehoy waters best in the early spring. The "highland" ones were wonderful in autumn when the heather was still in flower and the bracken was yellowing, and the rowans flamed scarlet from the rocks. Beautiful were the "lowland" streams in high summer when the banks were feathered with meadowsweet and the pastures bright with rock-rose and thyme. But I liked them best when the turf was still yellow, like old court velvet, or just beginning to green after the winter:

> "A month before the month of May,
> And the spring comes slowly up this way."

In April there was an ineffable freshness and purity in the cold grey waters and the austere shores. Also one had more generously than at any other season the companionship of birds. In a glen in Morvern I have looked down from the edge of a little ravine at the nest and eggs of a golden eagle in a sprawling birch. In the

grassy glens the angler could scarcely avoid stumbling
on the nests of lapwing and grouse, snipe and sand-
piper; with a little trouble he could find those of the
redshank and the curlew, and one notable day in
Sutherland I added a greenshank to my list. Also
spring is the time when the hill lambs are born, and
one day there is a bleating in the valleys, and presently
the hillsides are sprinkled with vociferous younglings
which, if of the Cheviots breed, are white as a snowdrift.

In such places I never felt the awesome solitude that
belonged to the uppermost green "hopes." There was
evidence of human occupation everywhere—a drove
road, a field of roots in the midst of heather, a moorland
farm-town with horses and cows at graze, a farm road
with a postman on it, even a hamlet where old women
washed the family clothes in the burn. Yet they were
quiet places and in their own fashion very lonely—
lonely because the world had never known them, or
had forgotten them. There were no fields, as in
England, each called by an ancient name; the slender
tributaries were often innominate, or described in the
large-scale maps as "Ugly Grain" or "Middle Grain";
they mattered only to the farmer as the feeding-ground
for his hirsels. They were unvisited, except by a rare
angler or a shepherd "looking" his sheep. No legend
was intertwined with them, and no ballad gave them
fame, or if they had a ballad the local application was
forgotten. The Douglas Burn in Yarrow is the reputed
scene of a famous ballad story, but I never thought of
that when I fished its waters. In Tweedsmuir Kingle-
dores Burn saw the slaying of Lord Fleming by those
red-handed bandits, the Tweedies of Drummelzier,
but it is a tale known only to the antiquary. Those
moorland waters have to flow further down the haughs
before they properly enter human life.

U

My time for the "hopes" was the morning, for at
that distance I had to put up my rod in the early afternoon to be home for tea. But to many of the burns
the journey was short, and with them I associated
especially the summer twilights when the dew had
begun to fall and the hill pastures were incense-breaking
like Araby, with mint and meadowsweet and thyme
and heather. I noticed then something which I have
often since observed, that there was a short spell just
before the dark when no fish would take. I have caught
trout when the pools were red and gold with the
pageant in the west, and I have caught them when dusk
had fallen and there was scarcely light enough to cast
by. But there would come a time when there seemed
to be a sudden hush in the world, when nature was
"breathless with adoration" and the trout had halted
to reflect on their sins. It was a time which I associated
with that magical word εὐφημία which Plato uses in
the *Phaedo* when he describes Socrates making ready for
death.[1] It was the hour to which Wordsworth no
doubt referred as the "light of setting suns" which was
the dwelling of "something far more deeply inter-
fused." It was the time when in earlier ages devout
men in the Hebrides would see far in the western sea
the shadowy outline of St. Brandan's isles. When that
hour came I would lay down my rod until the flop of a
rising fish told me that the wheels of the world were
going round again. With salmon it made no difference,
they being brazen creatures from the outer seas, but the
humble and pious trout observe the holy season. It was
not for nothing that in the Sixteenth *Iliad* Homer
applied the epithet ἱερὸς to fish.

[1] § 65.

CHAPTER II

THE MIDDLE COURSES

I

BY the middle courses I mean what in Scotland and northern England is described as a "water." It may be the middle course of a considerable stream which presently reaches the dignity of a river. Old folk in Tweedsmuir used to speak of the "water of Tweed." So in the ballads:

> "Annan waters wadin' deep,
> And my love Annie's wondrous bonny."

> .　　.　　.　　.　　.　　.

> "The roar of the Clyde water
> Wad hae dar'd a hundred men."

Or it may be only a substantial tributary, like Ettrick or Teviot. Or it may be a river on its own account, finding its end in sea or lake, but a river on a modest scale, no bigger than those affluents I have named. Such are the Lune and the Coquet, the Usk in Wales, and those pleasant streams of the west which derive from Exmoor and Dartmoor. My measure is not only by size, for in this chapter I do not take account of the smaller Highland rivers like the Brora and the Helmsdale, the Thurso and the Laxford, whose business is with salmon, or the famous dry-fly streams of the south. I am still concerned with trout, and with waters which have not lost the scent of the hills.

It is in this class that I find the river of my dreams. I have two landscapes in my mind which have always ravished my fancy. One is a morning scene. It is spring—say mid-April; a small fresh wind is blowing; my viewpoint is somewhere among the foothills where a mountain land breaks down to the plains. Below me is a glen with green fields and the smoke of hearth-fires and running water, and a far-off echo of human bustle, including the clack of a mill wheel. The glen runs out into the blue dimness of a great champaign, with the spires of cities in it, and on the far rim a silver belt of sea. A white road winds down the valley and into the plain, and I know that it will take me past a hundred blessed nooks into an April world of adventure and youth.

The other scene belongs to the afternoon, not the languorous afternoon of the poets, but a season which is only the mellowing of the freshness of morning. It is a wide tract of pasture, backed by little wooded hills, mostly oaks and beeches, but with clumps of tall Scots firs. Behind, fading into the sunset, are round-shouldered blue mountains. In the pasture there are shapely little coverts, as in the park of a great mansion. Through it winds a little river, very clear and very quiet, with long smooth streams and pools edged with fine gravel. The banks are open so that there is nothing to impede the angler. There are cattle at graze, and a faithful company of birds and bees. It is a place long-settled and cared for, with the flavour of a demesne, a place in close contact with human life.

My little rivers are also in touch with history. It is along their courses that you will find the chief memorials of the past. In the Borders it is rare to find a famous castle in the glen of a burn—Hermitage is one of the few I can call to mind; but the valleys of the "waters" are strewn with shards of old masonry, each on its promontory of hill, and each linked with some resounding name. In some parts these ruins are in sight of each other, for in their day of pride it was their business by lit beacons to pass the news that the enemy was marching. Rede and Coquet and Till, Esk and Eden, Liddel and Teviot, Ettrick and Yarrow and Leader; Lyne and Manor and Tweed itself—each mile almost of their course has its tower, now mostly a jagged stone tooth hung with ivy; and it is the same with the tributaries of Tay and the streams of Angus, and northern waters like the Don (the Scottish Loire), the Ythan and the Findhorn. With the castles go the ballads, the most famous are strung on a thread of little streams.

I like a place where history can be easily reconstructed, and except for a few dry-stone dykes and some planting, those glens have not greatly changed since the ancient days of sturt and strife. The peel-tower had a massy stone foundation which could not be destroyed, but the roof-tree and thatch and wooden outbuildings must have been constantly flaming to heaven. We can picture stormy dawns when the plenishing of a farm moved southward under the prick of raiders' spears, and moonlit nights when in the "hot-trod" men died for half a dozen lean cattle. It was a life which bred hardy fighters and fine poets, for from it came some of the world's greatest ballads, and it taught a stiff creed of honour and loyalty. But it had few of the gentler graces, and neither Roman Pope nor Scottish King could teach it decorum. Archbishops might lay on the malefactors their most terrible curse—"I condemn them perpetually to the deep pit of hell, to remain with Lucifer and all his fellows, and their bodies to the gallows on the Barrow Mure, first to be hangit, syne riven and ruggit with dogs, swine, and other wild beasts abominable to all the world." But to hang a Borderer you had first to catch him—no easy matter, and for the thunders of the Church he and his kind cared not a straw.

I have called those valleys my favourite kind of landscape, and they are also the places linked with my happiest fishing memories. But I have in mind one tract of country where the prospect is most pleasing but the fishing is vile. It is the land which lies roughly between Llandovery in the south and Plinlimmon in the north, Rhayader in the east and the valley of Teify in the west. Giraldus Cambrensis, who travelled in those parts with Archbishop Baldwin at the end of the twelfth century, and incidentally found beavers in the Teify, called it the "mountains of Elanydd." It is a land of sheep-walks rising at one point to a height of two thousand feet, with shallow vales, and wide stretches of bent and bog. There are no highways, no villages, no inns, and the postman visits the moorland farms perhaps twice a week. Especially it is the cradle of rivers, Elan, Towey, Teify, Ystwyth, and a dozen lesser ones, and their vales are the very flower of moorland peace. But there are few fish in those bright waters till they have left the uplands. Take the Towey, which in its lower reaches is a respectable sea-trout river. In its upper valley, above the cave of Tom Tym Katti, it flows in noble streams and long deep pools through a pastoral paradise. There you will find air like mid-ocean, and curious bog plants, and if you are fortunate you may see the honey buzzard and the last kites left in Britain. But you will be luckier than me if you get more than a few meagre trout.

II

In the middle courses I have done most of my fishing for trout and my 'prentice days were spent on streams which ran swift and open and very clear. It was wet-fly fishing, though, after I had been entered to the dry-fly, I often tried that mode with success on waters very unlike the Hampshire chalk streams. On two occasions only have I forsaken the artificial fly. In low water, fishing upstream, I have sometimes in my youth had good baskets with the red worm. In the may-fly season I followed the local practice, and in the small hours just before dawn had considerable success dapping with the natural fly.

These chapters are not a practical manual, for I have no special arts to expound or secrets to reveal. Also in my attitude to the sport I am lamentably unscientific. I admire the shooter who has theories about the ballistics of his craft, but I have no wish to imitate him. Nor am I inclined to follow the angler who has elaborate views on optics—how the light strikes the fish's eye, and at what angle the fly is seen—or on entomology, for insects are a part of nature for which I have no taste—or on ichthyology—or on that mysterious subject, the working of a fish's mind. Some even connect the habits of fish with the phases of the moon ; which seems to me a more promising line, for astrology may well be relevant, since the Fishes are a sign of the zodiac. I do not want to know too much about trout, for I like to leave some room for mystery. Indeed, I should prefer to keep science out of the business altogether. Izaak Walton gave us reams of the variety, popular in his day, but they are not his best chapters. I am not interested either in the elaborate gadgets with which the angler is now fitted out. Indeed, my disinclination to fish with bait, natural or artificial, is largely due to my dislike of its complex apparatus. I have few theories, and I want only a modest equipment. For trout, wet-fly or dry-fly. I do not use more than a dozen patterns, though

I believe in varying the size; for salmon about the same. I like old and well-tried rods and reels—everything old except the gut. When I see the bursting fly-books and tackle boxes of my friends I do not envy them:

"Perish the wish, for inly satisfied,
Above their pomps I hold my ragged pride."

I have few maxims, and they are all deductions from experience. Keep well back from the water, for trout are extraordinarily susceptible, not to noise but to vibration. Trout are voracious; a very young trout will eat its own weight every ten days—and therefore, though there is no rise apparent, they are probably somehow and somewhere on the feed. Your fly must show signs of life, for a trout does not feed on dead meat. A fish cannot detect delicate shades of colour and must see a fly as more or less a grey silhouette against the background of the sky. Therefore to achieve this silhouette, you must use a light-coloured fly on a dark day and a dark fly on a bright one. But what may matter a great deal is the size of the fly and the fineness of your tackle. Finally, when you are fishing for a rising trout, do not cast at him but at some point in the air above him. These are a few of the rules which I believe I have proved by experience, but I am ready to admit that they all have their exceptions. Indeed, except for the "dark day, light fly and *vice versa*" principle, I am very chary of dogmatising.

What makes the difference between a successful and a less successful angler? Scarcely the length and delicacy of his casting. In salmon fishing the length of a cast may be important, and in certain Welsh, Devonian and Highland streams, where the banks are thickly wooded and one must wade up the channel, it may be necessary to cast fine and far. But, generally speaking, most fishermen of experience attain to a fair level of expert casting. Nor is it the ability to select the appropriate fly. I do not believe there is ever any completely appropriate fly, except on the broad principle I have stated above, with the rider that in the twilight, when moths are glimmering, a little fantasy may be permitted. Nor is it any extra skill in striking and playing a fish. The *differentia* in my view is knowledge of the particular water and the habits of the trout in it—where and at what season are the likeliest lies. In the bare pasturelands of my youth that was all important. I have had a good basket on a stream where my companion not only caught no fish but saw none. If a man knows his stream he will know that the haunts of fish will be different in April and in August, in low water and in full water. So, both for trout and salmon, I would maintain that, after a certain standard of technique has been attained, what makes the difference among anglers is just knowledge, local knowledge—as Alan Breck defined courage, "great penetration and knowledge of affairs."

To-day, in Britain at any rate, one has to work hard for one's fish, except in jealously preserved and fully stocked waters. Most Scottish and north-country streams are free to the public, and new methods of transport have made them accessible to the dwellers in distant cities. When I was a boy I must have fished burns which did not see an angler once in a decade. Andrew Lang used to say that you might be certain you had found your happy valley when the shepherd begged the bit of daily paper which wrapped your luncheon that he might learn the news. To-day you might as well look in the same countryside for the nest of the sea-eagle which used to haunt it. The Ettrick Shepherd tells of filling a cart with trout out of Megget of about the size of a herring; the angler would be lucky now if out of Megget on most days he got a dozen half-pounders. On a once famous Lowland stream I have seen on a Bank Holiday anglers as thick as the gudgeon fishers on Thames.

III

I do not regret it. I would be glad to see angling clubs more widely organised, so that there was a certain amount of restocking, a decent limit to a day's catch, and an insistence on lawful lures. But I am glad to think that so many of my fellow mortals have the chance of this honest sport.

In my youth I formed a deep attachment to the democracy of the waterside. There was the ragged weaver out of work, with his ancient home-made rod, who was out to catch his dinner and kept the smallest fingerlings. He was partial to lures like salmon-roe, and was not above "sniggling" a fish. But he knew his job, for he knew where trout were to be had, and often he was an expert practitioner in the orthodox parts. But the commonest objects of the waterside were miners from the Lothian and Lanarkshire coalfields. They would come by train on a summer evening to some wayside station on Tweed or Clyde, fish all night and get back to their work in the early morning. Somehow or other they never left with an empty creel. Most were unorthodox in their methods, but not all. I remember one man whose casting with an indifferent rod first taught me what fly-fishing could be. I had many friends among them, and I have shared their supper of bread and cheese, and exchanged a respectable gut cast for one of their strange home-made contraptions, designed for the "parr-tail," that deadliest of lawless devices. I think pleasantly of my old comrades, who were kind to an inquisitive boy. Like the Black Douglas, they preferred to hear the lark sing rather than to hear the mouse cheep, and there must have been a strong passion for sport and wild nature in their hearts to drive them to spend laborious nights after laborious days. I remember hearing Andrew Lang say that some of Theocritus could best be rendered in Lowland Scots, so I tried my hand at it and turned the twenty-first Idyll into a tale of two such anglers. Here is the result—a sketch of two of the clan.

"'Tis puirtith sooples heid and hand
And gars inventions fill the land;
And dreams come fast to folk that lie
Wi' nocht atween them and the sky.

Twae collier lads frae near Lasswade,
Auld skeely fishers, fand their bed
Ae simmer's nicht aside the shaw
Whaur Manor rins by Cademuir Law.
Dry flowe-moss made them pillows fine,
And, for a bield to kep the win',
A muckle craig owerhung the burn,
A' thacked wi' blaeberry and fern.
Aside them lay their rods and reels,
Their flee-books and their auncient creels.
The pooches o' their moleskin breeks
Contained unlawfu' things like cleeks,
For folk that fish to fill their waume
Are no fasteedious at the game.

The twae aye took their jaunts thegither;
Geordie was ane and Tam the ither.
Their chaumer was the mune-bricht sky,
The siller stream their lullaby."

Then there were the local poachers. For them trout were small beer; their quarry was the salmon out of season. They would net or spear the big red fish in the autumn streams, and salt them down for winter use. The thing was in defiance of the law, and the water-bailiffs were always on their trail, so that there were many affrays by the waterside which ended in broken heads. I have assisted in "burning the water," which was a favourite pursuit of Sir Walter Scott's, and apparently in his day not illegal. It was an exciting business, for the shallows would be reddened by torches made of barrel staves dipped in tar, and wild figures with a three-pronged fork, called a leister, speared the fish as they blundered upstream. Once I was arrested by the bailiffs along with the others, but in consideration of my youth was released with a hearty kick! The story got about and was remembered many years after when I stood as parliamentary candidate for the county. I was assured that I had the poaching vote to a man! Dour, sardonic folk they were, but with their own dry humour. I once met one of them tramping the high-road on a very hot day and greeted him with an enquiry after his health. "Bearin' up," was the reply, "in the hope that if I can thole [1] it here I'll be able to thole it Yonder."

But the true angling democracy were the local anglers who fished legitimately. They were generally small tradesmen from the little burghs. But it was rare that a countryman became an expert. I have only known two, the son of a schoolmaster and the son of an inn-keeper. Angling was the breath of their life; every hour they could spare they were on a stream, and they attained often a remarkable skill. They would fill a basket in the tiniest runlets among the heather, and they would catch fish from a low water, in an east wind, in a thunder-storm, and in drifting snow. Angling to such

[1] Stand.

was not only a sport, but a social institution, for they had their little fraternities, their suppers and their songs. Meg Dods in *St. Ronan's Well* has spoken their *apologia*:

"Pawky auld carles, that kend whilk side their bread was buttered upon. . . . They were up in the morning—had their parritch, wi' maybe a thimble-full of brandy, and then awa' up into the hills; eat their bit cauld meat on the heather, and cam' hame at e'en wi' their creel full of caller trouts, and had them to their dinner, and their quiet cogue of ale, and their drap punch, and were set singing their catches and glees, as they ca'd them, till ten o'clock, and then to bed, wi' God bless ye—and what for no?"

Sometimes they ventured into verse. There is a little piscatorial eclogue which I used to hear repeated in my youth, but the source of which I have never been able to trace. The Kips mentioned in it are the Shielgreen Kips to the north-east of Peebles which look down on the head of Leithen Water.

JUVENIS AND PISCATOR

Juv. Canny Fisher Jamie, comin' hame at e'en,
Canny Fisher Jamie, whaur hae ye been?

Pisc. Mony lang miles, laddie, ower the Kips sae green.

Juv. Fishin' Leithen Water?

Pisc.   Nay, laddie, nay,
Just a wee burnie rinnin' doun a brae,
Fishin' a wee burnie bigger than a sheugh.

Juv. Gat ye mony troots, Jamie?

Pisc.   I gat eneugh—
Eneugh to buy my baccy, snuff, and pickle tea,
And lea' me tippence for a gill, and that's eneugh for me.

he describes a spring meadow he writes almost the best cheerful prose in our literature, prose which is all air and dew and light. His seventeenth-century rival is John Bunyan when he tells of the rare amenities of the Pilgrim's Way.

I say "cheerful" advisedly, for it is notable that most of our great prose is solemn prose, the prose of mortality. Instances crowd in on the mind. There is Bunyan when he talks of the passing of Mr. Valiant-for-Truth, and Walton when he writes of Donne :

> "that body which was once the temple of the Holy Ghost and is now become a small quantity of Christian dust."

There is the Authorised Version of the Bible. There are a dozen passages in Sir Thomas Browne. There is Sir William Temple, a passage which Goldsmith in *The Good-natured Man* puts into the mouth of the preposterous Croaker :

> "When all is done human life is, at the greatest and best, but like a froward child that must be played with and humoured a little till it falls asleep, and then the care is over."

There is the famous passage from the "Æsop and Rhodope" chapter in Landor's *Imaginary Conversations*. There is Lockhart on the death of Scott, and Colonel Henderson on the death of Stonewall Jackson. There is the last paragraph of Thomas Hardy's *Woodlanders*. And not least there is Emily Brontë :

> "I lingered round them under that benign sky; watched the moths fluttering among the heath and the harebells, listened to the soft wind breathing through the grass, and wondered how anyone could ever imagine unquiet slumbers for the sleepers in that quiet earth."

INDEX